Corporate Training

for Effective Performance

Evaluation in Education and Human Services

Other books in the series:

Madaus, G. and Stufflebeam, D.:
Education Evaluation: Classic Works of Ralph W. Tyler
Gifford, B:
Test Policy and Test Performance
Osterlind, S.:
Constructing Test Items
Smith, M.:
Evaluability Assessment
Ayers, J. and Berney, M.:
A Practical Guide to Teacher Education Evaluation
Hambleton, R. and Zaal, J.:
Advances in Educational and Psychological Testing
Gifford, B. and O'Connor, M.:
Changing Assessments
Gifford, B.:
Policy Perspectives on Educational Testing
Basarab, D. and Root, D.:
The Training Evaluation Process
Haney, W.M., Madaus, G.F. and Lyons, R.:
The Fractured Marketplace for Standardized Testing
Wing, L.C. and Gifford, B.:
Policy Issues in Employment Testing
Gable, R.E.:
Instrument Development in the Affective Domain (2nd Edition)
Kremer-Hayon, L.:
Teacher Self-Evaluation
Payne, David A.:
Designing Educational Project and Program Evaluations
Oakland T. and Hambleton, R.:
International Perspectives on Academic Assessment
Nettles, M.T. and Nettles, A.L.:
Equity and Excellence in Educational Testing and Assessment
Shinkfield, A.J. and Stufflebeam, D.L.:
Teacher Evaluation: Guide to Effective Practice
Birenbaum, M. and Dochy, Filip J.R.C.:
Alternatives in Assessment of Achievements, Learning Processes and Prior Knowledge

Corporate Training for Effective Performance

Martin Mulder
University of Twente, the Netherlands
Wim J. Nijhof
University of Twente, the Netherlands
Robert O. Brinkerhoff
Western Michigan University, Kalamazoo, MI, U.S.A.

Kluwer Academic Publishers
Boston/Dordrecht/London

Distributors for North America:
Kluwer Academic Publishers
101 Philip Drive
Assinippi Park
Norwell, Massachusetts 02061 USA

Distributors for all other countries:
Kluwer Academic Publishers Group
Distribution Centre
Post Office Box 322
3300 AH Dordrecht, THE NETHERLANDS

Library of Congress Cataloging-in-Publication Data
Corporate training for effective performance / Martin Mulder, Wim J.
Nijhof, Robert O. Brinkerhoff, eds.
p. cm.
Includes indexes.
ISBN 0-7923-9599-9
1. Employees--Training of. 2. Competency based education.
I. Mulder, Martin, 1951- . II. Nijhof, Wim J., 1941- .
III. Brinkerhoff, Robert O.
HF5549.5.T7C63 1995
658.3'124--dc20 95-4791
CIP

Printed on acid-free paper.

Printed in the United States of America

Contents

List of Figures

List of Tables

List of Contributors

Dr. Jean-Claude Asselborn is a professor of Computer Science at the Centre Universitaire in Luxembourg. His research field is enterprise modeling and related topics. He was involved in the development of several expert systems in the financial domain and is currently working on methods for modeling work-flows in document imaging systems; moreover he is leading a project on the modeling of cooperative work.

Dr. Uschi Backes-Gellner graduated in economics at Trier University in 1984. She finished her dissertation in 1987. She was visiting scholar at the Northwestern University in 1988, and at the University of California Berkeley in 1990. Since 1988 she is senior research fellow at the Institute of Labour Law and Industrial Relations at Trier University.

Dr. Klaus Breuer is a professor of Vocational Education with the Department of Law and Economics at the Johannes Gutenberg-Universität in Mainz, in the Fed. Republic of Germany. He holds a PhD in Education (1979) from the Institute of Technology at Aachen (RWTH Aachen).

Dr. Robert O. Brinkerhoff is a professor of Education at Western Michigan University. He is an international expert in training effectiveness and evaluation, as well als a consultant to corporations and agencies worldwide. He is author of nine books on training and evaluation.

Dr. Stephen Carter is head of development at the Institute of Management. Responsible for the development of competency based programs, programs for mentors, assessors and workshop leaders, he is particularly interested in the integration of training to national standards with specific organizational needs.

Dr. Stephen F. Foster received his PhD from the University of Illinois and is professor of Behavioral Sciences at the RVB-Maastricht School of Management, in the Netherlands. He is also active in private practice as a management consultant specializing in learning, motivation and change processes, and is external MD consultant to MOG-Management Development Group, The Hague.

Marcel R. Gmelich Meijling, M.Ed, is an educational scientist. He studied at the University of Twente at the Faculty of Educational Science and Technology. He designed the CBT materials for Brine Purification.

Dr. Geert W.J. Heling received his PhD from the University of Nijmegen and is Senior Management Consultant associated with Goossens Management and Organization (GMO), a consultancy based in The Hague, in the Netherlands. He specialized in HRM, management and organizational development, change processes, training and personal coaching.

Dr. Jean-Marie Jans is a computer scientist. He works as a teacher at the Centre Universitaire and as a researcher at the Centre de Recherche Public - Centre Universitaire in Luxembourg. His domains of interest are mainly information systems engineering, especially modeling and computer based learning, especially on-the-job learning.

Dr. Nico L. Krijger is a Dutch organization psychologist. He is a pioneer in the field of Personal Management Coaching. His special interests are: the transfer of learning and training designs that create lasting effects. He published several articles on those topics.

Dr. Philippe Méhaut is a labor economist. His main fields of studies are youth unemployment and youth training policies, adult vocational training and companies' human resource and training policies, evaluation of public training and employment policies. He is deputy director of CEREQ (Centre d'Etude et de Recherche sur les Qualifications) in Marseille.

Dr. Ir. Rik Min received his PhD from the Medical Faculty of the University of Limburg, in the Netherlands. He lectures at the University of Twente at Enschede in the Netherlands and conducts research into educational computer simulation techniques and teaches courses about designing methods and techniques for educational software. He is the designer of the MacThesis system.

Dr. Martin Mulder is associate professor at the University of Twente within a group of faculty who are interested in Human Resource Development (HRD). He teaches courses on HRD issues, and managed several research projects in this field.

Dr. Wim J. Nijhof, is a professor in Education, Faculty of Educational Science and Technology, Twente University, the Netherlands. His specialty is training research and development in corporate training and vocational education.

Jeroen H.A.M. Onstenk, M.Ed, is a senior researcher in the Centre for the Study of Culture, Inequality, Vocation and Education at the SCO-Kohnstamm Institute for Educational Research (University of Amsterdam). Recent topics include broadly applicable skills, apprenticeships in secondary vocational education, in-company training for poorly educated and older employees, and concepts and practices of on-the-job learning.

Silvia M. Pol, M.Ed, , M.A., studied organizational and clinical psychology at the University of Utrecht. She was part of the consulting group of Kryger Consulting for training, coaching and research. She is especially interested in research in the field of learning processes and the change mechanisms involved.

Ing. Ben Reimerink is working on computer simulation projects at the University of Twente in the laboratory of the Faculty of Educational Science and Technology. He is the programmer of the MacThesis system.

Dr. Alexander J. Romiszowski is a professor of Instructional Design, Development and Evaluation and the technical director of Training Systems Institute at Syracuse University. He has worked as consultant to many private and public education and training organizations all over the world. He has published extensively in the field, including the *trilogy*: Designing Instructional Systems; Producing Instructional Systems; and Developing Auto-Instructional materials.

Dr. Darlene F. Russ-Eft is division director of Research Services at Zenger-Miller. Previously, with the American Institutes for Research and with the Human Performance Center at the University of Michigan, she published numerous articles and books on the topic of adult learning. She has continued this research with an emphasis on learning through worker, supervisor, middle management, team, and total quality management training.

Dr. Pieter G. van Schaick Zillesen studied at the Universities of Utrecht and Twente. After the completing his dissertation, he worked for the Agricultural University of Wageningen, where he conducted research on the potential of educational software for process engineering education. He is with the Prof. H.C. van Hall Instituut in Groningen, where he manages several projects in the field of the production of educational simulations.

Afina C. Steinvoort, M.Ed, graduated in 1991 at the faculty of Educational Science and Technology of the University of Twente. Since then she is working at the National Centre for the Hotel and Catering Industry as project manager. She develops training materials for professions in the hotel industry, and besides that she is working on a new qualification system for the entire training system for the hotel and catering industry.

Dr. Siegfried Streufert is a professor of Behavioral Science and Psychology with the Department of Behavioral Science at Pennsylvania State University, College of Medicine (Hershey), and the Department of Psychology at Pennsylvania State University (Main Campus), Pennsylvania (USA). He holds a PhD in Experimental Psychology (1962) from Princeton University.

John E. Thompson lectures at the Ulster Business School, University of Ulster. He has been a senior manager in industry and a senior management developer in the Public Service. His research interests are in training evaluation, top team development and competence development. He developed one of the first competence based postgraduate programmes in the United Kingdom.

Dr. John H. (Jack) Zenger is a group vice president of Times Mirror responsible for the Training Group. He was an early user of behavior modeling and co-founder of Zenger-Miller, an international supplier of training programs and services, headquartered in San Jose, California, that support organization change efforts.

Preface

Corporate training and effective performance have become major issues in the last decade. Surveys showed that corporate training was a booming business in the eighties and the beginning of the nineties. Many professionals in the field of corporate training became aware of the tremendous volume of the market. Consecutive reviews of the training reseach literature have shown that parallel to the growing attention for corporate training, research in this field increased. Looking back to the fifties and sixties, it can be concluded that corporate training research also boomed. This development is appreciated widely amongst researchers. It gives an opportunity for further understanding the field of corporate training. And practitioners receive fundamental expertise on which they can build their practices.

This book contains a selected number of research studies. The studies were presented at the second international conference on Corporate Training and Development at the University of Twente in 1991. They were selected for publication and have been updated and rewritten since then. The studies are divided in three parts of the book: Part I on Changing Environments of Training and Development, Part II on Models, Stategies and Evaluation, and Part III on New Training and Development Devices. The various chapters differ to the degree in which they are related to performance issues. But all chapters underline the necessity of thinking from the perspective of effective performance. Today corporate training departments are held accountable for human resource results, which is quite different compared to the sixties and early seventies, when operator training and management training were mainly held accountable for training activities. The three parts reflect the changes in the field of corporate training, and they are broad areas of interest.

The book is composed for those interested in research on corporate training and effective performance. Doctoral students and practitioners may also find the book useful.

The authors wish to express their gratitude to the Dutch Ministry of Economic Affairs, the Dutch Association of Training Organizations (the VETRON), various other companies and training organizations, and the International Research Network for Training and Development (IRNETD) for their interest in the theme *Corporate Training for Effective Performance.* They sponsored the development of the book. For scholars and researchers in the field of

Human Resource Development, it is very helpful to receive this kind of support. It enables them to show the professional community what progress has been made, and what knowledge can be used in the daily professional practice.

The editors would like to acknowledgde Zachary Rolnik, publisher at Kluwer Academic Publishers, and the authors of the chapters in this book for kind cooperation.

Enschede, The Netherlands

Martin Mulder
Wim J. Nijhof
Robert O. Brinkerhoff

1 Linking Corporate Training and Effective Performance

Martin Mulder, Wim J. Nijhof and Robert O. Brinkerhoff

Effective performance has become critical throughout the global economy. In view of the severe competition within this global economy, organizations focus on their performance. They analyze their results and problems, and try to find solutions that may improve their results (Swanson, 1994). Organizations need to do so for the sake of continuing their existence in the future. They constantly need to adapt to new circumstances. In the process of focusing on performance, learning plays a critical role. Organizations have to learn from their failures and successes, and they should be able to analyze causes and effects of decisions and results. Much of the necessary learning can be facilitated by corporate training.

1.1 Conceptualizing Corporate Training and Effective Performance

There are various ways to conceptualize corporate training. In this book, the concept of corporate training has a broad meaning. Corporate training is conceived of as the entirety of provisions which are linked to the corporate policy, and aimed at realizing learning processes of employees within the organization, that directly or indirectly improve the effective performance and the development of the employees and the organization.

Conceptualized in this way, corporate training is related to the concept of Human Resource Development (HRD). HRD is defined as "... the integrated use of training and development, organization development, and career development to improve individual, group, and organizational effectiveness" (McLagan, 1989). Corporate training is part of HRD in the sense that it focuses on learning processes that enable effectiveness of individuals, groups, and organizations. As such it can support organization and career development.

The critical element in the definition of corporate training is that it is aimed at effective performance, at the development of the employees, and the organization. Effective performance can be influenced directly by corporate training when training programs are aimed at contemporary job specific skills and near transfer. Quite often, however, training programs are aimed at generic skills and far transfer, and when this is the case, effective performance will not be possible then in future work processes. Thus, corporate training for individual and organizational development will indirectly influence effective performance, but its impact in a later stage may be equally or even more significant than short term results of specific skills oriented training programs.

What is meant by *performance*? Stolovitch and Keeps (1992) refer to it in terms of outcomes, accomplishments, results or achievements of indidivuals. In a corporate context, performance comprises both the conducting of an action and its accomplishment, and it consists of the content of an action ("what?"), the way this activity is executed ("how?"), and the result of the action ("effect?"). In systems terminology, performance is related to the process and output of the action. The effectiveness of performance is the level to which the process and outputs of the action reach the standards that are set for jobs, work groups, and entire organizations ("how good?"). The standards are derived from the corporation's vision, mission, strategy, personnel policy, and management targets, and these elements are operationalized for departments and work units within the organization.

Including the notion of effective performance in the definition of corporate training is regarded as essential. It reflects its legitimacy as a support function in the organization. When corporate training contributes to effective performance, and corporate executives are convinced of that, corporate training may receive considerable attention, a high status, and sufficient funds. Corporate training that does not prove its worth for the organization, on the other hand, is an easy budget item that can be deleted when cost reductions are necessary.

1.2 Measuring Effective Performance

Effective performance can be measured in several ways. Two important issues have to be distinguished in this respect. First of all the kind of effects has to be defined. Secondly, the design of the study needs to allow the claims that are being made by the researcher.

With respect to the definition of the effects of corporate training, the most fertile approach is to start thinking in terms of customer requirements. Customers of corporate training departments are manifold. Depending on their hierarchy within the organization, they need a certain amount of aggregation in performance measurement. Coaches are mostly interested in the specific job performance of the persons they guide. First line supervisors are also interested in individual performance of workers, but they also want to know the performance of the group as a whole. The higher the position of the stakeholders, the more they are interested in performance indicators that reflect consolidated added value of corporate training. When measuring effective performance, a distinction has to be made between systems levels, which has been proposed already by Gilbert (1978), or between performance levels, organization, process, and job level, which is advocated by Rummler and Brache (1992). With this distinction the definition and operationalization of effects that need to be measured is being facilitated.

As to the design of the study, it should be noted that the definition of effectiveness is related to the concept of causality. A causal relationship is assumed between corporate training and effective performance. But effective performance of individuals, work groups and organizations is not exclusively determined by corporate training. Professionals in the corporate training department only control the acquisition of knowledge, skills, and attitudes. Whether they are being used in the workplace depends on factors like job design, human resource planning, culture, ergonomics, workload, compensation, employee assistance, intelligence, self efficacy, motivation, ambition, age, and experience. And use of newly acquired knowledge, skills and attitudes in the workplace is only one factor in establishing corporate effectiveness. Various other factors influence that, such as developments in international trade and politics. In short: corporate training programs are interventions aimed at improving effective performance, but there are other internal and external factors that co-influence the variation in performance (Camp, Blanchard and Huszczo, 1986). Studies in which the effects of corporate training on performance are measured should be designed in such a way that intervening variables, that may influence the dependant variable(s), are controlled. This is by no means an easy task.

1.3 The Need for Multi-Disciplinary Research

Solving complex problems in organizations often requires interventions of a multi-disciplinary nature. Corporate training alone is not sufficient in many instances; in most cases it serves as a necessary condition for effective performance, rarely as a sufficient condition. Full understanding of corporate training, therefore, requires a multi-disciplinary orientation on the field.

Studies from different perspectives, such as economics, policy, culture, management, and HRD itself, can help in this respect. To name just a few examples: studies in the field of economics have revealed macro and micro economic factors that influence the benefits of training; policy studies have shown that the division of responsibility between private and public organizations influence the distribution of expertise at the labor market; cultural studies point at the issue that the appreciation of effects of corporate training is culturally diverse; and management studies stress the role of managers in achieving results with training programs.

More of this research is needed, as the results of these studies provide guidelines for practitioners in the field of corporate training. Studies in which the causal relationships between process and outcome variables are tested, are especially needed. These studies, although they are hard to realize in practice, result in the most powerful guidelines for practice. As said, these studies are hard to realize in practice, because in most cases the conditions under which they have to be conducted are not very supportive. Nevertheless, researchers have to try to conduct such studies to further develop the field of corporate training. This does not mean that other research should not be done. In most cases other research serves other purposes, such as consulting, training process support, and information provision. In this book, the reader will find examples of various studies with different designs from several disciplines. It will be noted that the research methods used in the various chapters are quite different. Literature reviews, theoretical analyses, case studies, experiments, and other methods have been used. We value this methodological pluralism, as the reality of training and development in organizations is far too complex to capture with just one methodological approach from one perspective.

Studies in the first part of the book deal with various changes in the external environment of the organization. Profound economic, social demographic, and technological changes create the need for more and other training and development activities to facilitate the change in the structure and content of labor.

Studies in the second part go into models, strategies, and evaluation. New models and strategies are needed to develop training and development activities that reflect the requirements of the profound changes just mentioned. Traditional courses remotely organized for groups of employees, do not reflect the tremendously varied combinations of knowledge and skills needs, learning styles, and other preferences that go along with adult learning processes. New evaluation procedures are needed to determine the effectiveness of different approaches, and new evaluation procedures are needed that are cost-effective and viable in corporate settings.

In the last part, studies go into new training and development devices. Because of the potential of new media in supporting learning processes in changing environments, the chapters in this part focus on computer-based systems like computer simulation. The importance of this book is that it provides insight in a number of key issues in the field of training and development. It helps professionals in grounding their practical decisions in theory and research, and it helps researchers in communicating about their findings. As such it serves as a bridge between theory and practice.

References

Camp, R.R., Blanchard, P.N. and Huszczo, G.E. (1986). *Toward a more organizationally effective training strategy & practice.* Englewood Cliffs: Prentice-Hall.

Gilbert, T.F. (1978). *Human Competence: Engineering Worthy Performance.* New York: McGraw-Hill.

McLagan, P.A. (1989). *Models for HRD Practice.* Alexandria: American Society for Training and Development.

Rummler, G.A. en Brache, A.P. (1992). Transforming Organizations Through Human Performance Technology. Stolovitch, H.D. and Keeps, E.J. (1992) (Eds.). *Handbook of Human Performance Technology.* San Francisco: Jossey-Bass, 32-49.

Stolovitch, H.D. and Keeps, E.J. (1992) (Eds.). *Handbook of Human Performance Technology.* San Francisco: Jossey-Bass.

Swanson, R.A. (1994). *Analysis for Improving Performance. Tools for Diagnosing Organizations and Documenting Workplace Expertise.* San Francisco: Berrett-Koehler.

PART I

Changing Environments of Training and Development

Introduction to Part I

Wim J. Nijhof

The performance of companies and of training departments are influenced by a set of contextual factors. Looking at the world economy today with its extreme dynamics between east and west, and between north and south, we see an enormous impact on the behavior of people in companies and outside of them. Migration is one of the economic factors undergoing uncertainties. Migration itself will cause effects in the demographic composition of different countries and has a substantial effect on the skill formation of a country, and also within a company. Processes of migration in Europe, for instance, lead to cultural conflicts, changes in the workforce, multilingual settings and thus communication problems.

Developments in technology, although of a quite different character, do have an impact on organizational structures and patterns of cooperation. There will be no end to the technological revolution, and what we have seen so far is a pressure on people to act more precisely, at a higher level of cognition, with good communication skills and a natural tendency towards flexibility.

The need to survive in a global market-place puts a lot of pressure on a company to do the best it can, and this means training in a permanent way at the highest level of performance. National governments, like those in France, the United Kingdom (U.K.) and Germany, have recognized the importance of well-developed and maintained training-systems. Germany is known for the dual system, ruled by regulations set up by unions, employers and states. This system fully determines the vocational track and training system within companies, such as the content of a training program, the professionalism of the trainer, and the type of testing in order to deliver certifications.

France has a regulation system which is based on a 2% investment of the net wages. Every company however is free to set up a training system. Many policies are visible which are related to the organizational pattern of the company and its needs.

The U.K. began to set up a system of national standards in the eighties. Not having a fully developed system of vocational education, the U.K. is now trying to find a way of competing with its European partners.

The small sketch of frame factors allows us to see training within a systems concept at two levels: the first one is a macro level, where national governments see training as a tool for skill formation at the national level, as a strategy for coping with strategic and competitive challenges. By means of laws and regulations, they try to influence and to mold the skills of people, and indirectly to arrange a skills economy.

The second level is the micro level of the company. This is a system too in which the conditions, the clients and the needs of the company prescribe or condition the way of handling training. Training is only effective when it creates an impact on people and organizations, when it changes performance at the individual and collective level, and when it adds value to the company.

In this first part of the book three chapters are devoted to the macro level and one to the micro level illustrating the frames of training and their consequences.

Thompson and Carter (chapter 2) portray the development of a system of national qualifications for vocational education in the United Kingdom and illustrate this competence based approach with the development of national standards for managers. This highly informative and instructive text shows the essential differences in definitions on competencies between the U.S. and U.K. approaches, procedures and promising results of this national innovation in a number of case studies (large companies). The huge operation involved in implementing national standards is a landmark of an innovation in corporate training and vocational education, because the additional setting of formal teaching and/or training is not dominant. It is not the input which is important: the demonstrated competence at a certain job level is the key criterion for measuring the effect of prior learning, experience, and training. Training systems in Europe and the U.S. can learn from, and compare their results with, the U.K. experiment.

In chapter 3 Backes-Gellner presents an economic and policy analysis of the training systems in Germany and Great Britain. In trying to find the effects of policy regulations pertaining to corporate training, she sets up a model of costs and deduces some hypotheses of which the main thesis is that *overage* costs in combination with national regulations on the vocational/training systems prove to be very effective in Germany in terms of numbers of participants, costs and presumably qualification structure. On the basis of preliminary data there is some evidence for this. However, a recent cost analysis of the whole system in Germany revealed a lowering trend in the number of contracts in the dual system. So the question is whether other factors and regulations are going to play a role now that unification has taken place. One of these could be lower wages versus higher skills. We don't yet know if this trend will increase. If it should take place then a drastic change in the dual system will return the situation to what it was before World War II.

More empirical survey research has to be done in order to understand the mechanisms of regulations, competitiveness and institutional differences.

The relationship between wages, training and skill formation is an important topic being handled nowadays. Méhaut analyzes (chapter 4) a number of case studies he carried out in France. He wanted to know whether the old Fordist model, the Taylorian concept of division of labor, could match in an optimal way the new challenges of flexibility, competitiveness, variability and customized production. What he wants to know is whether the old regulation principles, like seniority, would hinder or foster new types of training. On the basis of a model of relations between wages, mobility and organizational patterns, he discusses the main outcome of the case studies: upgrading policies directed at skill formation with high mobility on the basis of general and technical knowledge. In this sense the French case is an example of a movement towards broad conceptions of training, which can be distorted by recession or conservative policies. Méhaut makes a plea for furthering training as an organic component of a production organization striving for new productivity gains on the one hand, and new patterns for distribution and consumption on the other.

At the micro level is portrayed the function of training within a systems concept. Globalization of industries brings inevitable cross cultural combinations, as Foster and Heling conclude at the end of chapter 5. It is not only combinations that will arise, but even problems, generally communication problems. In this case study of an international company in the Netherlands, Dutch and American cultures are coming together in management and leadership styles following a period of mergers. The case study is an illustration of an Organization Development approach, mixed with consultancy and Management Development interventions, on the basis of a thorough analysis of peoples' motives, expectations and attributions, and proves to be of value for the company itself. In using objective instruments for role analysis and profile analysis of the top management of the company, a process of understanding and exchange of information was set up to lead the organization into a future of common learning, interaction and cooperation. How we should bridge the gap between cultures has not been resolved by this study. The inevitable cross-cultural combinations will force us to find workable solutions. This chapter helps us to understand the problem and shows how OD and HRD professionals are using a systemic approach for changing corporate culture.

What do we learn from the studies? In a methodological sense all studies are case studies illustrating regulations and rules at the macro and micro level. The study of Backes-Gellner is comparative in nature and shows some preliminary data on the effects of regulations with a positive effect for Germany. It would be interesting to make comparisons after the implementation of the U.K.'s national standards for vocational education. In that case two completely different but well-developed systems of training, under different regulation systems, could have different effects. Where Germany has a long standing system with a highly regarded impact, the U.K. is trying to regulate the youth in such a way that a minimum qualification prevents young people from suffering unemployment. Méhaut's study proves to be an interesting example of the development of a typology of training policies related to organizational and production patterns. We would encourage Méhaut to validate and underscore these policies with empirical data in order to get insight into the effects of policies. The study carried out in France shows a model that has yet to be tested. In principle the wage earning relations pertaining to mobility and organizational patterns will show some considerable differences between large and small companies, and possibly also within and between branches.

What we have learned from these studies too is the effect of national regulations on the workshop. The dual system in Germany regulates time, content, contract and certification. The U.K. is setting up a system of certification of training institutes, not necessarily of the trainees. But the design of the system will guarantee a qualification at five possible levels and give young people the opportunity to get a foothold in the workplace.

From the micro study we learn that training is embedded in the social context of a company and that a total quality management system is necessary to have impact at all the levels of the organization. Foster and Heling portray an Organization Development process, basically oriented to solving communication problems caused by cultural differences and mergers. Traditional training does not help, it helps only to understand partial problems, but it does not help to change the behavior patterns of people. The model they present is a valuable tool for HRD personnel together with the instruments to analyze the basic problems of the organization and the workforce.

The present most important question to be asked is whether regulations, laws, tools and models really lead to effective performance of companies and people? The macro studies show how difficult it is to predict effectiveness and to implement new systems. In all cases, however, authors have tried to find some substantial evidence of the effects of regulations and interventions.

Delivering proof of effectiveness may be the weak point of most of the studies. We should try to foster survey designs for national comparisons, to reconstruct cases and try to set up multiple case studies with replication logic, in order to test the underlying assumptions and hypotheses, and to do studies into the effects of quality management training. If we can prove the added value of those studies to governments and companies, the HRD profession will have a real impact in the near future.

2 The Development of Competence: National Standards for Managers

John E. Thompson and Stephen Carter

Management education and training in the United Kingdom (U.K.) have been characterized as "too little, too late for too few" (Handy, 1987). The pressure for change in this tradition is highlighted by the dissatisfaction with current practice in shop floor and management training, made evident by many reports in the 1980s which compared the U.K. unfavorably with more economically competitive trading nations. This pressure led to government action to implement a national system of vocational training. The lack of any comprehensive training strategy resulted in the creation of the National Council for Vocational Qualifications (NCVQ) in 1986 with an aim of promoting standards based development and training within every sphere of industry in the U.K. economy. The national standards for managers, produced in 1990, define in output terms the standards of performance expected in employment. Concerns about national standards have been in two areas: the reduction of management to an atomistic list of skills and the fallibility of functional analysis used to determine the standards. On the positive side, studies of programs based on the national standards show benefits for both the individual and the organization. Managers are reported to have found the national standards reflective of their management role, enhancing teambuilding and problem solving, improving communications and clarifying objectives. Organizations involved in the programs found that managers made better decisions, maximized staff potential and generally improved the quality of operations.

If competency based management is to improve the quality of U.K. management practice, it is necessary for the national standards to be developed to ensure that they do not simply reflect historical management practices. Government should promote support of training programs and increased research into the effectiveness of standards based education. The initial results are encouraging. If this national experiment is a proven success, it will alter the shape of management development in the U.K.

2.1 Managerial Competence

The *notion* of competence in management has become a key topic in management development in the 1980s, and is likely to remain so in the 1990s. Organizations are increasingly taking a strategic approach to human resource management and to the human resource processes which can play a key role in generating and supporting change (Iles, 1992; Ashton and Felstead, 1995). A major emphasis in this area has been the integration of individuals and organizational goals. For managers, development and training based on a common set of competences is a key method of promoting the necessary integration. The competency approach is given further impetus by the view that organizational effectiveness is in part related to the performance of the managers in the organization (Boyatsis, 1982).

Two differing approaches to competence have evolved. One model, largely developed in the U.S.A. but now widely exported through multinational companies, is based on competences defined primarily in terms of characteristics of the job holder. The second model, currently only in use in the U.K., focuses on the occupation rather than the person and produces competences which are expressed in terms of job purposes and the standards expected to be met within the job.

The U.S. model is characterized by two pieces of work: the McBer Corporation study as reported by Boyatsis, and the later work of Schroder (1989). The McBer work sets out to examine, in the American Management Association's definition of competency, the underlying characteristics of a manager, causally related to superior performance in the job. A criterion related study produced eighteen management competencies grouped into four clusters, defined as characteristics which result in superior performance. Schroder derived eleven competences from experimental simulation which had a cognitive as well as interpersonal flavor. Many companies have developed their own approaches, incorporating these models, or developed a specific list using as a start point a *universal* set, produced by consultants such as McBer or Hay.

The Training, Enterprise and Education Directorate (TEED), the government body responsible for standards development in the U.K., takes a different approach. In what is perhaps the classic understatement of the British, the TEED does not look for *superior performance* but rather competence defined as:

> "The ability to perform activities within an occupation or function to the standards expected in employment. Competence is a wide concept which embodies the ability to transfer skills and knowledge to new situations within the organizational area. It encompasses organization and planning of work, innovation and coping with non-routine activities. It includes those qualities of personal effectiveness that are required in the

workplace to deal with co-workers, management and customers." (Training Agency, 1990, 2)

Table 2.1 Main differences between the U.S.A. and U.K. competence based assessment systems (Fletcher, 1992, 22).

Criterion-referenced (U.K.)	*Criterion-validated (U.S.A.)*
Standards of performance (competences) developed and agreed by industry	Competency clusters developed by research using 'excellent' performers
Assessment of workplace performance	Learning and development of competence
Competence = expectations of employment	Competence = personal characteristics
Standards outcome-based (criterion-referenced)	Standards output-oriented (criterion-validated)
Standards of occupational competence (actual performance at work)	Educational process (competence development)
Sectorally agreed benchmark of competent performance	Specifications of 'superior' performance defined by educational research

The comparison in table 2.1 shows that the U.K. competence approach is significantly different. The standards of performance are agreed and developed by industry rather than based on individual performance. These standards determine what actual job performance should be rather than focus on the development of the competences. The outputs of the process are statements of performance, such as, "Create and maintain the necessary conditions for productive work" (MCI, 1990a) as compared to the characteristics of individuals. Examples of characteristics are accurate self-assessment, self control, stamina and adaptability (from the Human Resource Cluster (Boyatsis, 1982)).

The remainder of this chapter is divided into two sections. The first section details the background to the U.K. Occupational Standards for Managers, the process by which they have been developed, their structure, and finally the debate concerning the initiative. The second section is offered as a case study which gives details of the earliest uses of the Occupational Standards as a basis for management development using a Certificate in Management offered in-company by the Institute of Management (IM), Europe's largest membership organization for managers. Conclusions on the usefulness of the U.K. competence approach and directions for future development are given.

2.2 The Pressures for Change

Management training and development in the U.K. are undergoing a revolution. There are two major forces for change: a widespread dissatisfaction with the quantity and quality of management development, and the government's active pressure for the implementation of a national system of vocational qualifications, both of which emerged in the second half of the 1980s.

Management education in the U.K. since the 1950s is summarized well by Handy as "too little, too late for too few" (Handy, 1987, 11). Other influential research underlines the extreme poverty of U.K. practice in the training of managers. (Constable and McCormick, 1987; Coopers and Lybrand, 1986; Handy, 1987; Mangham and Silver, 1986).

Mangham and Silver point out that "over half of U.K. companies appear to make no formal provision for the training of their managers" (1986, 1). Handy (1987, 10) reports another survey which indicates that 36% of middle managers has had no management training since starting work. Constable and McCormick's report "The Making of British Managers", concentrated on the policy and procedures for management education and training in the U.K. They concluded that although there was a willingness to consider new approaches, U.K. managers lacked the opportunities provided for their overseas competitors. The average U.K. manager received only about one day's formal training per annum and the majority received none. Handy examined management education training and development in the U.S.A., West Germany, France, Japan and the U.K. He found that management groups overseas were more likely to have been educated to a higher level, and more likely to have taken part in systematic and formal training and development processes. Handy's observation was that compared to the other countries, established traditions of management training and development, the U.K. system is badly organized. A key element in his suggested solution was that leading organizations should act as role models of good practice.

This recommendation led to the creation of the Management Charter Initiative (MCI) in 1988 which, by 1992, has brought together 240 companies representing over 25% of the U.K. work force. MCI produced a three part program which aimed for chartered status for managers (under a Royal Charter); the foundation of a mass movement committed to a code of practice providing the development and application of high standards of modern management practice; and the development of a widely recognized system of professional management qualifications as a source of motivation to individuals undergoing continuous management development.

A parallel movement has been the creation of vocational education and training systems with an emphasis on occupational standards. During the 1980s many reports in the U.K. outlined demographic changes, and a "skills gap" which contributed to a lack of economic competitiveness compared to other European countries. For example, Steedman and Wagner (1987) in a study of matched manufacturing plants in the U.K. and West Germany, show that only 10% of the British workforce held any kind of vocational qualification against 90% of the West German workforce which had passed through a three year period of craft training. This imbalance had been noted much earlier and had resulted in the Manpower Services Commission's (MSC) White Paper A New Training Initiative: An Agenda for Action (MSC, 1981) which highlighted two critical components, a comprehensive training strategy and standards of a new kind. The development of these standards was to be the result of a partnership between the providers of education and its users, mainly seen as employers. (This partnership was in itself an innovation.) There were some attempts to develop standards in the early years of the decade, but a major re-emphasis came with the Review of Vocational Qualifications (MSC, 1986) which described a system in which there was no clear, readily understandable patterns of provision and that there was limited take-up of vocational qualifications. The National Council for Vocational Qualifications (NCVQ) was formed in October 1986 to create the framework. The success of NCVQ is that it met a target to have National Vocational Qualifications (NVQs) in place for 80% of the workforce by the end of 1992. NVQs have become part of the National Targets adopted by the National Training Task Force, which see 50% of the workforce aiming for NVQs by 1996 and 50% to have attained NVQs at level III or equivalent by 2000 (CBI, 1989). Considerable progress has been made. 38% of the workforce by 1994 possessed NVQ III or equivalent (Employment Department, 1994). The NVQs are awarded at five levels, with management and other professional and similar roles occupying levels four and five.

The keystone to National Vocational Qualifications is effective assessment (Hager, Gonzi and Athanasov, 1994; Pedreschi, Connor, Thackray and Wolstencroft, 1994). Competence and hence the award of a qualification is based on demonstration through evidence that an individual has met all the standards. Importantly, therefore, NCVQ do not prescribe specific programs of instruction and indeed encourage a variety of approaches that will allow individuals to do only the amount of study and development they actually need to demonstrate competence. Implicit in this approach is the encouragement for the accreditation of prior learning. Where someone can already demonstrate a level of competence, no further study or development is required, even to the point where they can achieve the complete qualification purely on the basis of the submission of current evidence derived from work activity.

The government actively promotes NVQ based training (Command 2563, 1994). Tax relief has been made available on training towards NVQs but not for other qualifications. This is the first time that educational programs have so qualified in the U.K. Government funding for company training is now commonly given only for programs which lead to the award of an

NVQ. These two forces have created a demand for management training which is based on the award of NVQs.

2.3 The Development of the Standards

There are two main elements which have been adopted for the development of all the standards for NVQs: functional analysis and the job competence model. Standards are produced by lead bodies which are collaborative groups consisting of employers and experts in the area. The development of the management standards began in October 1988 and finished in July 1990 and the work was completed by seven project teams and two sets of consultants. The model was tested in the field on hundreds of managers (MCI, 1990a).

Functional analysis is the process of identifying the functions which an individual carries out which lead to organizational effectiveness (Training Agency, 1990). The functions are broken down with sufficient detail to be used as standards. The key features in this process are a focus on work roles rather than a series of tasks and on outcomes rather than input processes and methods. The process is as follows:

- Describe the key purpose of the occupational area.
- Ask what needs to happen for this to be achieved.
- Repeat the process until the functions being identified are at unit level.
- Repeat the process for each unit until the functions are at element level.

Unit level is reached when the functions are carried out in their entirety by an individual rather than by a team, and the range of units facilitates recognition of differences in the functions performed by groups of individuals in similar jobs or occupations. Element level is reached when performance criteria can be written for the function, describing adequately the performance required of an individual. Each element has associated performance criteria and range indicators. The elements and performance criteria should be stated with sufficient precision to allow unambiguous interpretation by different users and not be so detailed that they only relate to a specific job or task, employer or organization, location or equipment.

The standards are then checked for completeness using the Job Competence Model (Mansfield and Matthews, 1985), which views competence definition in terms of four components:

- task skills – for the performance of relevant tasks;
- task management skills – for management of the groups of tasks to achieve the overall job functions;
- contingency management skills – for responding to breakdowns in routines, procedures and sequences;
- job/role environment skills – for responding to general aspects of the work role and the environment.

The resultant standard states in output terms what is expected from an individual performing a particular occupational role. They do not look at the underlying abilities or traits of the individual.

The U.K. standards do make some recognition of the contribution to performance of the qualities and attributes of managers themselves. The Personal Competence Model (MCI, 1990b) was published simultaneously with the Standards. The model identifies four clusters of personal competence: planning to achieve the optimization of results; managing others to optimize results; managing oneself to optimize results; and, using intellect to optimize results. These are not assessed in the U.K. competence based approach, and do not have statements of performance but are assumed to exist if the output standards are met.

It should be noted that functional analysis as developed by the Training Agency, is different from functional job analysis (Fine, Holt and Hutchinson, 1974), which is a method of categorizing a large number of occupations using a limited number of key worker functions.

2.4 The Occupational Standards for Managers

The Occupational Standards for Managers at entry level M1, and at middle management level M2, have four key roles: Manage Operations, Manage People, Manage Information, and Manage Finance (MCI, 1990a). The roles are broken into units and elements, as shown in table 2.2.

Table 2.2 Dimensions of occupational standards for managers (MCI, 1990a).

Level	*Units of Competence*	*Elements of Competence*	*Performance Criteria*	*Range Indicators*
Entry (M1)	9	26	183	126
Middle (M2)	10	36	240	166

As an example at level M1, within the key role – Manage Operations – there are two units and four elements as shown in table 2.3.

Table 2.3 Breakdown of key role - manage operations into units and elements (MCI, 1990a).

Units	*Elements*
I.1 Maintain and improve service and product operations	1.1 Maintain operations to meet quality standards
	1.2 Create and maintain the necessary conditions for productive work
I.2 Contribute to the implementation of change in services, products and systems	2.1 Contribute to the evaluation of proposed changes to services, products and systems
	2.2 Implement and evaluate changes to services, products and systems.

There is not an even spread of units and elements between the four key roles. Manage People has four units and fifteen elements, with Manage Finance, one and two, and Manage Information two and five, respectively. The spread reflects the emphasis on managing people at this level and also the greater differentiation of managing people which functional analysis reveals.

The elements are described by performance criteria which vary in number from 10 to 3, with a related variation in range indicators. An example of one unit with performance criteria and related units is shown in table 2.4.

2.5 Concerns about the Standards

The task of establishing national standards is a large undertaking and it is not surprising that there have been many criticisms of the approach. Burgoyne (1989a, 2) raises eight issues of which he believes point to the "inappropriateness of the universal, mechanistic, differentiated list of managerial competences." His solution is to move to a method of measurement based on a managerial portfolio (like an artist's or creative designer's portfolio). His commentary has often been heralded as a damning criticism of the approach, but in another contribution Burgoyne (1989b) states that he is a fan and supporter of the competence approach which he views as very useful – but also that he is a critic and that the approach is not a cure all. Finn (1994) echoes these concerns and is particularly concerned that the standards are threshold measures which do not recognize continuous development.

Silver (1991) echoes many of Burgoyne's criticisms, emphasizing that management is a holistic activity and must not degenerate into skills training. The use of the job competence model in standards development should alleviate this concern with the model's emphasis on contingency management skills. Silver highlights three other significant concerns: Constable and McCormick's (1987) report which identifies a shortage of qualified training providers to implement any initiative, the loss of the essence of management, and the structure and process which makes management happen. This is described elegantly by Pye (1991, 101) as "The Flower in the Mirror and the Moon on the Water, that which can be seen but cannot be grasped." The final concern is the danger of organizational rigidity, that the defined competences do not change as necessary across organizations and over time.

Table 2.4 – Element 2.1 – with performance criteria and range indicators (MCI, 1990).

Performance Criteria	*Range Indicators*
(a) Feedback from subordinates, customers and users is assessed and passed on together with a reasoned evaluation to the appropriate people. (b) Proposals for improvements are passed to the appropriate people with minimum delay. (c) The advantages and disadvantages of introducing changes are assessed against current operational standards and the information forwarded to the appropriate people.	Proposed changes are received from, and information fed back to: • immediate line manager • specialists • subordinates Feedback is gathered: • informally • formally Proposed changes involve: • personnel requirements/team composition • employment/work practices • nature and availability of services and products • quality of services and products • methods to reduce waste • new equipment/technology • work methods Change may have an impact on: • profitability • productivity • quality of service/product • working conditions

Holmes (1992) raises concern that functional analysis is not sufficiently robust to understand and analyze professional competence. His major concern is that the functional analysis fails to provide guidance on how we can infer competence which is concerned with anticipated future performance by observation of past performance. This is especially difficult as the nature of professional work is distinguished by its reference to a framework of fundamental concepts linked with experience rather than by impromptu reaction to events. Other recent reports on the standards have reflected these concerns. Glasgow Business School (Paton, Boddy and MacDonald, 1993; Watson, 1994) feels that the generic approach did not suit all organizations, and the Glasgow Business School report states that MCI standards seemed better suited to measuring competences at the lower levels which include M1 for entry level managers. A Roffey Park Management Institute survey (Lewis, 1992) found that while over 73% of the 267 organizations surveyed used a competence approach, only 10% followed MCI guidelines. One explanation for this disparity is that the larger organizations surveyed had already utilized competence frameworks based on the McBer and derivative competence approach, and as there is a natural reluctance to disregard this investment even though the emphasis of the two competence approaches is different, as shown in table 2.1.

These are legitimate concerns which reflect on the current use of the standards as a basis for management development. On the positive side, the Roffey Park Report shows that 10% of the organizations surveyed had taken on board a complex system of standards within two years of their publication, and another 15% used the standards in conjunction with another source. More persuasive is the view of the managers who have undertaken the programs. The Glasgow Business School study showed positive results with the emphasis on skills and decision implementation with the practical requirements of the management level M1. In-depth studies (Evans and Kerrison, 1994; Janes and Burgess, 1992) across public and private industries show that practicing managers find the standards robust, and cross differing roles easily. They are easy to understand, and their use helps to promote better practice in management through the clarification of personal expectations.

These findings are reflected in a project involving all providers of MCI standards-based programs in the U.K. with the objective of providing guidance to higher education providers on the integration of competence objectives into academic awards (Thompson and Stephenson, 1992). The research design consisted of workshops and discussions with the large majority of institutions in the U.K. who are engaged in competence training. The findings were generally supportive of the standards approach as a sound educational experience. In respect of the standards "there is little fundamental critique of the standards of competence" (op cit, 12). It was accepted, though, that the standards were a good starting point but as they were barely two years old, it was necessary to continue with their development.

The concerns about the standards are generally raised by trainers rather than managers. The reports above indicate that managers understand and value the standards in their *own* work role. One explanation of the trainer apprehension is that the trainer attempts to develop a general theory of implementation where, because of the complexity of the job role, there is no readily accessible template.

The remainder of this chapter discusses the design consideration of the IM Certificate in Management from the viewpoint of the accrediting body, employer and learner. The design of the program is described and research findings are presented on company and individual views of the program.

2.6 The Design Considerations for the Certificate

In designing an award bearing program suitable for delivery *in-company*, IM was mindful of the needs of a number of stakeholders, the NVQ system, the employer, and the employee/learner.

2.6.1 The Needs of NCVQ

The NCVQ gives criteria which a program must meet to qualify for the award of an NVQ. These criteria reflect the concern about the provision of conventional education as discussed above. The criteria are that any program must be:

- based on national standards required for performance in employment, and take proper account of future needs with particular regard to technology, markets and employment patterns;
- based on assessments of the outcomes of learning, arrived at independently of any particular mode, duration or location of learning;
- awarded on the basis of valid and reliable assessments made in such a way as to ensure that performance to the national standard can be achieved at work;
- free from barriers which restrict access and progression, and available to all those who are able to reach the required standard by whatever means;
- free from overt or covert discriminatory practices with regard to gender, age, race or creed and designed to pay due regard to the special needs of individuals. (NCVQ, 1991, 1).

The main implication for any competence based program is freedom from barriers, which means that proposed qualifications which have a tightly defined course of study, with set time commitment and a particular place of study, are unlikely to qualify for the award of an NVQ.

2.6.2 Needs of Employer

This is an area traditionally least well addressed by providers. Employers have long held suspicions of management development programs whose content and timetable have been primarily designed to meet the needs of the provider with some acknowledgement of those of the learner, and with those of the sponsoring organization. Market research by the IM identified a number of key issues that a program should address:

- A program should be flexible enough to recognize that a manager's work is not regular and that such traditional features as regular weekly attendance on part-time courses run counter to commercial reality.
- The less a program has integrated the goals, culture and specific needs of an organization, the less relevant it is to that organization.
- Organizations are interested in their managers improving their performance, not in gaining theoretical knowledge which does not lead to such improvement.
- As with all investments, organizations require the greatest degree of control.

2.6.3 Needs of Employee

Many of the needs of the employee/learner are reflected in the requirements of NCVQ, but it was a central tenet of IM design philosophy that in order for transfer of learning to occur between any materials or tuition provided on the one hand and performance in the workplace on the other hand, the employee should recognize a high degree of congruence between the content, context and processes described in the learning materials and his/her work role. This clearly echoes the idea of "high reality design" suggested by Stuart and Binsted (1981) who view reality in the learning experience as a subjective property conferred on a learning event, whose source of reference is the sum total of his/her past, present and conceived future work experience. The greater the degree of congruence between the two, the greater the degree of transfer. This is of crucial importance in a program designed to improve performance in the workplace.

2.7 Program Design

The IM Certificate in Management is modular. Each module consists of three elements: self-study material, one or two day workshops, and subsequent work-based activity. The self-study material is designed to provide the underpinning knowledge required to develop competence in a particular functional area of the standards. It is also designed to place this knowledge and understanding within the framework of the learner's organization. The major advantage of self-study materials is that they allow the learning to take place at a time that suits the learner rather than the provider. The workshops are not designed as further information inputs, but as a means of providing developmental experiences for learners in the competences they are wishing to develop. They also enhance and maintain learner motivation, a problem with pure distance learning programs. The development of the competences is undertaken through agreed activities in the workplace.

The IM Certificate addresses the design needs identified above in the following ways:

- The timing of the modules is decided by the organization.
- The first and second elements of each module can be customized to meet specific organizational requirements. The third element is as far as possible directly related to a particular manager's job and decided by that manager and his/her employer.
- The timing and place of the workshops are decided by the organization. Moreover the tutors on these workshops can be drawn from the organization and trained by IM. These tutors will have a far greater understanding of how the standards and the program as a whole will integrate into the organization.
- The program is output assessed. Managers gain credit on a module by module basis towards the final award, through the submission of portfolios of evidence. These are demonstrations – arising out of the work based activity – of a manager's competence directly related to the standards. Where a manager can already prove existing competence in a functional area, he/she can submit a portfolio without undertaking a period of study.
- Assessment is developmental. Managers can submit evidence at any time. Those deemed *not yet competent* receive counseling and advice and the opportunity for further developmental activities followed by re-submission of evidence.
- The efficient integration of the learning into the workplace is the responsibility of an in-company *mentor* trained by IM.
- The transfer of the ownership of learning from the provider to the employer is usually a progressive one. Initially each organization requires a greater or lesser degree of support from IM, but over time, each takes more and more control as their confidence and internal structures develop. The goal is for IM to provide the means and quality control systems for an organization eventually to run a program that meets both the new national standards and their own specific management development needs.

2.8 The Effect of the Program: an Organization's View

Five large national companies and public sector bodies were contacted with four replies. They represented 100% of the organizations which had started the Certificate Program in 1991 as an in-company program. Employee numbers ranged from 4,000 in a printing and publishing company to 16,000 in a food retailing organization. The number of managers ranged from 500 to 5,000. Two are in local government and one in tele-communications.

The organizations were asked questions based on the five key areas from MCI's Principles for Management Development (MCI, 1988). These principles are those which organizations, on joining the Charter Movement, must grasp, and they are designed to incorporate *best practice* in management training. The Certificate Program should meet the requirements of this best practice. All companies were in the initial stages of their first Certificate program. A structured questionnaire was followed up by telephone contact, and in three cases by personal interview. The findings are case studies from large organizations' initial foray into competence learning.

Open Access – the removal of any unnecessary barriers which prevent managers embarking on learning programs and ensuring that practicing or experienced managers have access to assessment for MCI endorsed awards.

The introduction of certificated in-house programs is new to all the organizations and would be expected to have an attraction to all managers. In the publishing company 10% of the total population of managers (in a typically *hands on* organization) requested the program which is encouraging for the management development specialists. In another, it was a positive feature that the ordinary people, other than the targeted high fliers, could now get on the management development ladder. The other organizations operate a superior nomination system. In all cases those attracted were experienced managers who were already successful in the organization.

Corporate and Individual Development – requires that a coherent framework for individual development is provided within the context of the organizational goals.

In all cases, attendance on the Certificate has forced the organization to consider how individual and group goals interact. In one organization with highly differentiated skills there was a clear need to provide potential replacements to fill a potential *void* if a manager left. Interestingly, one participant now had the confidence to apply for a management position across the specialist boundaries. In the local government organization the Certificate was seen as a main vehicle for the move from a well-administered bureaucracy to a well-led organization which achieves results. In all cases, there was a view that the program would break down internal communication barriers.

Flexibility and Innovation in Delivery – to ensure choice in the approaches to learning and to make effective use of the workplace for developing managers.

The flexibility is given by the use of distance learning packs for the majority of delivery. In all cases this has caused difficulties. In the retailing organization with a sixty hour week workload, managers see themselves as having no time to direct their own learning and have become frustrated. The material is seen as too *onerous*, and one organization has added in eight additional one day *lecturing* sessions to deliver the theory content.

All organizational concerns focus on the level of knowledge input – perhaps a reflection on past experience of input dominated management education. Clearly there is a need to provide not only the opportunity of managing your own learning, but also to provide time in which to do it.

A Competence Approach – requires assessment of effective performance at work with evidence of the necessary underpinning knowledge and understanding to ensure that managers have transferable competencies and are capable of working in a variety of situations. Individuals will need to demonstrate that they have met the appropriate national standards for managers and supervisors established by the MCI.

The key finding is that the standards have a validity to the organizations and the managers. They are understood as an accurate description of the current management role and as examples of desired behavior. There are no perceived barriers to demonstration of competences within the workplace.

The demonstration of competence in the key roles has been viewed as effective management behavior within the organization. One concern was that the newly demonstrated competence was not shared by peer managers and the individual was in the difficult position of the *missionary*.

Where organizations view management responsibility as less than those in the standards, it is being challenged by participant managers. Organizations find it uncomfortable when managers ask "Why do I not have responsibility for recruiting my staff?" or "Why do I not have full responsibility for my budget?"

Credit Accumulation – through the proposed structure which enables assessment, element by element, at a time suited to the needs of the individual and independent of the methods of learning.

All organizations found it met their needs that their managers could *drop in and out* of the program and still be able to move towards an external recognition of their accomplishment. This opportunity never to have to throw any benefit away was seen as important.

2.9 The Effect of the Program: Participant's View

Fifty students who completed the program were debriefed using a semi-structured questionnaire and were asked to identify benefits to themselves and their organizations. Their view indicated that the program produces competent managers who:

- deal more effectively with uncertainty;
- maximize the potential of their staff;
- make better decisions;
- improve the quality of their operations;
- save money/ create wealth .

When asked what impact the program had as an in-company program, the participants stated that it produced a climate which:

- enhances teambuilding;
- creates sharing of problems;
- improves communication;
- clarifies objectives;
- enhances cross functional awareness.

2.10 Conclusions

The introduction of competence based education, based on national standards, is very much in its infancy. This chapter has reported on one of the first programs to incorporate the standards. Evaluation of the benefits of any training intervention is notoriously difficult, and to assess the benefits at a national level, even more so. It is (and will be) difficult to distinguish the beneficial effects which accrue from the delivery of the IM, or any program and those which accrue from the standards. Evaluation is further complicated on the Certificate Program in that there is considerable freedom on the modes and methods of input whilst the outputs and methods of assessment are specified quite explicitly. It is encouraging that at an individual level, participants found the standards reflective of their management role, and the development processes for standard achievement useful.

It is at the organizational level that the success of the standards approach is more easily judged. If organizations adopt the standards, it can be assumed that they contribute to successful development of the managers for the 1990s and beyond. In general NVQs at levels 1-5 have proved their worth to employers and individuals (CBI, 1994). Evidence on the management standards is limited. Many organizations which adopt standard-based programs have had, as reflects the dearth of management development in the U.K., no development. Competence based programs are filling a vacuum. Other organizations claim that the standards do not meet their particular needs (for example, Bognanno, 1991; Lee 1991). Yet these views often come from organizations which have invested much time and effort on the development of their own standards, which process has naturally produced a level of ownership and custom which they do not wish to negate. A positive note is that the original five organizations involved in the research increased to 30 by 1992, and the number of participants increased from 90 to over 1000. Current experience confirms that standards-based programs do produce measurable results as discussed above and organizations who use these programs remained committed to this approach. More positive is that the number of providers of competence training based on the MCI standards at the end of 1992 was 297, reflecting the potential demand.

Evaluation is further complicated by debate over the derivations of the standards. There was an enormous effort to produce the initial standards in 1989. It is critical that those standards are not accepted as fixed and that further work continues to validate and refine them. Standards based on the past will fix or reinforce current or historical practice. This will not reflect well the current view of managers, especially at a senior level, as "riding the waves of change" (Morgan, 1988), or as a manager of "chaos" (Peters, 1987). There is a very real danger that "inward looking competence approaches will produce managers unable to open their minds to new markets, ideas and techniques" (Paton, Boddy and MacDonald, 1993).

The Northern Regional Management Centre (Thompson and Stephenson, 1992) report describes those who promote competence based development as "pioneers." If the pioneers are to succeed and prosper, those involved have indicated that awareness of standards must be promoted, development of programs should have greater support, funds should be switched from traditional input based courses to competence courses (at least on an experimental basis), and that there is far greater evidence of the credibility of the competence approach. The initial results of this approach are good. It is a national experiment which will alter dramatically the shape of management development in the U.K. and other countries if it is shown to be a success.

References

Ashton, D. and Felstead, A. (1995). Training and Development. Storey, J. (Ed.) *Human Resource Management: A Critical Text.* London: Routledge.

Bognanno, M. (1991). *Facilitating Cultural Change by Identifying the New Competences Required.* Paper presented at I.R.R. Conference on Effective Strategies for Defining and Applying Competences in London.

Boyatsis, R.E. (1982). *The Competent Manager: A Model for Effective Performance.* New York: John Wiley.

Burgoyne, J. (1989a). Opinion, *Transition.* Year not applicable, issue not applicable, 2-3.

Burgoyne, J. (1989b). *The Concept of Management Competencies,* Paper presented "What is Management Competence?" in London. British Psychological Society - Occupational Psychology Section Conference.

CBI (1989). *Towards a Skills Revolution - Report of the Vocational Education and Training Task Force*. London: Confederation of British Industry.

CBI (1994). *Quality Assessed: The CBI Review of NVQs and SVQs*. London: Confederation of British Industry.

Command 2563 (1994). *Competitiveness: Helping Business to win*. London: HMSO.

Constable, J. and McCormick, R. (1987). *The Making of British Managers, A Report for the BIM and CBI into Management Training, Education, and Development*. London: British Institute of Management and Confederation of British Industry.

Coopers and Lybrand (1986). *A Challenge to Complacency: Changing Attitudes to Training*. London: National Economic Development Office and Manpower Services Commission.

Employment Department (1994). *National Advisory Council for Education and Training Targets*. Report on Progress. Sheffield: Employment Department.

Evans, K. and Kerrison, S. (1994). *MCI Personal Competence Model: Uses and Implementation*. Technical Report No. 24. Sheffield: Employment Department.

Fine, S.A., Holt, M., and Hutchinson, M. (1974). *Functional Job Analysis - How to Standardize Task Statements*, Michigan: W.E. Upjohn Institute for Employment Research.

Finn, F. (1994). *A synthesis of current research on Management*. Working Paper. Henly: The Management College.

Fletcher, S. (1992). *Competence Based Assessment Techniques*. London: Kogan Page.

Hager, P., Gonzi, A. and Athanasov, J. (1994). General Issues about Assessment of Competence. *Assesment and Evaluation in Higher Education, 19,* 1, 3-16.

Handy, C. (1987). *The Making of Managers*. London: National Economic Development Office.

Holmes, L. (1992). Taking the Load on Professional Standards. *Personnel Management,* November, 35-38.

Iles, P. (1992). Centres of Excellence? Assessment and Development Centres, Management Competence, and Human Resource Strategies. *British Journal of Management, 3,* 2, 79-90.

Janes, J. and Burgess, C. (1992). *Applying the Management Standards within Organizations*. Sheffield: Employment Department.

Lee, J. (1991). *The Competency Approach in I.C.I. - 6 Years On and Still Learning*. Paper presented at the I.R.R. Conference, Effective Strategies for Defining and Applying Competences, London.

Lewis, A. (1992). *Use of Competence in Organizations*. West Sussex, England: Roffey Park Management Institute.

Mangham, I.L. and Silver, M.S. (1986). *Management Training: Context and Practice*. London: Economic Social and Research Council/Department of Trade and Industry.

Mansfield, B. and Matthews, D. (1985). *Job Competence - A Description for Use in Vocational Education and Training*. Bristol: Further Education Staff College.

MC (1988). *The Management Charter Code of Practice*. London: Management Charter Initiative.

MCI (1990a). *Management Competences: The Standards Project - Final Report*. London: Management Charter Initiative.

MCI (1990b). *Personal Competence Project: Summary Report*. London: Management Charter Initiative.

Morgan, G. (1988). *Riding the Waves of Change: Developing Managerial Competencies for a Turbulent World*. San Francisco: Jossey-Bass.

MSC (1986). *Review of Vocational Qualifications in England and Wales*. London: HMSO.

MSC (1981). *A New Training Initiative: Agenda for Action*. London : Her Majesty's Stationery Office.

National Council for Vocational Qualification (1991). *Criteria for National Vocational Qualification.* London: NCVQ.

Paton, R.A., Boddy, D. and MacDonald, S. (1992). Crediting Management Competence: Right or Wrong? *Management Development Review* (April). Mentor Management Digest, Vol. 1, 8-20.

Pedreschi, T., Connor, J., Thackray, D. and Wolstencroft, E. (1994). *Effective Practice in Assessment against the Management Standards.* Sheffield: Employment Department.

Peters, T. (1987). *Thriving on Chaos: A Handbook for the Management Revolution.* London: McMillan.

Pye, A. (1991). Management Competence: The Flower in the Mirror and the Moon on the Water. Silver, M.S (Ed.) *Competent to Manage: Approaches to Management Training and Development.* London: Routledge, 101-117.

Schroder, M. (1989). *Managerial Competence: The Key to Excellence.* Dubuque: Kendall and Hunt.

Silver, M.S. (1991) (Ed.). *Competent to Manage: Approaches to Management Training and Development.* London: Routledge.

Steedman, H. and Wagner, K. (1987). A Second Look at Productivity, Machinery and Skills in Britain and Germany. *National Institute Economic Review* (November), Issue 122, pp. 84-96.

Stuart, R. and Binsted, D. (1981). The Transfer of Learning. Nixon, B. (Ed.) *New Approaches to Management Development.* London: Gower, 70-111.

Thompson, D. and Stephenson, M. (1992). *Management Standards in Further Education/Higher Education Programs: Interim Report.* Washington, England: Northern Regional Management Centre.

Training Agency (1990). *Development of Assessable Standards for National Certification (Guidance Note 2).* Sheffield: Training Agency.

Watson, T. (1994). *In Search of Competence: Culture, Chaos and Control in Managerial Work.* London: Routledge

3 The Role of Regulations in Corporate Training Strategies

Uschi Backes-Gellner

Comparing the qualification strategies of companies in industrialized countries, one can observe systematic national differences: otherwise comparable companies (as to similar size and industry) show differences in the amount of internal and external training, the specificity of training, the length of training units and the target groups of training efforts (Marsden, 1986; Maurice, Sellier and Silvestre, 1986). Additionally, workforce qualification differences vary with the systematic differences in companies' personnel policies.

The aim of this chapter is to analyze whether and how these systematic differences in corporate decisions among countries are influenced by legal regulations of vocational education and other labor market institutions. Therefore the likelihood of realizing active, far-sighted corporate training strategies is the focus of the study. In an environment where changes constantly accelerate[1] the adaptation potential or the innovation rate of a company depend heavily on the availability of excess qualifications that can be quickly drawn from in the case of changing production demands (cf. Mulder, Romiszowski and Van der Sijde, 1990; Piore and Sabel, 1984; Reich, 1983; Sorge, 1990; Stern, 1990). The major question to answer is, under what circumstances are excess qualifications more or less likely to occur? To model this company decision an analogy is used to inventory decisions (here an inventory of excess qualifications), in which external regulations determine the cost of providing and holding excess qualifications as well as the shortage costs in cases of acute under-supply.

To explain the differences in companies' investment in training, and not in state or private vocational school education, two countries with similar structures in their systems of vocational education and training will be selected: Great Britain and Germany. In both countries state and private vocational school education is only a minor phenomenon. In both countries the burden of providing vocational qualifications rests mainly on the shoulders of the companies themselves (Marsden and Ryan, 1991, 251; Training in Britain 1989, 69).

Firstly, an economic model for the companies' decision on the amount of training to be undertaken is designed. This model is used to derive the relevant determinants of the institutional framework. The second step is to compare the vocational education systems of Germany and Great Britain and to derive a hypothesis about the expected qualification structure in companies in the two countries. In the third section of the chapter some preliminary empirical evidence is delivered. Some conclusions for corporate and national vocational education are formulated at the end.

3.1 The Company's Decision to Train

Generally a company has a wide spectrum of possible qualification strategies. At one end a company can follow an active qualification strategy, meaning that people are trained today for a possible need in the future. A qualification stock is built in the hope that it guarantees more flexibility for future decisions. At the other end a company can follow a reactive strategy, that is, people are trained if and only if there is an acute need for additional qualifications. In cases of technological innovation or varying needs on the product market the company reacts and looks for incremental solutions to the problem. Between these two poles there is a whole spectrum of different qualification strategies.

To illustrate this decision an analogy is used between an inventory of products and an inventory of qualifications. In both cases companies try to handle an uncertain future and look for a cost optimal strategy.

3.1.1 The Model

The basic idea of all kinds of inventory models is that the stock depends on two cost components. Firstly, there are costs if the firm keeps too many products or qualifications in stock. They are called overage costs (C_o). Secondly, there are costs if the demand for products or qualifications is higher than stock. They are called underage costs (C_u). Overage costs grow and underage costs decrease with an increasing stock. Thus there will be one optimal inventory level that minimizes the sum of the costs[2].

A formalization leads to the following condition for the optimal inventory level[3]:

$$\phi(Y_o) = \frac{c_u}{c_o + c_u}$$

3.1.2 Application

Overage costs: The analogy

Vegetables can spoil if they are stored for too long; qualifications can become obsolete or may be forgotten in time, if not used. Products may be stolen from a stock; qualifications or qualified workers may be poached from labor market competitors. Products in stock need upkeep and maintenance, qualifications may need updating and sometimes must be paid for, even if they are not used. Finally, products as well as qualifications in stock cause opportunity costs, because the capital cannot be invested elsewhere.

Thus, overage costs are in general: 1. costs of obsolescence; 2. poaching costs; 3. holding costs; and 4. opportunity costs. To reveal the influence of national institutions on the company's overage costs, one has to find out and analyze which kind of institutional regulation influences one of the four cost components.

Costs of obsolescence

The costs of obsolescence mainly depend on the actuality of qualifications and their orientation towards future needs. This is determined by the content, particularly by the curriculum of a training measure. The risk of obsolescence is also dependent on whether or not the workers are able to use their qualifications in the workplace (cf. Thurley and Ling Lam, 1990).

The question of whether a qualification measure guarantees an orientation towards future needs depends largely on how and where its content is decided upon. If the content of a training measure is a result of the everyday requirements of a workplace, the qualification is not likely to be oriented towards the future. If on the other hand the content of a training measure is developed for example, in close connection with the R&D department of a company or even specialized institutions considering relevant research in setting up a curriculum, it is more likely that the qualification will be valuable for a longer time span.

The possibilities of using new qualifications in the workplace mainly depend on job demarcation rules. If jobs are classified very narrowly it is likely that broad qualifications cannot be used in everyday work. If jobs are classified according to qualifications, it is very likely that there will be possibilities to use new qualifications.

Thus, to analyze systematic differences in the costs of obsolescence for German companies in comparison with British companies one has firstly to study institutional rules that determine training curricula and secondly institutions that regulate job demarcations.

Poaching costs

The poaching costs depend on how labor market competitors train their workforces. This depends largely on whether there are efficient institutional regulations to ensure an overall high level of training of companies in a common labor market. Assuming that future oriented skills are very likely to be marketable, one has to expect a significant poaching risk in a non-regulated situation (as human capital theory has shown extensively). If on the other hand there are institutions that ensure an almost equal amount of investment in training and at the same time guarantee a common quality standard of training, the poaching risk and thereby poaching costs may be kept at a minimum[4].

Thus, to reveal systematic differences in poaching costs one has to analyze institutions that regulate the quantity and the quality of companies' investment in training.

Holding costs

The holding costs are determined by the dominating criteria in employees' pay schedules. If qualifications (even if not used in the production process) are a major criterion for the wage level this immediately leads to high holding costs. If on the other hand only those qualifications that are used in the production process are paid for, holding costs are kept at a minimum.

Thus, to answer the question of whether there are systematic differences in holding costs between British and German companies one has to study collective agreements or other regulations of pay schedules for qualified workers.

Opportunity costs

The opportunity costs depend on the interest rate and the cost of training an employee. As regards interest rates one can assume international interest parity and concentrate on training costs in the following. An important part of the training costs is the wages paid to trainees. Depending on special regulations for trainees pay, training costs can be almost negligible, or significantly high.

Thus, to discover systematic differences in opportunity costs one has to study collective agreements or state regulations of trainees pay.

Underage costs: The analogy

If a stock is too low and products cannot be delivered in time, companies may have to pay conventional penalties; if there are insufficient adequately qualified employees, new technologies cannot be used efficiently from the beginning and/or one can expect a higher rate of rejects or a below average flexibility of production. If demands for products cannot be satisfied, customers may go to competitors and the company loses goodwill; if new technologies cannot be used efficiently, or cause quality problems at the beginning, one can also expect a loss of customers and goodwill.

To solve delivery shortages a company can buy products externally at a higher price; to solve qualification shortages a company can *buy* (poach) qualified workers on the external labor market and pay them higher wages.

Underage costs are thus costs of inefficiency and delaying costs. To simplify the analysis one may assume that because of internationalization and globalized markets there are no significant differences in product market reactions in the countries analyzed: customers and clients behave similarly in Great Britain and Germany (delaying costs). In the same way, one can assume that there are no significant differences in technology induced efficiency losses where a less well qualified workforce (costs of inefficiency) is concerned. Thus, the costs of being short of qualifications should be very similar for German and British companies. Therefore a concentration on overage cost differences in the institutional analysis is adequate.

3.2 Vocational Educational and Training in Great Britain and Germany

3.2.1 Institutions Regulating Vocational Education and Training

As already explained in the introduction vocational education and training is mainly the task of the companies themselves. Vocational education in Germany is dominated by the so-called *dual education* system, which consists of training in a company plus part-time vocational education at a public vocational school. Apprenticeships in the dual system are strongly regulated by a whole set of institutional regulations and rules.

The most important part of this set is the Vocational Training Act of 1969 (Berufsbildungsgesetz BBiG). It regulates the content as well as the examination procedures in 377 recognized occupations (BIBB 1991, 173). Its objective is to orientate the contents and requirements of vocational training to future mobility and the acquisition of professional experience, skills and knowledge which are necessary for a qualified occupational activity (§1 BBiG). The title of the occupation, the period of training, the contents and timetables of the courses (*Ausbildungsrahmenplan*, which means, curricular framework), and the requirements for examinations are determined by federal training directives (*Ausbildungsordnungen*). The aim is to ensure ordered and uniform vocational training (Haase, Richard and Wagner, 1979, 105). During the vocational training, the apprentice must attend a part-time vocational school and the employer must exempt the apprentice from work to attend the school. Planning, implementation and further development of vocational training are carried out in cooperation with employers' associations, trade unions and federal institutions. The craft chambers and the chambers of commerce and industry counsel and control vocational training (§§44, 45 BBiG); they register training contracts and they conduct mid-course and final examinations. The chambers are public institutions, in which membership of the companies is compulsory.

The chambers as well as industry and employers' associations insist on a broad supply of apprenticeships in a sector an/or region. To ensure this aim they exercise different kinds of influence. Inter-company training centers, run by chambers, boards, employers' associations or trade unions, complement in-company training especially in the craft sector. Their aim is to ensure the quality standards of recognized vocational education. Another institution involved in regulating the dual education is the Bundesinstitut für Berufsbildung BIBB (Federal Institute of Vocational Training). The central committee (Hauptausschuss) of the BIBB, in which employers, unions, the States and the Federal Government are represented, develops training curricula and proposes recommendations for the further development of vocational training. For the development of training curricula the BIBB initiates research projects and takes into account experiences and the knowledge of large, technology intensive, trend setting German companies. Another important element of the dual system is the so-called German *Meister*. A company is only allowed to train apprentices if it has at least one *Meister* in its workforce. To become a *Meister* one has to progress through a significant amount of pedagogic and professional further education and take a standardized final examination. This should ensure relatively high minimum standards of in-company training[5].

This consistent set of institutional regulations not only guarantees that companies invest their fair share in vocational education,[6] but also that they keep up with required quality standards (low poaching risk, because companies not investing adequately in training are very rare). As regards curricula, the institutional setting promotes up-to-date and future-oriented training contents (low risk of obsolescence).

By guaranteeing high minimum quality and nation-wide recognition of a dual vocational education, the strongly regulated dual system also has a positive side effect: It makes apprenticeships attractive to young adults[7]. This encourages youths with high levels of initial qualifications to enter into apprenticeships. Through this the effectiveness of in-company training is supported[8].

In Great Britain vocational education is also dominated by company training and not by full-time school education. But the regulation of initial vocational education in companies is in stark contrast to that of Germany[9]. In Germany the system of vocational education can be characterized as a consistent set of rules and enforcement agencies. In Great Britain the system of vocational education can be characterized as a selective, unstable and inconsistent set of rules[10]. Some major developments during the last decades will explain this assessment.

As in Germany, apprenticeships in Great Britain traditionally had been the major way of educating youths for the world of work. However, important characteristics of British apprenticeships were the strong regulation of entrance by unions, the definition of qualification levels by years of training (up to seven years), the absence of controls or examinations on a national level, and missing guarantees of off-the-job training parts (Finegold and Soskice,1988, 27).

Because of an insufficient involvement of companies in apprenticeships in the 50s and 60s the Industrial Training Act was released in 1964. A major innovation was the establishment of Industrial Training Boards which imposed levies to guarantee an acceptable and equally distributed amount of company training. As early as 1973 the first exceptions in the levy system were enacted. Also in 1973 the tripartite Manpower Services Commission (MSC) was established. The initial idea was to control and coordinate the subsidized training activities of companies. However, in reality the MSC concentrated very quickly on the increasing problems of unemployed youths (Finegold and Soskice, 1988, 33).

A radical interruption of these developments was made by the conservative government in 1981. The ITB and the levy system were substituted by voluntary *Non Statutory Training Organizations.* State initiatives and the MSC concentrated in the following on the so-called *Youth Training Scheme* (YTS). Under this program one-year training measures for unemployed youths were created (since 1986 two-year-training measures as well). Some of the important characteristics of these YTS's are firstly a minimum amount of off-the-job training of 13 weeks in one-year and of 20 weeks in two-year programs. Secondly, the wages for trainees in these programs were held at a minimum in comparison to apprenticeship pay or youth wages (e.g., 118 Pounds Sterling per month in the first year). Thirdly, the content and the quality of the training measures were not controlled or regulated. And last but not least, the companies received some subsidies for overhead costs and off-the-job training periods (Finegold and Soskice, 1988, 29; Jones, 1988, 57; Keep and Mayhew, 1988, IXff; Marsden and Ryan, 1991, 268ff).

Neither employers' associations, nor the state, nor unions have a role similar to their counterparts in the German Vocational Education System.

A consequence of the complex but not very clear or consistent system of Vocational Education in Britain is that neither similar quantities nor similar, nationally recognized qualities of apprenticeships and YTS's are guaranteed (so creating high poaching risk for companies investing in high quality training). There are no institutions that develop unique future-oriented training curricula; the training content is determined very closely by everyday requirements of the workplace (high risk of obsolescence).

The British system of vocational education that can be characterized as unstable and fragmented at best, and induces the side effect of not being very attractive to youths. Youngsters prefer either to go into higher education or to start working as soon as they leave school. The qualifications of youths entering into apprenticeships or YTS programs are thus not very high[11], which has a negative impact on the effectiveness of company training measures.

3.2.2 Trainee Pay

Table 3.1 shows the basic trainee pay as a proportion of the basic pay of skilled adult workers in Great Britain and Germany.

Table 3.1 Basic or standard trainees pay as a proportion of the basic pay of adult skilled workers in certain British (1981) and German (1979) collective agreements.

	Britain by Age						German by Year				
	16	*17*	*18*	*19*	*20*	*Average*	*1*	*2*	*3*	*4*	*Average*
Chemicals	56	65	82	88	94	78	31	36	41	46	37
Engineering:											
metals (a)	47	60	75	90	100	75	29	32	35	40	33
building/construction (b)	43	70	90	--	--	68	24	37	47	--	36
Motor mechanic	43	50	65	85	100	68	21	22	25	--	23
Textiles	50	63	75	90	--	72	32	37	42	46	38
Clothing	67	79	88	92	--	83	30	33	38	--	34
Electrical	40	45	50	65	80	55	17	21	24	28	22

Notes:

(a) Engineering in Britain, metal working industries in Germany

(b) By year of apprenticeship in Britain

Source:

Skill Formation and Pay Relativities by L.J. Jones in *Education and Economic Performance*. Ed. G.D. Worswick, 1985, and national sources, quoted according to Training in Britain (1989, 28).

It can be seen that trainee pay in Germany is significantly lower than in Great Britain: average trainee pay to adult pay mostly ranged around 30% to 35% in Germany and around 68% to 75% in Great Britain. Similar evidence is given by Jones (1984). He showed that the pay of trainees in comparison to the pay of adults is 2.5 times higher in Great Britain than in Germany[12]. The costs of building a qualification stock, and thereby the opportunity costs of holding stocks are higher in Great Britain than in Germany.

The situation differs slightly for YTS programs. As mentioned in chapter 3.2.1 one of the important characteristics of YTS training measures is low trainee pay. The cost of qualifying a young adult in YTS is significantly lower than in apprenticeships, which should cp. lead to greater efforts by companies in YTS qualification measures. However, under the given institutional framework these qualification measures have no particular attraction for young people (cf. Marsden and Ryan 1991, 255f), which should cause a restraining effect on the number of YTS candidates.

3.2.3 Job Demarcation Rules

Because of the historically grown structure of craft unions, job demarcations were traditionally very narrow and rigid in Great Britain (Finegold and Soskice, 1988, 28). Workplaces or the kind of work to be done by a worker are defined by a set of tasks, the so called job territories, but not (or to a much lower extent) according to the qualifications a worker holds. Workers within a job territory are represented by *their* union and they are the only group allowed to do this kind of task (Marsden, 1987, 199f).

In contrast, the German structure of workplaces is shaped by the structure of vocational education. Workplaces, or the kind of work to be done by a worker, are structured according to occupations, that is, based on exactly defined and recognized worker qualifications (Blossfeld, 1992; Hotz-Hart, 1989, 116f; Marsden, 1987, 200). Evidence for this is the relatively large occupational labor market segment in Germany which Sengenberger (1987, 147f) showed in his international comparisons.

To summarize, due to typical job demarcations workers in Germany have workplaces containing a greater variety of different tasks. Thus, it is likely that they have more possibilities to use broad or excess qualifications than their British counterparts, which reduces the risk of obsolescence for companies investing in a stock of qualifications in Germany

3.2.4 Criteria for Wage Schedules

Even though the criteria for wage schedules vary substantially between Great Britain and Germany (Finegold and Soskice 1988; Marsden, 1987), wages in both countries are not significantly determined by qualifications which are not used in the workplace[13]. Thus, for further analysis it is assumed that there are no systematic differences in this kind of holding costs between Great Britain and Germany.

3.2.5 Hypotheses

Taking together all the systematic differences in the overage costs the conclusion is clear-cut: it is less risky or costly for German than for British companies to invest in apprenticeships. Overage costs for this kind of training are substantially higher in Great Britain than in Germany. Underage costs can be assumed to be almost equal. Thus hypothesis 1 is: German companies engage more in apprenticeship training than their British counterparts. Additionally, the British YTS programs have some advantages over classical British apprenticeships. Thus one may expect the British situation to be some-what better for companies' investments in YTS training. At the same time, the institutional setting of YTS training leaves some important problems unsolved (particularly quality issues). Thus hypotheses 2 is: British companies train more youths in YTS than in classical apprenticeships but the quantity of YTS training in Great Britain does not reach the level of apprenticeship training in Germany.

3.3 Preliminary Empirical Evidence

3.3.1 Germany

The number of apprenticeships was 1.77 million in 1988, 1.8 million in 1986 and 1.4 million in 1977[14]. The ratio of apprenticeships to the overall workforce (including the unemployed)[15] was about 6% in 1988. The ratio of apprenticeships to the number of youths between 15 and 20 years who are not on a higher education track was about two thirds. The proportion of the workforce without any vocational education was about 27.3% in 1985 (Zedler, 1988, 87).

3.3.2 Great Britain

The number of apprenticeships was 328,000 in 1988 (79,000 of them were in public programs) and 367,000 in 1979. The ratio of apprenticeships to the workforce[16] was about 1.1% in 1988. The ratio of trainees in YTS to the number of youths between 16 and 18 was 16% in 1988 (against 9% in 1983)[17]. The proportion of the workforce with no vocational education was about 42% (Training in Britain 1989).

3.3.3 Result

Although not all the figures are exactly comparable, it is still obvious that British companies invest significantly less in apprenticeships than their German counterparts. As expected, the number of YTS training measures is substantial, but they still do not reach the German level of apprenticeship-figures.

3.4 Conclusions

In this chapter it is shown that legal regulations and other labor market institutions play a significant role in corporate training. By modeling the corporate training decision in analogy to an inventory decision the important aspects and dimensions of the institutional framework are systematically derived. The costs of obsolescence are influenced by institutional regulations that guarantee the adaptation of technological developments into training curricula and the rigidity of job demarcations. Poaching costs are determined by institutions regulating the quantity and quality of corporate training within a common labor market. Holding costs depend on the weight of qualification potentials in pay schedules and opportunity costs depend on regulations of trainee wages or minimum youth wages. Penalty costs are loss of market shares or additional costs of hiring qualified personnel from the external labor market. Penalty costs were assumed to be similar in Great Britain and Germany. For all the other cost components it could be shown that the British regulation of vocational education leads to systematically higher costs than the German net of regulations in vocational education. Thus, differences in corporate training decisions have to be seen as a result of institutional differences. This leads to the conclusion that it is not only companies which compete, there is also significant competition between national systems of vocational education and labor market institutions. The study shows furthermore that a major condition for the success of a system is its internal consistency, that is, the completeness of institutional regulations on one side and their consistency on the other side. This is not to say that the German version of vocational education is the only successful way of regulating vocational education, but rather that every other alternative would need to have functional equivalents for the problems of vocational education derived above. To discover such alternative solutions more research, particularly empirical research on the effects of varying institutional rules is needed. Keep and Mayhew (1988, V) plead for a comparative systems approach and an economic approach which contains a "careful marriage of analysis with knowledge of detail and of institutions" (op cit, XIII).

References

Backes-Gellner, U (1992). Berufsausbildungssysteme und die Logik betrieblicher Qualifizierungsstrategien im internationalen Vergleich - Gibt es einen 'Wettbewerb der Systems'? *Jahrbuch für Neue Politische Ökonomie*. Tübingen: Mohr, 245-271.

BIBB (1991). *Verzeichnis der anerkannten Ausbildungsberufe und Verzeichnis der zuständigen Stellen*. Bonn: BIBB.

Blossfeld, H. (1992). Unterschiedliche Systeme der Berufsausbildung und Anpassung an Strukturveränderungen im internationalen Vergleich. Sadowski, D. and Timmesfeld, A. (Eds.) *Ökonomie und Politik beruflicher Bildung*. Berlin: Duncker and Humblot, 45-60.

BMBW (1987/88). *Grund- und Strukturdaten 1984/85*. Bad Honnef: Bock.

Bundesanstalt für Arbeit (1989). Der Arbeitsmarkt. Textberichte - Statistische Übersichten. *Amtliche Nachrichten der BA*, 37.

CEDEFOP (1981). *Rechts- und Organisationsstruktur der Berufsbildung. Bundesrepublik Deutschland, Frankreich, Italien, Vereinigtes Königreich*. Berlin: CEDEFOP.

CEDEFOP (1984). *Guide Vocational Training Systems in the Member States of the European Community. Comparative Study.* Berlin: CEDEFOP.

CEDEFOP (1988). *Der soziale Dialog in den Mitgliedstaaten der Europäischen Gemeinschaft auf dem Gebiet der beruflichen Bildung und Weiterbildung - ein zusammenfassender Bericht.* Berlin: CEDEFOP.

Degen, U., Seyfried, B. and Wordelmann, P. (1991) (Eds.). *Qualitätsverbesserungen in der betrieblichen Ausbildungsgestaltung. Fragen und Antworten.* Berlin: BIBB.

Finegold, D. and Soskice, D. (1988). The Failure of Training in Britain: Analysis and Prescription. *Oxford Review of Economic Policy, 3,* 21-53.

Haase, H., Richard, H. and Wagner, H. (1979). *Berufsbildungsgesetz mit Erläuterungen.* Köln: Bund.

Hotz-Hart, B. (1989). *Modernisierung von Unternehmen und Industrien bei unterschiedlichen industriellen Beziehungen: Ein Vergleich bei der verarbeitenden Industrie der USA, Grossbritannien und Deutschland im Hinblick auf eine institutionenorientierte Theorie.* Bern: Haupt.

Institut der deutschen Wirtschaft (1991). *Internationale Wirtschaftszahlen.* Köln: Deutscher Institutsverlag.

Jones, I. (1984). Pay Relativities and the Provision of Training. *National Institute Discussion Paper,* 77.

Jones, I. (1985). Skill Formation and Pay Relativities. Worswick, G.D. (Ed) *Education and Economic Performance.* (quoted according to Training in Britain, 1989.)

Jones, I. (1988). An Evaluation of YTS. *Oxford Review of Economic Policy, 3,* 54-71.

Keep, E. and Mayhew, K. (1988). The Assessment: Education, Training and Economic Performance. *Oxford Review of Economic Policy, 3,* I-XV.

Kushner, S. (1985). Vocational 'Chic'. An Historical and Curriculum Context to the Field of Transition in England. Fiddy, R. (Ed.) *Youth Unemployment and Training: A Collection of National Perspectives.* Brighton: Falmer Press.

Marsden, D. (1986). *The End of Economic Man? Custom and Competition in Labour Markets.* Brighton: Wheatsheaf Books.

Marsden, D. (1987). Collective bargaining and industrial adjustment in Britain, France, Italy and West Germany. Duchêne, F. and Shepherd G. (Eds.) *Managing Industrial Change in Western Europe.* London: Frances Pinter.

Marsden, D. (1988). Institutions and labour mobility: occupational and internal labour markets in Britain, France, Italy and West Germany. Brunetta R. and Dell'Aringa, C. (Eds.) *Markets, Institutions and Cooperation.* London: MacMillan.

Marsden, D. and Ryan, P. (1991). Initial Training, Labour Market Structures and Public Policy: Intermediate Skills in British and German Industry. Ryan, P. (Ed.) *International Comparisons of Vocational Education and Training for Intermediate Skills.* London: New York, Philadelphia: Falmer Press, 251-285.

Maurice, M., Sellier, F. and Silvestre, J.J. (1986). *The Social Foundations of Industrial Power. A Comparison of France and Germany.* Cambridge, Mass.: MIT Press.

Mulder, M., Romiszowski, A.J. and Van der Sijde, P.C. (1990) (Eds). *Strategic Human Resource Development.* Amsterdam: Swets & Zeitlinger.

Piore, M.J. and Sabel, C.F. (1984). *The Second Industrial Divide.* New York: Basic Books.

Reich, R.B. (1983). *The next American Frontier.* New York: Times Books.

Sadowski, D. (1980). *Berufliche Bildung und betriebliches Bildungsbudget.* Stuttgart: Poeschel.

Sadowski, D. and Decker, S. (1992). *Contractual Regulations on Continuing Vocational Education and Training in Germany*. Trier: mimeo.

Sengenberger, W. (1987). *Struktur und Funktionsweise von Arbeitsmärkten: die Bundesrepublik Deutschland im internationalen Vergleich*. Frankfurt: Campus.

Sorge, A. (1990). Unternehmensstrategien, Qualifikationsentwicklung und Erfolge von Wirtschaftszweigen. Aufschlüsse aus zwischengesellschaftlichen Vergleichen über industrielle Mikroeletronikanwendungen. Sadowski, D. and Backes-Gellner, U. (Eds.) *Unternehmerische Qualifikationsstrategien im internationalen Wettbewerb*. Berlin: Duncker & Humblot, 75-97.

Stern, D. (1990). *Institutions and Incentives for Developing Work-Related Knowledge and Skill*. Paper prepared for the Conference on 'Technology and the Future of Work', Stanford, March 28-29, 1990.

Streeck, W. (1989). Skills and the limits of neo-liberalism: The enterprise of the future as a place of learning. *Work, Employment & Society, 3*, 89-104.

Strikker, F. & Timmerman, D. (1990) (Eds.). *Berufsausbildung und Arbeidsmarkt in den 90er Jahren*. Frankfurt: Lang.

Thurley, K. and Ling Lam, C. (1990). Improving the Skill Formation Process of Electronic Engineers and Information Technologies in the UK and Japan. Sadowski, D. and Backes-Gellner, U. (Eds.) *Unternehmerische Qualifikationsstrategien im internationalen Wettbewerb*. Berlin: Duncker & Humblot, 59-74.

Timmermann, D. (1990). Zukunftsprobleme der Dualen Systems unter Bedingungen Verschärften Wettbewerbs. Sadowski, D. and Backes-Gellner U. (Eds.) *Unternehmerische Qualifikationsstrategien im internationalen Wettbewerb* (37-58). Berlin: Duncker & Humblot.

Training in Britain (1989). *A Study of Funding, Activity and Attitudes. The Main Report*. London: HMSO.

White, M. (1988). Educational Policy and Economic Goals. *Oxford Review of Economic Policy, 3*, 1-20.

Zedler, R. (1988). Standortvorteil: Berufsausbildung. Lenske, W. (Ed.) *Qualified in Germany. Ein Standortvorteil für die Bundesrepublik Deutschland*. Köln: Deutscher Instituts-Verlag, 75-98.

Notes

1 Piore and Sabel (1984) derive as a consequence a need of *flexible specialization*; Streeck (1989) uses the term "diversified quality production".

2 This implies that cost minimizing is the only or the dominant criterion in the company's training decision. This seems reasonable because empirical surveys of Von Bardeleben, Böll and Kühn (1986) in Germany and Training in Britain (1989) in Great Britain revealed a dominance of the costs of training measures for training decisions in companies.

3 Detailed information about the model is given in Backes-Gellner (1992, 266f).

4 Marsden (1988) uses the term "occupational labor markets".

5 Further information is given by Sadowski and Decker (1992).

6 Sadowski (1980) shows that another reason for companies to invest extensively in dual education is to build up a high reputation on the labor market, which makes recruiting of qualified labor easier.

7 CEDEFOP (1988, 51) emphasizes the importance of the participation of unions and employers' associations in the organization of vocational education for the attractiveness of vocational training to youths.

8 This is not to say that there are no problems in the German system of vocational education. They are well documented in Timmerman (1990, 39f), Strikker and Timmerman (1990) and Degen, Seyfried and Wordelmann (1991).

9 Cf. CEDEFOP (1981), CEDEFOP (1984).

10 See also Keep and Mayhew (1988), Kushner (1985), Training in Britain (1989).

11 White (1988, 9) and Finegold and Soskice (1988, 23) give further evidence on the low education level of newcomers to the British labor market.

12 Marsden and Ryan (1991, 259) presented figures for 1989, which showed a rate of trainee to adult pay in the metalworking sector (engineering) of 35,2% for Germany and 72,5% for Great Britain.

13 In Germany there is one noteworth exception: a collective agreement in the metal industry (Metalltarifvertrag Nordwürttemberg/Nordbaden). It contains pay for qualification potentials, that is, if workers cannot use qualifications they gained during further education, employers still have to pay for these after a certain time-span. However, this kind of collective agreement is still an exception.

14 BMBW (1987/88), Bundesanstalt für Arbeit (1989, 550).

15 29.6 millions in 1988 (Institut der deutschen Wirtschaft 1991, 23).

16 28.3 millions in 1988 (Institut der deutschen Wirtschaft, 1991, 23).

17 However, one should keep in mind that 77% of the participants in one-year-programs and 46% in two-year-programs did not get any accredited vocational qualification (Jones, 1988, 65f). Usually the qualifications were of a "mostly fairly basic character" (Jones, 1988, 65). YTS training measures are thus not really comparable with German apprenticeships (cf. also White, 1988, 9).

4 The Challenge of Competence and Further Training Policies

Philippe Méhaut

Since the mid-eighties, further training policies of large companies have been evolving in France both in quantity and in nature. This change is linked to the setting up of new production and organization patterns. At a micro level, it could be analyzed as an attempt to build new organic relationships between training, job organization, mobility rules and wages regulations. Based on case studies of large innovating companies, this chapter analyzes under what conditions the new training policies may become an organic component of the flexible and *learning* organization. It proposes a theoretical model integrating training within multidimensional human resource policies components. At a macro level, the shift in companies human resource management contributes to designing the new lines of a wage-earning relationship breaking with the previous Tayloristic-Fordist characteristics. Here, we discuss the theoretical assumptions for a non-merchant analysis of training and *labor market* and for the stabilization of a new macro model in the French situation.

It is well known that in France, since the beginning of the eighties, participation in further training by firms is rapidly increasing. From 1982 to 1991, the percentage of wage costs spent for training activities increased from 1.81 to 3.12 (in companies with 500-2000 employees) and from 3.06 to 4.67 (in companies with more than 2000 employees) (Berton and Podevin, 1991).

Training policies today seem to be more embodied in the global strategies of the firms, as a tool for managing change in job organization and in mobility patterns.

The Human Capital theory regards training as an investment for the individual or for the company (Becker, 1964). It lies on the hypothesis of a direct link between education (or training), productivity and wages. In the basic model, the labor market is classed as any market for commodities run by the prices, in this case, wages. The investment of a company in training is explained by the differential between training costs, productivity growth, and wage increase when training is specific to the company (to a job), avoiding the risk that employees quit and get rewards outside for the increase in their human capital.

The model has been frequently discussed, both on empirical evidence and on theoretical bases. On the former, empirical link between education, training and productivity is not so clear, neither at a micro level (Koning and Gelderblom, 1992) nor at the macro level (Auer, 1994) and evidence of companies' investment in general education and training are yet to be found, for example in the German dual system. On the latter, the equivalence between the labor market and any market for a commodity is discussed inside the standard economic theory and outside, by institutional analysis or by heterodox analysis (Bazzoli, Kirat and Villeval, 1992).

In this chapter, we develop a model to analyze companies' training investment in a changing environment.

- First, it is based on the assumption of a deep change in the production model (post-Tayloristic or post-Fordist model), renewing the question of the competences and the place of education and training in the organizations.
- Second, it assumes the heterodox hypothesis that what is usually called *labor market* does not run as a market but is made up of a set of institution rules and social relationships, particularly in the case of large companies developing internal rules and regulations.
- Third, in that framework, we consider the relationship between training, job organization, mobility and wages as multidimensional with no direct link with technology, productivity or wages.

In 16 case studies of large companies, both the global patterns of change and the various training policies were analyzed (Méhaut, 1989). In this chapter, we will present some results of this study: in the first section, we propose a theoretical framework to analyze corporate training; in the second section, we present various cases of policies chosen by the firms and in the last section we discuss the issue of passing from micro to macro level.

4.1 Micro Considerations on Training in Big Firms

4.1.1 Wage-Earning Relationship and Training

Analysis in terms of *wage-earning relationship* are principally developed by two French schools: the "Régulation" school (Boyer, 1986) and the "Aix group" (Maurice, Sellier and

Silvestre, 1986; Rose, 1989). They disagree on a lot of questions but share in common some points of view on the so-called labor market.

The Régulation school aims to analyze and explain the historical development of capitalism by building a theory of its institutional forms. At each stage of its development, there is an organic coherence between the dominant way of capital accumulation and some basic economic and social institutions (the wage labor nexus or wage-earning relationship, the State configuration, the forms of competition and the international regime of exchanges) which guarantee the coherence of the whole and the regularity of the growth model.

The concept of wage-earning relationship denotes one of the fundamental social relationships of the system. It concerns:

> "The mutual relationships between different types of work organization, way of life and modes of labor force reproduction. In analytical terms, five components are used in order to characterize the historical configurations of the relationships between capital and labor: the means of production and the form taken by the social and technical division of labor; the ways in which wage earners are mobilized and attached to the firm; the determinants of direct or indirect wage income; and lastly, the wage-earner's way of life, which is more or less linked to the acquisition of goods and the use of non-market collective services" (Boyer, 1986, 49).

At each historical stage of the accumulation, a dominant pattern of the wage-earning relationship is attached. A structural crisis implies an evolution in the basic institutions, including major changes of the five components of the wage-earning relationship and of their internal coherence.

For example, during the Fordist post-war period (and for France until the middle of the seventies), the wage-earning relationship coherence was based on: an increasing Tayloristic work organization, a stabilization of contractual relationships between employer and employees (including the prevailing seniority rules), a relative inelasticity of direct wages, a strong State intervention to provide public goods (including education and training, social security system) in order to guarantee close relationships between production and consumption norms (Michon, 1992).

In the present crisis, the model of production is put in question on both sides: on the accumulation side, the question is to find new bases to enhance productivity and to restart the process of accumulation; on the *institutional side*, the question is to reshape the pattern of the wage-earning relationship (and of the other basic institutions, such as State intervention) in order to develop a new flexibility coherent with the accumulation path.

The purpose of the Aix group is different. Rather than to develop historically based analysis, they aim at explaining the differences between national patterns of the wage-earning relationship, even if the economic constraints appear to be similar. So they fundamentally disagree with the hypothesis of a strong and direct connection between the characteristics of the accumulation and of the wage earning relationship (Maurice, Sellier and Silvestre, 1986).

But they share at least three common hypotheses and conclusions:

- The wage-earning relationship is a set of social relationships and institutions produced by and producing the individuals and the social actors' behavior.
- There is a national (*societal*) configuration (historical rather than national in the case of the Régulation school) of the wage-earning relationship which cannot be analyzed through universalistic market rules and hypotheses.
- The wage-earning relationship is a nexus of social relationships: of five components in the Régulation approach; of three basic dimensions in the societal approach (the formation of the labor force – namely the role of the educational and training system – and its mobility pattern, the work organization and the form of the cooperation and hierarchy within the teams, and lastly the forms of the industrial relations and the wage structure). Whatever the differences are, the common point of view is a multidimensional approach, putting emphasis on the one hand on the use of the labor force and on the other hand on its allocation and exchange, and lastly on its way of production and reproduction.

As the regulation approach is mainly a macro-economic analysis, the question of education and training is usually not highly developed. Conversely, the societal approach, mixing a macro analysis with micro considerations on the firms' behaviors embodied education and training in the building of the wage-earning components. For example, in the analysis of the difference between Germany and France, the national patterns of mobility, defined both as individuals' projects and as a strategy of the firms (which indicates the opposite relationship between occupational versus seniority rules), are explained by the structure of education and training. Similar considerations are developed about job organization where they oppose a *qualificational space* in the German case (i.e., hierarchical and team structure allowing apprenticeship and further training) and a *hierarchical space* in France (with longer hierarchical lines, fewer cooperative relationships within and between teams and no room for training).

That kind of hypothesis appears workable for understanding the international variety of education, training and retraining institutions and their dynamics. If we retain the hypothesis of a dominant pattern of the wage-earning relationship, we can shift from a macro analysis to a micro one, assuming that, in the dominant firms, we are able to build also a multidimensional analysis of work and employment relationships, including education and further training considerations.

A Model of the Embodiment of Training

Large French companies are often conceived of as organizations where internal labor markets prevail (Silvestre, 1986). According to various non-standard economic theories (Doeringer and Piore, 1971; Marsden, 1989) the process of use and allocation of the work force is not mainly driven by the level of wages. Other considerations such as seniority rules play an important role in the structuring of the labor market.

Following the proposals of the regulation theory about the wage-earning relationship and its components, we can distinguish three relations between the training and mobilization of the work force within an organization (see figure 4.1).

Figure 4.1 Multidimensional relationships between continuing vocational training and the labor force mobilization.

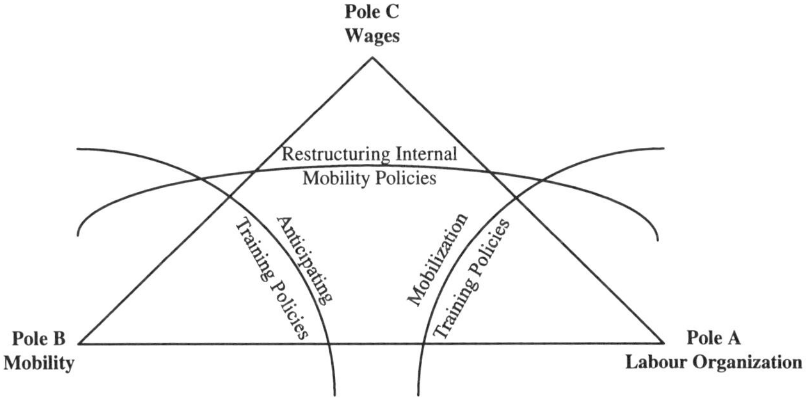

For the management of the company, training could be regarded as:

- A tool to build (and change) the job organization and ameliorate its efficiency by giving to the work-force some knowledge and ability according to the characteristics of their jobs and teams (this comprises for instance technical knowledge, but also an ability to communicate with other workers within the team or with other teams and behavioral characteristics). The distance of training from job contents and job organization is given by the characteristics both of the division of work and of training itself. General education and training are far away from pole *A*. On-the-job training or apprenticeship is close to pole *A*. A strong Tayloristic organization of work does not endeavor to attain the interaction of work and training; conversely, some new forms of work organization (autonomous team with no direct and a priori time control) strengthen the links (the *learning organization*).

- A tool to organize the allocation of the work-force and to manage mobility flows: it facilitates internal mobility by providing new skills and channeling the work-force in to new jobs; it provides management with information on the competence of the trainees. Here also, the distance to pole *B* is a complex structure. When internal mobility is driven by seniority, training could be said to be far away from pole *B*, used only as an a posteriori adjustment tool. When internal mobility is driven by competences and/or by certifications, training acts as an internal principle, building the mobility rules. Two formal similar positions on pole *A* could have different meaning on pole *B*: some kinds of apprenticeship or on-the-job training counteract mobility; in the case of occupational rules (such as the German form of apprenticeship) they are embodied in mobility rules. The search for new kinds of flexibility probably implies a renewal of both internal and external mobility rules with a more active role devoted to education and training.
- A component of wage policy: on the one hand, training (when paid by the company) is a part of wage costs; on the other hand, it is method of achieving hierachisation of the workers and of their distribution across the wage scale. Again, the distance from pole *C* is highly variable. In some organizations, there is a direct link between the level of training (or its evaluation through competences) and wages. In others, the link is either cut or is non-existent.

But training should not only be considered from the management point of view. Training is not only a constitutive fact within an organization, it serves as a function of *socialization* as well, contributing to building individuals' behavior and to their belonging to social or occupational groups. On the one hand, by the mediation of the individual embedding of knowledge and know-how, training produces not only competences but also the capability of cooperating within groups, to identify oneself to the group; on the other hand, as defining the possible mobility patterns, it enhances individual *mobility projects*.

So we should establish a relationship as depicted in figure 4.2 between training as a tool for the organization and as a fact of socialization for the individual. The way by which this relationship is accomplished is embodied inside educational national traditions, namely, social rules (Dubar, 1991).

For example the actual belonging to the group of foremen is driven by occupational rules in Germany (the necessity of *Meister* training and certificate) and the social behavior of the foreman. Its hierarchical situation cannot be understood without the socialization due to the training (including its former position as skilled blue collar and apprenticeship experience). But it is out of the scope of this chapter to develop the right side analysis of figure 4.2. We focus only on its left side.

Figure 4.2 Continuing vocational training, organization and socialization.

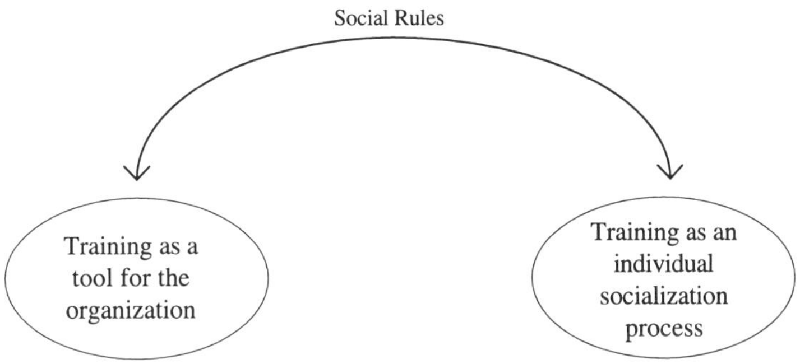

In the French case, and before the changes of the 1980s, we can speak of a kind of *externality* of the training to the organization. As a matter of fact, in our case studies, seniority rules prevailed in internal labor markets; the classifications were mainly built on job analyses; the use of further training was mainly to reinforce previous characteristics of the mobility rules (with training used *a posteriori*) and of job organization which was mainly Tayloristic and left no room for training within working time: training was mainly directed towards the narrow adaptation to job requirements (Méhaut, 1990).

4.2 The Changing Pattern of Organizations and Training Policies

Since the mid 1980s, some companies seem to have shifted from one production and organization model to another. In that process of change, training is used as an active tool to reshape their human resource policies. We selected a sample of large innovative companies and tried to analyze their training policies and the way in which they were moving from a position where training was rather external to the organization to another where we can speak of an organic integration of training, embodied within the three dimensions of figure 4.1. The study was based on deep monographic analysis, implying interviews at the various hierarchical levels and the collection of data on training, human resources, mobility and technical choices.

4.2.1 General Considerations

The changing pattern of the production organization that was observed in the case studies can be summarized in three ways:

- a process of change with respect to both the technology of the products and of production technology (computerization), with more attention paid to the use value of the goods (quality control, variability according to the demand), with strong consequences for job organization (for instance team work and closer relationships between maintenance and production);
- a relative shift in the base of the productivity: if the reduction of the immediate productive time remains a goal, more attention is given to a global saving of time within the whole production cycle (based on the *zero stock* principle, preventative maintenance, computerized management of production), which implies a greater *systemic* integration at the level of the company (Zarifian, 1987);
- a stricter management at the employment level: on the one hand, and by analogy to the zero stock production management, one can speak of a zero stock management at the level of employment; on the other hand, as internal flexibility becomes a major goal in that respect, there is a growing need for internal mobility, according to the variations in the quantity of work within the whole production process.

Returning to the three poles of figure 4.1, what are the consequences of such changes for the nature of the training policies? Three main groups of policies have been isolated. But before we go into these, we have to point at some general trends.

In all the cases, the level of expenditure for training doubled; four firms are now spending more than 6% of the wage bill on corporate training; but if we choose a broader definition of training than in the French legal framework, we have to add between 20 and 30% to this figure as it is increasingly difficult to set up a boundary between formal training activities (courses) and informal ones (for instance on-the-job training and training within quality circles).

Management of training plans evolves: on the one hand, decisions about training policies are taken at a the top level of the firm, in relationship with the strategic plans of the firms; on the other hand, concrete decisions about training activities are spreading to all levels of the companies; for example, trainers could be technicians, foremen, skilled workers. Another characteristic is the shift from short-term training plans to medium or long term ones.

The relationship between training and working time is more complex: previously, in France, due to the legal framework and to the union's claims, training was mainly included in the total working time, but off-the-job; a first trend is to partly reintegrate training and the job; but a second trend is to divide the total duration of the training, partly over working and free time (as evening courses). The following three groups of training policies are developed within this general framework; they are sometimes co-existing at various degrees in the same firm, and are more or less pure. In the following description we place emphasis on the *ideal-types.*

4.2.2 Mobilization Training Policies

This first group is often said by the firm as aiming to build new behavior patterns and new attitudes for job places. It is made of a series of short sequences, mixing and alternating for instance formal courses (on technical issues, economics, quality control), on-the-job training, visits of other departments within the company and meetings of the team to analyze and redefine the job organization. It concerns a large number of workers, sometimes all members of a shopfloor, and all categories: unskilled blue collars workers are mixed with skilled, technicians and foremen. It is mainly defined by the training department within the company and realized by internal trainers, including members of the staff.

It could be analyzed as a revival of the *on-the-job training*, but it exceeds this, as it relates not only to the job but to the general organization of the department or the company and aims at changing the job organization.

Training in this sense is enlargement of job contents: new techniques, ability to perform first degree maintenance, quality control, but also ability to cooperate within the team, to dispatch information to other teams. So this kind of policy is close to the pole *A* in figure 4.1. But it includes also considerations about mainly horizontal mobilization by multi-skilling and the ability of the individuals to rotate from on job to another and eventually, for the whole team to be displaced along the line, according to the quantitative flexibility of the work. The relationship to the wage structure remains weak: in most of the cases there is no change in the wage regulation; eventually a slight increase in the level of wages as a reward for polyvalency, given at the level of the team.

4.2.3 General Upgrading Skill Level Anticipating the Changes

This kind of policy could be defined as the opposite of the first one. It concerns also companies or departments where semi or skilled workers (blue or white collar) prevail. Due to their age and seniority, they often have a low level of formal education and no initial vocational training. The choice is to change the skill structure avoiding or postponing dismissals. The company is looking for internal flexibility, by breaking down the lines, introducing a new team organization, a decrease of the number of tiers in the hierarchical structure and the development of quality control. The market strategy is to introduce technical innovations in the product. It implies frequently technical innovations in the production technology. But it is viewed as a general process of change, without a precise forecast of the timing and of the future job structure: the evolution of the skills is a prerequisite on which organizational and technical flexibility largely depends.

The training strategy places emphasis on basic knowledge, general (communication, mathematics) or technical (for instance mechanics, electricity and automation). The structure of the courses resemble academic curricula and the teachers and trainers are drawn partly from the staff and partly from external training bodies (including public ones). The courses often result in a certificate or an officially recognized qualification. As the goal is a global change of the skill structure, courses are not selective at the entry stage; they are designated for all the workers of a shopfloor or a department, although on a voluntary basis, and could be given partly in working time. But selection does occur at the end of the course: as a matter of fact, those who fail probably would be dismissed at a latter stage.

The consequences of training for job organization, mobility and wages will be great: a general change is forecasted in the job structure, implying a general process of upgrading; the wage structure will be based more on training considerations. But at present there is no strong and immediate relationship between job and training content. Training clearly anticipates the changing patterns, aiming to build new mobility and wage rules; the concrete choices of a new job organization will rely on the success of the training policy and on the opportunities that it will provide. In that sense, training policy is close to pole *B* and *C* in figure 4.1 but rather far away from pole *A*.

4.2.4 Training for the Restructuring of Internal Mobility

If we consider the formal structure of the courses only, this last policy group is similar to the previous one: formal courses with officially recognized qualifications, with a considerable degree of general and theoretical knowledges. But other characteristics can help us to distinguish this particular group.

The curricula are not copied from an external school-line, but are specifically designed for the firm: they try to connect the specific requirements of the company with workers' skills and experience. So one can say that training is an original set of knowledge and know-how, including evaluation and acknowledgement of the workers' competences.

Training is meant to accompany the process of change and is highly embodied within the changing pattern of the job organization and of the mobility structure: workers are selected a priori, by means of skill evaluations and tests. They undergo the courses and, at the same time or very soon afterwards, they are occupying highly classified new jobs. The mobility goals are very important as the question is to change the traditional mobility patterns and to channel employees into new mobility clusters. The job definition and the wage rules clearly embodied individual characteristics and training specifications. A new organizational structure is set up parallel to the provision of training. Such training devices enhance the fusing of external knowledge, in more or less academic form, with internal knowledge, recombining various topics with the experience of the job and of organization. It is the clearest case of an organic integration of training within the three dimensions of the model, designing a *learning organization*. This kind of training policy is located at the center of figure 4.1.

4.2.5 Synthesis

With different intensity according to the type of policies, one of the common consequences of the change is the embodiment of training in the setting up of the organizational rules; training could not be regarded as external to the structuring of the labor market:

- In the first case, job organization, rules of multi-skilling and internal functioning of teams are partly defined during and by the training sessions, by the trainees themselves.
- In the second and in the third case, training acts as a catalyst of the job restructuring process; it becomes a structural way of defining the mobility channels and of selecting individuals to enter these channels; it also contributes to the process of individualization of wages.

In all cases, one of the goals is the evolution of the behavior patterns and attitudes of the workers, due mainly to the reorganization of the hierarchical structure and of control of tasks: there is a shift from a mode of hierarchical prescription of labor, with a strict definition of tasks of individuals, towards a collective prescription to teams, defining the goals, but with more opportunities to choose the way of achieving them.

4.2.6 Strategical Changes, Choice of Training Policies and Evaluation

If we try now to set up some relationships between the paths of production chosen by the firm and the training strategies, we can use the classification defined by Salais and Storper (1993) in a study of the modernization process of a sample of French firms. According to him, firms could be located on a two axis plan, one axis is the "product" axis, the other is the "market" axis.

The first one opposes a standardized type of product for a market with a low level of uncertainty to a specific production adapted to uncertain individual demand.

The second one opposes two kinds of process of production which could be summarized by, on the one hand, *a mass production*, using general knowledge, aiming at economy of scales (competition of the costs) and on the other hand, *flexible production* with specific knowledge (competition through the quality). So it is possible to define four types of strategies according to each quarter of the plan. We go now through three of these, as the fourth one was not represented in our sample.

The classical type of firm, in the *Fordist model*, combines cost competition through mass production and standardized products. It is coherent with the French classical framework of internal labor market, job evaluation, prescription of tasks (in quantity and quality) by hierarchy according to the forecast of risk. This model could be regarded as the point of departure of the majority of the firms in our sample.

Another model could be defined as a *merchant* one. Here the firms retain the characteristics of mass production and are always looking for economy of scale; but their products are less standardized and fit more to the variety of the demand; so the degree of uncertainty (both on prices and on the nature of the product) is higher. The companies need a higher degree of internal flexibility to adjust themselves to this uncertainty: this means both quantitative and qualitative flexibility (changes in the range of products, technical change of the product); they need workers with a high degree of availability, capable of facing the change and adapting themselves; so the level of skill requirements is higher, embodying general knowledge and specific skills according to the firms' know-how and to the internal process of learning by doing.

The third model could be called an *immaterial model*: it characterizes innovating firms, creating and developing new products (and in the same movement, the demand and the market). In the production process, economy of variety is more important than economy of scale. On the market, the uncertainty is nowadays very high, but will be reduced later. The trust of the individuals in the firm and of the firm in the employees is a prerequisite of the immaterial nature of the process of production in its first stages. The nature of skills could be called *scientific*, with a large amount of general knowledge.

In our sample, the majority of the companies is trying to escape from the first model (the industrial one). The paths of evolution of those companies could be described as follows.

Some of them are trying to build a kind of compromise between the *industrial* and the *merchant* model. But they do not really break with their previous industrial characteristics. It is in those cases that we find mainly the *mobilization policies* (excluding the others) and the success does not seem to be guaranteed. Since our investigations began, two companies have fallen again into deep crisis; one of them is now closed.

The majority of companies is now close to the merchant model. To realize and achieve the changes, they use mainly the training policies of the two other kinds, combining general upgrading of the skills and specific vocational courses aiming at the building of new mobility channels. In such cases, the degree of internal coherence of the strategy (various components of the management of the work force, economic and organizational choices) seems to lead to better economic and employment conditions.

Some other case studies are close to the immaterial model, or combine merchant and immaterial characteristics. In that case, they develop also the two last patterns of training strategies: on the one hand, they are looking for blue collar workers with a high level of general skills (for example the French baccalaureate) and provide general long term courses for that purpose; on the other hand, the need for technicians or engineers is high: they develop strong links with universities, to design curricula combining general technical skills and specific ones, to increase upgrading flows of highly skilled workers to technicians and of technicians to engineers. It does not avoid mobilization policies, but there come more through other managerial policies such as total quality control than by direct training policy.

4.3 From Micro Level to Macro Level

The evolutions analyzed above seems to show a deep restructuring of the relationship between training, employment and work, at the level of the company. But these considerations are based only on case studies. In this section, we discuss first the condition of an extension of a new model of relationship of the firm to training, second the question of the stabilization of this model as a new macro model of wage-earning relationship.

4.3.1 Extension of the Training Innovations

In the case of France, all the statistical data show that in recent years large companies are pursuing the growth of the training activity. Other surveys (Cereq, 1991) confirm our case studies. For example, in some big firms, we have studied one plant; since then new training devices have been extended to all plants.

Moreover, if we accept the hypothesis of a deep renewal of the social conditions of productivity, one can think that the method of restructuring we analyzed in our case studies have good chance of spreading through many big firms.

But this does not take place in a linear way. The cost of such policies is rather expensive and we have seen that success is not guaranteed: if the model is not sufficiently generalized, it could lead to a new recession in the use of training.

French public policy, by means of a credit of tax when the firm increases its training expenditures, and by means of special grants when the company bargains a long term pledge to develop training, could help to avoid adverse movements.

Another adverse trend could come from the actual condition of the labor market: the rather high level of unemployment and the growing level of schooling could lead the firms to prefer firing and hiring policies. But on the one hand, it implies high social costs and difficulties with the unions. On the other hand, a lot of studies show that firing and hiring could lead to a general loss of skill in the company and to the impossibility of building easily new collectives with young recruits (Villeval, 1992b).

So we can guess that in coming next years, the higher and new use of training could have an extensive growth in the large companies.

4.3.2 Towards a New Wage-Earning Relationship?

The question is not only of the spreading of the model, but also of its stabilization at a macro level. We go beyond the individual company and beyond the mere question of training. If the new training policies of the major companies became the dominant way of using training, under what conditions could we speak of the setting up of a new wage-earning relationship?

As we have seen in section I, the wage-earning relationship implies a double coherence: a macro-institutional one between its five components and another between its structure and the way of accumulation of the capital. Taking only the first question into account, we have to discuss the compatibility between such further training policies and initial education policies. In the French model, there are presently few links between initial and further training, and the social status of the vocational training remains low. New interactions between further training curricula and initial vocational training in a general framework of renewed recognition of the vocational training have to be developed. So the change in the educational system over the last ten years, with the trend to professionalisation and the growth of new links with the firms, allows a better coherence between initial education and further training.

Second, we have to discuss the compatibility between the growth of the corporate training and the global features of the labor market: on the one hand, the main classifications rules are still based on job analysis and seniority rules and not on occupational considerations; on the other hand, corporate policies do not necessarily lead to general diplomas; so there is a contradiction between the quest through training for higher internal and external voluntary mobility of the work force and the still dominant rules of the labor market. The development of corporate training in the view of a positive flexibility has to lead to general and transversal rules. If this is not the case, and in an increasing degree if a lot of firms choose hiring and firing policies, it could reinforce the seniority rules and decrease again the external mobility of the workers to prevent downgrading risks in case of external mobility. But again, some changes in the classification in certain branches of industries, some attempts to evaluate and recognize individuals' competences at the branch level indicates a trend towards more coherence (Jobert and Tallard, 1995).

Third, we have to discuss the relationships with the wage setting. This relates to the previous remarks about classification. But more broadly, how to ask the employees to accept a greater involvement in training courses and sharing of the burden of the training costs without any reward? In some cases, we have seen that there is a wage compensation; in other firms this is not the case. It is possible today to give no rewards due to the threat of unemployment; but it is not possible to stabilize on such a base. So the question of the wages rules remains open.

But according to the regulation theory, one can think that the movements we have analyzed are a part of the dynamics of the wage-earning relationship: it puts in question the Fordist model and acts towards a new kind of wage-earning relationship, allowing new productivity gains on the one hand and new patterns of distribution and of consumption on the other hand. It seems that this kind of wage-earning relationship will embody trainingconsiderations as an organic component.

References

Auer, P. (1994). Further education and training for the employed: systems and outcomes. Schmid, G. (Ed.) *Labor market Institutions in Europe. A socio economic evaluation of performance.* New York: Sharpe.

Bazzoli, L., Kirat, T. and Villeval, M.Cl. (1992). *Rules, contract and institution in the wage-labour relationship: a return to institutionalism?* Paper presented at the Fourth AELE conference, Warwick.

Becker, G. (1964). *Human Capital: a theoretical and empirical analysis with special reference to education.* Chicago: University of Chicago Press.

Berton, F. and Podevin, G. (1991). Vingt ans de formation professionnelle continue, de la promotion sociale à la gestion de l'emploi. *Formation emploi, 34*, 14-30.

Boyer, R. (1986). *La théorie de la régulation, une analyse critique.* Paris: La découverte.

Cereq (1991) *Les entreprises françaises et la formation continue, Natures, Financement, Fonctions, Usages.* Paris: Centre d'Etude et de Recherche sur les Qualifications.

Doeringer, P. and Piore, M.J. (1971). *Internal labor market and manpower analysis.* Lexington: Lexington Books.

Dubar, Cl. (1991). La Sociolisatien, Construction des identites sociales et professionelles. Paris: Armand Calin.

Jobert, A. and Tallard, M. (1995). Diplômes et certifications de branche dans les conventions collectives. In 'Formation emploi' (in press).

Koning, J. and Gelderblom, A. (1992). *Company training: volume, underinvestment and return.* Paper presented at the Fourth EALE Annual conference; Warwick.

Marsden, D. (1989). *Marchés du travail, limites sociales des nouvelles théories.* Paris: Economica.

Maurice, M., Sellier, F., Silvestre, J. J. (1986). *The social foundations of industrial power, a comparison between France and Germany.* Cambridge : MIT Press.

Méhaut, Ph. (1990). French corporate training: historical considerations and new prospects. Mulder, M., Romiszowski, A.J. and Van der Sijde, P.C. (Eds.) *Strategic Human Resource Development.* Amsterdam/Rockland: Swets & Zeitlinger, 119-130.

Méhaut, Ph. (1989) (Ed.). Production et usage de la formation par et dans l'entreprise. *Rapport de recherche PIRTTEM-CNRS, 3 tomes.* Nancy: GREE.

Michon, F. (1992). Institutional forms of work and employment. Castro, A., Méhaut, Ph. and Rubery, J. (Eds.) *International integration and labour market organization.* London: Academic Press, 222-243.

Rose, M. (1989). Universalism, culturalism and the Aix group: promise and problems of a societal approach to economic institutions. *European sociological Review, 1,* 1, 65-83.

Salais, R. and Storper, M. (1993). *Les Mondes de la production. Paris: Editions de l'Ecole des Hautes Etudes en Sciences Sociales.*

Silvestre, J.J. (1986), Marché du travail et crise économique: de la mobilité à la flexibilité. *Formation Emploi, 14,* 54-61.

Villeval, M.Cl. (1992a) (Eds.). *Mutations industrielles et reconversion des salariés.* Paris: L'harmattan.

Villeval, M.Cl. (1992b). The workforce reconversion in the crisis of fordism: element of break-up or element of transition. *International Contributions to Labour Studies, 2,* 61-75.

Zarifian, Ph. (1987). Du taylorisme au systémisme, une nouvelle approche de la qualification dans l'industrie. *Gip-Mi, Cahier n°8,* Paris.

5 Organization Development in a Changing Corporate Culture

Stephen F. Foster and Geert W.J. Heling[1]

In this chapter we report organizational development activities within a Dutch metals firm recently involved in an international merger. Initial diagnostic and follow-up procedures were applied to assess and improve aspects of management performance. Experiences are reported and discussed in light the of problems of organizational development, change, and culture.

The target company, that we will call *Castco* (a pseudonym), was recently merged into an American parent company, itself a product of a recent merger. Although business has been good, top management has been unhappy with some aspects of their situation. Top management perceived that management problems were holding the firm back from realizing its fullest potential. Thus all three divisions of the organization (two in North America and one in the Netherlands) have actively sought training and consultation from outside agencies. Virtually all managers within the organization have been involved in some form of management development activity within the past two years, and the firm is seeking to establish coherent management and organizational development policies and programs to meet their current and future needs in this area. As part of a systematic attempt to assess and address perceived organizational needs, a diagnostic procedure for assessing management effectiveness was applied to top and middle management and supervisory level staff. Follow-up seminars were held in English and in Dutch to assist the managers and supervisors to interpret their scores in terms of patterns of strengths and weaknesses, and to develop action plans for improving their managerial skills. Follow-up interventions including individual coaching and group training sessions covering team-building and communication skills were carried out. The current situation in the Dutch division of the organization is described with reference to the effects of the interventions performed. These are interpreted in the light of the problems of managing organizational change and changing organizational cultures.

5.1 Introduction: Organization Development and Culture

In the contemporary literature on organization development (OD) (e.g., Beer, 1980), the relationship between effectiveness of managers and leaders and the success of their organizations is assumed to be direct, positive and significant. Thus as organizations grow, becoming increasingly complex, the requirement for managerial competency will become ever more critical. This is especially the case when external factors (for instance global competition and mergers) challenge and override previously held policies. Creating and adjusting to changes in organizational culture require major efforts from all individuals involved and especially those having management responsibilities. The relationship assumed between management effectiveness and organizational success is in fact supported by research linking one popular approach to OD, management by objectives, to empirical measures of success as summarized by Rodgers and Hunter (1991). Their meta-analysis of 70 studies indicates that whereas top management commitment and support are key conditions for organization development, direct participation for example, through management development (MD) activities is often a prerequisite for greater productivity. Whereas the overall goal of the project described there is OD, the main methods we employed in achieving it can be regarded as MD activities.

Additionally, recent analyses (e.g., Burke, 1994) stress the reciprocal impact of culture and OD. That is OD necessarily involves influencing or changing the culture, and when organization culture changes, through merger or takeover, it becomes all the more important to adapt OD to the new conditions. Both of these processes are present in the case-in-progress described below.

This chapter is a progress report on a project in planned change through organizational development. A set of contemporary approaches to OD (cf. French and Bell, 1990) was systematically applied, including diagnostic activities using an instrument, the Management Effectiveness Analysis (MEA), confidential survey feedback, group training, intergroup activities, third party peace-making, process consultation, coaching, counselling and mentoring. Additionally, elements of other standard OD approaches – structural activities, life and career planning – were employed with mixed success. These are discussed in the context of the organization's situation before and during its OD process.

We describe the company, its recent history, and the key problems involved in section 5.2. In the third section we describe the structure of the project and the approaches taken. We then deal with the proceedings of the project, followed by results to date, the major events and current status. Practical and theoretical implications are discussed and preliminary conclusions are drawn in the last section.

5.2 The Problem, Context, and Objectives

Space limitations prevent us from listing here all features of the organizational context, aspects of the problem or program objectives. A summary of key issues is outlined in table 5.1.

Table 5.1 Context and aspects of the problem and objectives to address within the Castco project.

Description of Castco (context):
- *kind of business;*
- *international organization;*
- *internal structure.*

Problem aspects:
- *cultural discrepancy U.S.A. vs. Benelux;*
- *which demands are posed on this organization by the 'foreign' mother organization, and how to accommodate to them;*
- *mother organization has undergone organizational changes too;*
- *strategic planning;*
- *how to accommodate the Dutch organization as quickly as possible to the American culture;*
- *worldwide product delivery;*
- *measurability;*
- *internal logistic problems;*
- *personnel problems;*
- *dominant character of GM;*
- *future successor of GM;*
- *position of HRM.*

Objectives set for this consulting project:
- *setting individual MD goals;*
- *more responsibility for all managers;*
- *more team spirit;*
- *better and more open communication;*
- *more efficient, and more goal oriented working;*
- *formalize a mission statement.*

Basically Castco is a Benelux-based[2] specialty metal parts manufacturer and supply firm. Until recently it was one of the major independent players in the international market. Somewhat unexpectedly it was acquired by an American parent company, itself a product of recent mergers of two of the other majors. Thus change was thrust upon the Dutch managers, supervisors and workers from outside. New cultural issues became apparent as the Dutch managers now had to deal with and take orders from their U.S. counterparts, who until recently had been in competition with them. Indeed a few U.S. managers even joined the local Dutch team. Local sub-cultural variations were also present in the form of the generational contrast between for instance *old hand*, namely experienced managers, and younger people who were more open to modern automation techniques; between people having technical vs. business orientations; and between plant vs. *front office* jobs.

In recent years up to and since the merger, business was good and improving, but management expressed increasing concern about its own internal effectiveness. It should be noted that at the same time as our MD/OD activities in the Benelux, the parent company was independently experiencing similar activities with a U.S. firm of consultants. For various reasons we had no formal relationship, or direct communication with the firm's counterparts in America.

By the end of 1990, the local general manager (GM) approached our group with a request to assess and treat their situation. He described a group of individually talented managers who, among other things, lacked initiative and esprit de corps.

Using results from a set of diagnostic procedures, and in consultation with our clients, the Castco management, we developed a set of objectives and interventions to address their perceived and assessed problems.

Our objectives included diagnosis and, where indicated, remedial help for management effectiveness at Castco with a view to assisting the organization to develop into a self-learning/correcting group. The procedure taken to achieve this and the results to date are indicated in the sections that follow.

5.3 The Interventions

5.3.1 Diagnostic Activities: the Management Effectiveness Analysis[3]

We used a diagnostic method called "Management Effectiveness Analysis" (MEA) (Goossens, 1990; Mahoney, 1987; Rand, Mahoney and Mahoney, 1990; Van der Klauw and Van den IJssel, 1990) as starting and organizing points for the project. This method yields a Personal Feedback Profile of management behavior for each individual. For groups, combined group profiles can also be computed and compared.

A key part of the logic of beginning with diagnostic intervention is to provide the database for choosing and implementing further interventions. Although the MEA is in essence an individual diagnostic for MD, it can be used for related developmental purposes. It also has the benefit of offering possibilities to connect management development with organizational change and vice versa. The process of organizational change can be tailored to the needs and skills of the managers involved, and the MD program can be tuned to organizational demands. Thus we illustrate the use of this instrument in some detail to describe the project here, because we think it provides a good example of how an MD diagnostic instrument can be used in a process of management development and organizational change.

In using the MEA diagnostic we sought a clearer view of the problems underlying the organizational issues initially stated by the GM. The MEA outcomes would be intended to put individual managers on the trail of developing their own skills, and overall to indicate directions to take for the desired organizational changes.

Use of the MEA is based on the premise that optimal MD requires managers to know and understand what their developmental needs are. It purports to provide managers with the knowledge required to develop effective management practices. The MEA Personal Feedback Profile delivers an assessment of current management practices against 21 specific behavioral characteristics which comprise the management role (table 5.2).

Table 5.2 Functions and behavioral sets of the MEA.

1. Evaluation Function
   - *Traditional*
   - *Innovative*
   - *Technical*
2. Decision-Making Function
   - *Directive*
   - *Consensual*
   - *Strategic*
3. Implementation Function
   - *Tactical*
   - *Structuring*
   - *Delegation*
   - *Communication*
   - *Team*
   - *Individualist*
4. Leadership Function
   - *Management Focus*
   - *Production*
   - *People*
   - *Excitement*
   - *Restraint*
5. Follow Through Function
   - *Control*
   - *Feedback*
6. Public Relations Function
   - *Persuasive*
   - *Cooperation*

The MEA, however, goes beyond a mere description of how an individual approaches the management role. Utilizing proprietary questionnaire methodology, the MEA provides feedback to heighten awareness of one's management behaviors. It provides a detailed description of patterns of assets and liabilities. It also includes specific strategies to sustain strengths and confront weaknesses particular to the individual and his role in an organization.

The MEA feedback is used in a developmental format which directs the manager's attention to practices which require the greatest emphasis for behavioral change regarding the specific situational context. Once the manager's path for development has been visualized, there are outlines of specific strategies and actions to make changes. Participants develop their own action plans to address developmental needs through individualized strategies and approaches.

Planning, and taking action, and seeing change typically requires at least ten months after which a follow-up assessment is recommended to chart the individual's progress. This evaluation phase should occur after the main interventions.

The MEA provides a summary profile of the combined results for all managers within a group/team of an organization. This is called the Composite Profile. It allows an analysis of the prevailing management climate which diagnoses the developmental needs found to characterize the majority of the organization's managers. It is an inventory of management strengths and weaknesses which directs the organization's resources to the most critical training and developmental interventions. The method of Composite Profile Analysis was extensively used in the current case.

Every organization is unique. MD is thus unique to an organization's culture and business mission. At least two national cultures (Dutch and American) and three corporate cultures (representing the pre-merger companies) currently influence Castco. Additionally *subcultures* can be defined as: technical vs. administrative, manufacturing vs. business and older vs. younger personnel. While these are not the problem per se they contribute to stereotyping and misattributions in communications in Castco.

The MEA system uses an 111-item, empirically-derived and validated instrument for tapping self-reported management behaviors (Rand, Mahoney and Mahoney, 1990). In the MEA, management behavior is divided into six functional areas. Each area contains two or more *item-sets* or characteristics. These sets are used to define the role of the manager within each function. The six functions and the sets per function are shown in table 5.3. Feedback on these 21 sets gives a description of the way the manager fulfills his role (a management profile). Scores on these sets are expressed as percentile scores. For every set potential assets and liabilities are indicated for high as well as low scores. In addition the MEA computes 30 behavioral aspects based on set-score combinations. Insight is gained in the major managerial assets and liabilities by investigating the clustering of behavioral aspects. Though sometimes of a confrontational nature, this feedback is often easily recognized by participants because it is closely linked to their every day (problem) situations. It is important to note that the MEA questionnaire and the feedback are behavior-oriented even though they are self-reports. They do not reflect mere attitudinal aspects.

MEA feedback was given during two day seminars for the Management (N = 9) and Supervisory Staff (N = 10) separately. Each participant had filled out the MEA-questionnaire beforehand. The questionnaires were collected and processed to obtain the individual and group profiles. During the seminar the underlying theory about behavior attached to the management role is explained and participants receive their feedback step by step. Each participant wrote his/her own action plans based on the liabilities he recognized in his own feedback profile, and discussed these with a colleague.

Table 5.3 Composite profiles scores of management group and supervisors of Castco.

	Management Group (N = 9)	Supervisory Staff (N = 10)
1. Evaluation Function		
• *Traditional*	85	85
• *Innovative*	75	60
• *Technical*	55	45
2. Decision-Making Function		
• *Directive*	60	40
• *Consensual*	45	45
• *Strategic*	45	20
3. Implementation Function		
• *Tactical*	55	35
• *Structuring*	90	95
• *Delegation*	50	15
• *Communication*	60	75
• *Team*	50	40
• *Individualist*	60	20
4. Leadership Function		
• *Management Focus*	70	45
• *Production*	45	75
• *People*	50	65
• *Excitement*	55	50
• *Restraint*	55	80
5. Follow Through Function		
• *Control*	75	60
• *Feedback*	65	50
6. Public Relations Function		
• *Persuasive*	60	45
• *Cooperation*	65	90

(Scores are percentiles)

Process results of the MEA diagnostics

On the individual level MEA results and action plans led to a certain amount of individual coaching, counseling and mentoring (see section 5.3.4 below). Whereas some managers and supervisors seemed surprised at their profiles, most recognized themselves in the scores and were able to address action planning accordingly.

The MEA results can also be analyzed at the group level. Within the context of OD these analyses are most relevant. Inspecting the Composite Profiles of both groups several observations can be made:

a. The management team shows moderate positions on most behavioral sets.

b. The management as well as the supervisory staff strongly rely on past experience in facing problem situations (both 85 % on *Traditional*), and they prefer using rules and procedures to ensure that tasks are properly carried out (90 % and 95 % on *Structuring*).

c. The supervisors pay little attention to long-term planning and implications of decisions (20 % on *Strategic*).

d. The supervisors feel uncomfortable with those subordinates whose behavior deviates from group norms. They tend to reject the development of individual accountability, incentives and sanctions (20 % on *Individualist*).

e. There is generally a firm identification with the company's goals and objectives, and a willingness to adjust individual objectives in order to give assistance to other departments. This is especially characteristic of the supervisors (90 % on *Cooperation*).

f. Supervisors are reluctant to delegate task and decision responsibilities to their subordinates (15 % on *Delegation*).

Comparing the group profiles of management and supervisors some interesting differences can be noticed.[4]

g. Management accentuates being close to the action and is more inclined than supervisors to be involved in the way things are going *on the floor* (55 % vs. 35 % on *Tactical*).

h. The management is more willing to assume responsibility for their own decisions, and feel more comfortable in their role of manager (60 % vs. 40 % on *Directive*; 70 % vs. 45 % on *Management Focus*).

i. The supervisors stress a result-oriented approach and accentuate quantitative aspects more than does the management (75 % vs. 45 % on *Production*).

j. Supervisors are more inclined than management to emphasize the importance of being in control of one's own emotions and being patient and solid (80 % vs. 55 % on *Restraint*).

Assets revealed by MEA diagnoses

By analyzing clusters of behavioral aspects insight is gained into major managerial assets and liabilities. The three major assets of the Managers as revealed by MEA scores were:

- Consistent and Clear Performance Expectations:
  The Castco manager is capable of being decisive and explicit about his expectations regarding the execution of tasks. He will find ways of controlling the quality and the progress of the performance.
- Definitive Delegation:
  If the Castco manager delegates tasks, responsibility and authority to his subordinates, he knows what his expectations are and what is being delegated. The Castco manager generally checks that the subordinate has understood the orders properly and he gives feedback on the progress and the quality of the performance.
- Straightforward in Disagreement:
  The Castco manager does not avoid conflict and is willing to handle problems and disagreeable cases in definitive ways.

The three major assets of the Supervisors as revealed by MEA analysis were:

- Clear Performance Expectations:
  The Castco supervisor clarifies, without saying too much, his expectations about the way tasks should be executed. He ensures that systems exist to protect the progress and the quality of the delegated tasks.
- Manager as Master Teacher:
  The supervisor at Castco spends a certain amount of time in coaching his subordinates and he has a good view on the information subordinates actually need. In this way he is able to develop his people in desired directions.
- Definitive Delegation:
  If the Castco supervisor delegates tasks, responsibility and authority to his subordinates he is aware of the need to clarify his expectations and what is being delegated. The

Castco supervisor generally checks whether the subordinate has understood the question properly and he gives feedback on the progress and the quality of the performance.

Liabilities revealed by MEA diagnoses

The three major liabilities of the Managers revealed by MEA analysis were:

- Insensitive to Subordinate Needs:

  A Castco manager has to be careful in handling subordinates' emotions and motivations. This means that he has to be prepared to listen to his subordinates, to let them be involved in carrying out certain activities and to give them feedback about the ways they have executed some tasks.
- Provides Insufficient Autonomy:

  Subordinates need to have more autonomy (territory) so that they can develop their own capacities. A reason for this is that Castco managers' give too much attention to the ways they solve problems by working according to known methods and the managers' desire to control the delegated tasks.
- Too bureaucratic:

  The Castco managers are perceived as having rigid attitudes. This is consistent with close attention to the traditional ways of working as well as the flow of information aided by rules and procedures.

The major liabilities of the Supervisors revealed by MEA analyses were:

- Overly Cautious and Conventional:

  Castco supervisors maintain existing working methods without taking initiatives to propose and initiate possible improvements. They don't encourage themselves or their subordinates to be creative with new ideas or new developments. They aren't at home in the role of *innovator*.
- Provides Insufficient Autonomy:

  The supervisor doesn't allow his subordinates sufficient territory and autonomy to develop their own capacities. This can be explained firstly by the strong attention given by supervisors to applying past experience and proven methods as a way of solving problems and searching for solutions, and secondly by his strong attention to checking if things are going the way they are supposed to go.

- Too Bureaucratic:

  Both the managers and supervisors of Castco, the supervisors are seen as having rigid attitudes. This can be explained by responses indicating great attention to traditional ways of working, and the flow of information following fixed rules and procedures.

During the MEA seminars it also became clear that there were several serious problems in internal communication. The Management Group (MG) certainly did not create as a team. The Supervisory Staff considered the MG to have serious interpersonal problems, and to be backward in defending their department's positions during meetings. Communication between the two levels was poor and confusing at best, suggesting the potential value of intergroup activities.

Based largely on the MEA results and our discussions with the GM and his group, the structure of the rest of the project was designed.

The consulting team presented the MEA group results to the MG and discussed the impli-

Table 5.4 Structure of the Castco project.

PHASE 1	DIAGNOSIS	
	Intake	
	MEA Questionnaires + Feedback Seminars	
	Survey	
PHASE 2	INTERVENTIONS	
	Individual Level	Group Level
	Realization Individual	Composit Profile Sessions
	MEA Action Plans	
	Training Specific Skills	MEA Support Organization
	Mentor Counseling	Training Mentoring
	Individual Consultation	Team Building Sessions
	Training on the job	Group Training Sessions
	Training Consultation	Group Consultation
	Skills for HRM	
	Third Party Peacemaking	Internal Publicity
PHASE 3	RE-DIAGNOSIS	
	MEA Re-diagnosis Feedback Sessions	
PHASE 4	FURTHER ORGANIZATIONAL DEVELOPMENT	
	Strategic Planning	
	Conference on Strategic Development	
	Strategic Profile	
PHASE 5	ORGANIZATIONAL GOALS	
	Future MD Policy	
	New Mission Statement	
	Self Learning Organization	

cations for further action. Agreement was reached on overall plans for the management and organization development scheme. Among the conclusions of these talks, it was decided to conduct a series of OD activities including: survey feedback, group and intergroup (supervisors and managers) team building, third party peace-making, process consultation, coaching and counseling, mentoring training sessions with the management group, and related activities. Space does not permit a complete account of these activities, but important highlights are sketched in table 5.4.

5.3.2 Survey Feedback Results

In preparation for the first team building session each individual was asked to inform the trainers confidentially in writing about his or her main frustrations with regard to the current situation and ways of dealing with the organization's problems. From these written declarations some common complaints were derived:

- poor communication patterns;
- meetings and the GM's actions;
- mistrust within the group;
- decision making;
- feelings of powerlessness in the group.

Follow-up talks with each participant were held individually. It became clearer how some of the problems within this company could be explained. In essence it turned out that the core issue could be described as a complex of communication problems. To illustrate this situation we used the process description in figure 5.1. Each step in the process can be seen as influencing and being dependent on both the previous steps and those that follow. This illustration proved very useful in making clear that the situation consisted of a mixture of interrelated communication problems and misattributions.

Communication across languages and cultures

The Castco GM is the most fully bilingual (Dutch-English) of the group. Most members of the MG and supervisory staff are native Dutch speakers, while a small minority is either English or American. The working language in the plant is Dutch, whereas a small minority is either English or American. The working language in the plant is Dutch, whereas both Dutch and English are used in the *front office*. The *home* office in the U.S.A. is mainly an English (American) speaking group, and two of the nine Benelux MG members were from this American group.

The MEA, originally developed in the U.S.A., is available in Dutch translation thus aiding our work. Each participant completed the MEA and received feedback profiles in their mother tongue.

Due to a variety of factors, internal communication between and within the management levels was mainly oral, fragmentary, grapevine-like, and highly subjective. One could say internal information was frequently distorted, confusing and conflicting. Reports of proceedings of meetings (see below) typically were oral and fragmentary. The Supervisors' strong preference for written rules and procedures as indicated by their MEA scores is a correlation if not a direct result of this situation.

Figure 5.1 Scheme used to describe pattern of social processes within Castco MG.

It should be noted that more than language differences separate national groups. The Dutch and the Anglo-American culture are quite similar on two of Hofstede's (1980, 1991) four dimensions (power distance and individualism). They are very different on two others, masculinity (U.S. > NL) and uncertainty avoidance (NL > U.S.). Hofstede (1991) argues convincingly against using these group scores collected within one multinational organization (IBM) to make training decisions for individuals. We agree with this caution and used the information rather as background for formulating our training goals and a strong clue as to the nature of the cultural context within which we would be working.

Thus the cultural milieu Castco managers work in can be seen as likely being more homogeneous on power distance and individualism and more divergent on masculinity and uncertainty avoidance. Seen cross-culturally, the task becomes helping a group of Dutch managers to *deal more effectively with* their (likely) more masculine and less uncertainty-avoidant American counterparts.

As indicated above, sub-cultural differences along for example technical and administrative, production and management, older and younger can be observed among the employees of Castco. The potential for *in-* and *out-* groups and concurrent misattributions and apprehensions is thus high. The production group and their supervisors are located in a separate building (the plant) located *behind* the (front) office building which houses the managers and administrative supervisors. Thus physical *geography* reinforces sub-cultural differences at Castco, as indeed is the case for many firms.

Meetings and the GM's actions

Compounding the basic communication problems were difficulties associated with having an inefficient *meeting culture*. The MG meetings especially, were chaired by the GM who frequently behaved in a highly dominant manner. There was no agenda, neither were minutes taken. The GM's skills at chairing meetings can be best described as one-way communication. He used meetings solely to give information and to try to implement his (changing) vision of how managers should deal with the problems they encountered. From a psychological viewpoint he held the position of a dominant father, who supervised his children using an overload of (ideologically biased) information. The approach was an attacking style. After a few utterances from the manager whose topic was on the agenda, the GM would interrupt, confronting the person with information from other sources and then redefine the problem, explaining his ways of dealing with these kinds of problems, and ordering the manager involved to follow his instructions exactly. If the person resisted these recommendations, he threatened severe punishment of various kinds. The GM's words would give the impression of being a severe depreciation of the management skills of the person under attack. In the eyes of the other MG members attending, the person was being *rightfully slaughtered* (in their presence) because according to the information they had he was definitely wrong.

Decision making

Because no minutes were taken, problems with decision making and communicating the decision were all too obvious. Although most meetings were held in the same atmosphere, the process of decision making was not always the same. Sometimes the GM would make a decision without mentioning that he had done so, but afterwards he might refer to the meeting for justification. The absence of minutes made confirmation impossible. And the boss's memory prevailed in case of any disagreements. On other occasions a decision was made, but afterwards, in bilateral talks, these decisions were modified and often even reversed. As a consequence, during the period following a meeting, most people were uncertain about which decision was valid, and to which standard they had to perform. In the worst case they thought they were performing to agreed standards, unaware of decisions being subsequently altered.

Trust, motivation and commitment

Because of the uncertainties indicated above general commitment to the management team was very low. Managers began to distrust each other and, even worse, to mistrust themselves. If during the last meeting decision *A* was made and, later on, contrary procedure *B* was carried out with the GM's approval, how could this be possible other than through bilateral communication and without informing the others? This distrust led in turn to even poorer communication. The main motive for sending some messages was simply to secure one's position in terms of avoiding the punishing hand of *father GM*. The situation described above provided us with raw materials needed to set explicit goals for the training sessions covering communications and meeting skills.

Responsibility

One of the original complaints the GM expressed to us was lack of accepting responsibility by the managers. They did not see the company's problems as being their own, therefore they did not recognize solutions as being in their own interests. They just waited until he, the GM, would take up a problem and prescribe the solution. For instance, increased workload, internal cultural differences and changed external factors, all influenced this process dynamic in negative ways.

5.3.3 Team Building, Inter-group and Training Approaches

Given the objectives derived from the diagnostic and survey feedback procedures described above, a plan was created to address the management problems at Castco.

At the group level we introduced inter-group training in team building and several sessions on problem solving, communication skills, and presentation skills. Additionally, meeting skills training was planned but not completed. The training sessions resulted in an improved skill and morale and were generally met with enthusiastic participation of the participants, and were positively evaluated afterwards (structured evaluation feedback sheets were used after every session).

In the first Team Building session we worked with a group consisting of the managers plus three *promising* staff members who attended at the GM's request. It was later recognized that this led to an unequal status balance within the group, which sent mixed signals to all concerned on the status of the participating supervisory staff. Were they being promoted, tested for suitability, or in line to replace existing managers? Later sessions were addressed either to the groups separately, or explicitly as inter-group training involving both management and supervisory groups.

One of the inter-group sessions featured an alternative future scenario activity whereby managers and supervisors participated together in sketching and discussing best, worst and typical case scenarios for the organization over the coming ten years. This activity addressed the multiple goals of team building, group communication and long-term planning. Although it generated considerable spirited discussion and appeared to the trainers to be effective, it was one of the interventions (along with some of the coaching and mentoring training interventions) evaluated by the participants as being less effective. The timing of this activity, an evening session after a long day of team training, was one likely reason for its lower rating by the participants. Another could be related to the group MEA results that indicated that the supervisors in particular are not well-oriented to strategic planning.

5.3.4 Coaching and Counseling and Mentor Training

On an individual level the participants' written MEA action plans were carried out. Each participant had chosen his/her own *mentor* to help realize the stated goals. This part of the project was carried out with the supervision of the internal Human Resources Manager (HRM). Where necessary each participant would have the opportunity to receive individual training or group MD activities.

At the same time two of the managers were to be trained individually. Both had behaved in a *closed* manner and were clearly having great difficulties in coping with the cultural changes towards more businesslike operations. They reacted to the GM's style even more negatively than the others. In their cases a specific program was designed. For the *training on the spot* of these individuals, a third trainer was introduced.

In addition to the individual activities noted above, advising and coaching for the GM, HRM and some selected members of the management group were designed and conducted. These were met with mixed success, largely due to scheduling and other logistic problems. Although currently suspended, coaching is still regarded as being one of the means of continuing MD in the future. Additionally, mentor-training sessions were designed and conducted to provide managers with the opportunity to learn how to coach each other. These also received mixed acceptance. Whereas the idea seemed useful in the abstract, busy managers found other uses for their time and mentoring was generally considered to have a low priority. Moreover, the bulk of mentoring tasks fell to the HRM and the GM, the latter being the one who promoted the idea and who had the power to reward or discipline those who were mentored, a structural conflict-of-interest that was not really resolved.

5.3.5 Other OD Approaches Taken

Third party peace-making, structural activities, and process consultation intervention, all of which are other often cited OD approaches (French and Bell, 1990), occurred during the two year period in question.

The third party, an OD consultant, participated in mediating disputes between the GM and individual managers on two occasions. Process consultation also occurred in connection with an OD consultant sitting in on management meetings, later providing feedback and using the observations to design details of the training sessions. Structural activities occurred spontaneously, usually at the GM's behest. One that was tried in an attempt to balance power more evenly was the creation of a three person management committee which excluded the GM, to meet weekly and oversee daily operations. Other structural changes emerged from discussions in and following team training sessions. These seemed to gain more acceptance since they grew out of participation on the part of the full managerial team.

Life and career planning were not major parts of this project, but discussions with individual managers and the OD consultants and the coaching sessions often addressed these issues. Some of the managers have made important career decisions since this project began.

5.4 Project Results to Date

Among the chief contributions of our interventions were the institutionalization of MD activities in the written mission statement, increased participation in planning locally, and the improvement of communications with, and therefore acceptability of, ideas arriving from the home office. Management development activities became regular subjects for the in-house newsletter whereas they had previously been relegated to *grapevine* communication.

5.5 Current Project Status, Future Planning, and Discussion

The two rounds of coaching and training sessions took place in the first half of 1991 and in Spring 1992. There were subjective oral reports of progress from within the group and from observers. Some of the required skills, for example, listening skills, conduct and function in meetings, are fairly straightforward. Other skills and attitudes, for example, trust, personal confidence and responsibility, take more time to acquire and develop, not only from team training but from experience on the job. The contact with the consulting team and going through the MEA procedure heightened awareness of all participants to the need for and possibility of real progress in personal and management functioning. Awareness is taken as an initial step which is necessary but rarely sufficient in solving a variety of personal and interpersonal problems.

During the Team Building sessions several latent interpersonal tensions and frictions became manifest. These were discussed in depth. Also some internal personnel changes of management were suggested and decided upon. These matters were openly discussed. Clearing the air proved to be a necessary step towards improvement of communications and acquiring a true team spirit.

On the bright side, it should be emphasized that the original request for consultation came from the GM who continued to participate actively and support the change process overtly throughout the project. Any successes achieved must be attributed to a certain extent to this top-down participation and support (cf. Rodgers and Hunter, 1991; Rodgers, Hunter and Rodgers, 1993), enhancing the interventions of the consulting team.

On the other hand, changing old bad habits, especially attitudes, is neither easy nor quick to achieve. Awareness of problems may be necessary but it is often insufficient to resolve them. Having new skills alone rarely suffices without the attitudinal and motivational support to use them. If culture is as in Hofstede's (1991) terms a "collective programming of the mind", then what needs changing is not so much one's basic cultural orientation, but an acceptance of it, and of each other's culture and development of a set of skills to enable communication within but especially across cultures.

Because effective communication was a problem within Castco the project and its proceedings were deliberately publicized in the company's internal newsletter. From the very beginning internal information was regarded as a vital facet in this project. Ultimately organizational change affects everyone within the company, and there is the constant danger of lack of information evoking (misleading) grapevine communication, resulting in uncertainty, unrest and resistance.

By the second half of 1992, the effects of the international business recession were clearly being felt. Budgets were trimmed and expenditures for MD activities were put on hold for the rest of the year. In particular, the phase of re-diagnosis was postponed. The paradox of earlier business success coupled with management difficulties in contrast to the current business downturn and improved management skills became all the more obvious and chagrining.

Although the project was in an inactive phase in December 1992, some of the objectives set for OD could be taken to be met. Within Castco a general feeling of being on the right track has become evident, and OD is perceived as less threatening. The MEA proved to be a useful instrument to assess and address the needs of OD and MD. MD is now a formal part of Castco's written objectives and managers expect to take part in training every year. The project was due to be resumed at the beginning of 1993, but during that year a number of personnel changes occured within Castco including a change on GM, and this project was not restarted as planned.

An overall goal of the consulting team was to leave Castco as early as possible and in better shape than they found it; ideally as a self-correcting, self-learning organization more capable of realizing its potentials than before. This has occurred, at least partly. Sadly, we were not able to completely instill the value of strategic OD, that is continuing to develop managerial strengths during a period of economic downturn. Clearly, during difficult times other emphases are needed, for instance on boosting morale, planning for the turnaround, and making cuts carefully and with a strategic view to future plans. Taking a *strategic view* of OD does not come easily or naturally especially for smaller organizations. However, one practical lesson to be drawn for OD consultants is to include this prospect explicitly and early in goals for the mission statement.

In addition to national cultures on the one hand and (sub-) organizational cultures on the other, the interaction between these is an important issue for organizations like Castco. Globalization of industries bring inevitable cross cultural combinations. A better understanding of this and its implications for management practice and development will be necessary for both consultants and their clients in future.

Hofstede's caution on the danger of basing individual training on reported cultural norms of groups is well taken. On the other hand, we believe that an awareness of the cultural variations (likely) present in the group of managers to be trained/consulted is indispensable to the consultant in terms of understanding their potential communications problems.

Castco exemplifies in many ways other organizations where sudden growth results in a combination of business success on one hand, and management difficulties on the other. Wise GMs (like Castco's) recognize that management and organization development need to be institutionalized and prosperity is a good time to do it. Unfortunately, it is all too seductive to postpone or abandon MD and OD activities when times are tough. The good news is that Castco made a strong start. The bad news is that it has not been sustained, except on principle, during the current business recession.

References

Beer, M. (1980). *Organization Change and Development: A Systems View.* Santa Monica: Goodyear.

Burke, W.W. (1994). *Organization Development: Principles and Practices.* Boston: Little Brown.

French, W.L. and Bell, C.H.Jr. (1990). *Organizational Development: Behavioral Science Interventions for Organization Improvement.* (4th Ed.) Englewood Cliffs: Prentice-Hall.

Goossens, W. (1990). Management Effectiviteits Analyse. Van Haaren, P.W.M., De Lange, W.A.M., Meekel, W.J.M and Vinke R.H.W. (Eds.) *Methoden, technieken & analyses voor Personeelsmanagement, 13.* Alphen a/d Rijn: Kluwer.

Hofstede, G. (1980). *Culture's consequences: international differences in work-related values.* Beverly Hills: Sage.

Hofstede, G. (1991). *Cultures and Organizations: Software of the mind.* London: McGraw Hill.

Mahoney, J.T. (1987). *Management Effectiveness Analysis: Facilitator's guide.* Portland, ME.: Management Research Group.

Rand, T.M., Mahoney, J.T. and Mahoney F.C. (1990). *Management Effectiveness Analysis: Technical Considerations.* Portland, ME.: Management Research Group.

Rodgers, R. and Hunter, J.E. (1991). Impact of Management by Objectives on Organizational Productivity. *Journal of Applied Psychology Monograph, 76,* 322-336.

Rodgers, R., Hunter, J.E. and Rodgers, D.L. (1993). Influence of top management commitment on management program success. *Journal of Applied Psychology, 78,* 151-155.

Van der Klauw, M. and Van den IJssel, M. (1990). *De management effectiviteits analyse (MEA) in haar wetenschappelijke context.* Den Haag: Goossens Management en Organisatie.

Notes

1 The first author is Professor of Behavioral Sciences at RVB, The Maastricht School of Management, Maastricht. The second author is senior management consultant of the Management Ontwikkelings Groep, The Hague, The Netherlands.

2 Benelux: Belgium, Netherlands and Luxemburg.

3 Management Effectiveness Analysis, copyright © 1985, James Mahoney, Thomas Rand, Management Research Group, Portland Maine.

4 In this case only differences ≥ 20 % are considered.

PART II

Evaluation of

Models and Strategies

Introduction to Part II

Robert O. Brinkerhoff

Training and development is pursued in today's organization through an ever broadening array of methods and strategies. These diverse approaches vary on several dimensions: among the primary dimensions are training format, venue, objectives, content, and teaching method. Learning may be accomplished in groups, or individually. Learning sessions may be organized on the job-place, in nearby classrooms, at any variety of off-site locations, or alternatively as is characterized by the developing concept of the *learning organization*, can be structured into the activities of jobs themselves.

Learning objectives may be primarily focused on knowledge and information, cognitive skills such as problem solving and communications techniques, psychomotor skills such as use of machine tools, or attitude formation, such as the desire to please and serve customers, or commitment to organizational goals and strategy. Content of training is usually centered on the skills, knowledge, and attitudes needed for effective job performance, but may also be directed toward personal effectiveness topics such as conflict resolution abilities or communication skills, or primarily socialization and acculturation topics intended to help employees become better integrated with an organization.

The learning and teaching methods used in human resources development (HRD) represent probably the largest dimension along which approaches vary. Methods include mediated instruction, group interaction, lecture, role play, behavior modeling, trial and error, mentoring and tutorials, apprenticeships, simulation and gaming, to name only a few.

Given this tremendous diversity among formats, venues, objectives, content, and methods, this section of the book is exceedingly sparse, in that it highlights only a small handful of research projects.

The chapters in this section are representative, however, of the sort of action research and evaluation efforts that we believe are vitally important for the practice and profession of HRD. As we have noted earlier in this book, the need for effective HRD is growing dramatically, and the pressures on HRD to be more effective and cost efficient are likewise growing. The sharply competitive global business environment demands increasingly higher levels of competence and performance from employees, and thus effective HRD becomes more strategically important than ever. Given that there is a broad array of training models and strategies from which to choose, and given demands for increasingly effective performance, we believe that HRD practitioners must do more of the sorts of work that is reported on in this section: to evaluate and critically examine the effectiveness of chosen approaches, and to continuously improve them.

Darlene Russ-Eft and Jack Zenger have broad experience in training approaches based on behavior-modeling learning strategies. Thus, it is fitting that their research project has summarized North American research and evaluation on behavior modeling programs. Their chapter reviews and summarizes 30 recent studies, drawing conclusions and recommendations that are useful for HRD professionals to learn from and about the behavior modeling approach. Their study concludes that behavioral modeling is effective in changing specific managerial performance dimensions, but also that such changes are not always equal; some behaviors are more readily changed than others. They report, as well, that behavioral modeling approaches can positively affect attitudes toward organizational climate and management. Their study is full of very practical guidance in the design and format of behavioral modeling training, such as the use of multiple examples, individualized feedback, balanced (negative and positive) examples, and so forth.

Nico Krijger and Silvia Pol, in contrast, report on their research with a single leadership development training effort with which they have had long experience, and which has demonstrated (through prior research that they reference) to have had a lasting impact on trainees. The focus in their research is on the specific design variables and trainer interventions that can be associated with the impact of the training. As might be expected, their study reveals that a primary factor in the creation of lasting behavioral change is the presence, in the training design, of a systematic and comprehensive follow-up strategy. Action planning, individual analysis of needs, setting of specific learning and usage objectives, and so forth, contribute strongly to training transfer.

We see two benefits for readers of this study. First, the findings of their evaluation strike us as probably quite generalizable. The sorts of design variables and trainer interventions that have proven effective in their setting are highly likely to work in other similar settings. Secondly, the purpose and method of their study is likewise generalizable. HRD professionals should not strive only to assess impact and to *prove* worth, but need as well to conduct research to improve effectiveness and efficiency, seeking as did Krijger and Pol to learn what seems to make their program work, and improve it based on their findings.

Jeroen Onstenk's chapter departs from an investigation of training programs to a review and analysis of on-the-job *learning*, which is defined and discussed as an alternative to *training*, either on-the-job or in programs. The concept of on-the-job learning is that jobs themselves can be designed and managed so that job incumbents learn and develop competence as they work, thus reducing the frequency and imposition of training. It is not structured by pedagogical practices and theories, but is structured by the work activity itself, so that the work venue constitutes a learning environment. Onstenk reviews a comparison of on-the-job learning and on-the-job training in six countries, then proceeds to present a model for analyzing and defining on-the-job learning. The chapter makes important contributions for studying, planning, and assessing on-the-job learning.

The final contribution from Martin Mulder, Wim Nijhof and Afina Steinvoort is similar to the second and third chapters, in that it bases its research inquiry on a single training program. Like the first chapter in the section, however, it generalizes its findings to the type of intervention represented by the training effort, the professional seminar aiming at dissemination of expertise. The findings in this study note that there is partial effectiveness for the seminar format in disseminating expertise. But the findings indicate as well that the seminar design was neither directly nor completely responsive to needs, and that there was considerable "missing of the mark," in that many attendees reported content that they could not, or did not need to use. This study reminds us that effective training requires careful attention to needs analysis and other front-end procedures, and that general, large group training formats contain considerable risk for lack of transfer, excessive content, and lack of responsiveness to some individual and organizational needs.

As we noted, the selection of these five chapters represents only a tiny sample of the broad diversity of methods and strategies among which today's HRD professionals must choose and design, achieving for their organizations the effective results that all organizations vitally need. But the small sample is not, we think, a weakness. The task facing HRD professionals is not one of searching and scanning the plenitude of research in order to locate finally the solution that they will use, for such an approach would be logistically overwhelming in the first case, and probably not responsive to their organization's needs in any case. Rather, the task facing HRD professionals who wish to serve their organization's training needs is one of thoughtful design, followed by disciplined inquiry and continuous improvement.

Throughout this process, evaluative inquiry will play a key role. The design process begins with needs analysis, then progresses through evaluation of alternative solution strategies, thence to one or more design cycles, where evaluation of trials and pilots is often useful. Finally, as demonstrated by several of the chapters in this section, the thoughtful professional will inquire into impact and effectiveness, seeking to determine how well needs have been met, and what design variables add to or detract from effectiveness.

With respect to disciplined HRD practice and evaluation, the chapters here are exemplary, for they represent the sort of inquiry that we believe must become the rule rather than the exception. Methodologically, we find that these chapters provide good examples as well of the sort of tradeoffs that the action researcher must make between rigor and practicality. The methodology of the cases is rooted primarily in a psychological perspective, wherein the impact of training is presumed to be found in the reactions and cognitive and behavioral patterns of the recipients of training. The cases do not, for instance, employ methods from economic or political analysis, though surely training can also be viewed from and has consequences for the political and economic functioning of the organization. And, even within the psychological domain, we do not find the cases employing rigorous psychometrics.

More rigorous approaches have a role to play in the more basic research into learning models and techniques that are the domain of the university or scientific laboratory based researcher, and in these contexts, we would fault the methods of the cases for their lack of rigor. In the context of the HRD professional and practitioner, we find methods such as those used in the cases, survey questionnaires, interviews, and informal learning assessments, to be adequate and appropriate. The setting of practice is always fraught with many intervening and contaminating variables, and the practicalities are such that rigorous control is not always advisable nor possible. The case methods employed strike us as very reasonable, and are exemplary in that they can be emulated by virtually any HRD practitioner. We should also note that, at times and within resource constraints, more powerful quasi-experimental, or even experimental, designs may be appropriate. It is often possible to control some important intervening variables even in a corporate setting, and when this is possible, we advise it. On the other hand, we would advise that practitioners should not let their inability to control such variables or to use more rigorous designs keep them from conducting research, however rough and simple.

The cases are also noteworthy for their focus on the behavioral and organizational results of training, versus the more direct impact on learning of trainees. This focus reminds us that the purpose of training is to add value to organizational functions, services, and products, and is not simply to create new learning. Thus, the HRD practitioner-researcher should be concerned, as are these cases, with the instrumental value of training, and how effectively and efficiently it meets the needs of organizational performance.

6 Behavior Modeling Training in North America: a Research Summary

Darlene F. Russ-Eft and John H. Zenger[1]

American industry spends somewhere between $40 and $60 billion per year on training, an amount roughly equal to all public and private education expenditures at the college level. With this enormous investment, training professionals and corporate executives should be looking for ways to get a better payoff from expenditures.

One of the most popular methods for training is behavior modeling. It is now well known and widely discussed, with much of the research on this technique beginning in the 1960s and continuing into the present. According to Decker and Nathan (1985, 1), "The principles behind behavior modeling are ancient and were possibly best expressed over 2,000 years ago by the Chinese philosopher Confucius, when he wrote:

'I hear and I forget.

I see and I remember.

I do and I understand.'

... This is what behavior modeling is all about," Decker and Nathan continue, "seeing and remembering, doing and understanding." The key components of behavior modeling begin with learning simple rules of behavior, followed by demonstration, imitation, and feedback.

A unique feature of behavior modeling is that it can be considered "no-trial learning" (Bandura, 1965). Thus, unlike behavior modification, learning is not dependent upon direct experience and reinforcement. New behaviors can be acquired by observing the behavior of models. However, certain processes do facilitate learning using behavior modeling: attention, retention, motor reproduction, and motivation (Bandura, 1977). According to social learning theory, an observer cannot learn unless they attend to the behavior of the model. After having attended to the behavior, the observer must encode and store the behavior for later retention. Motor reproduction involves actually performing the behavior. Finally, reinforcement can increase or decrease the motivation for performing the behavior.

A second unique feature of behavior modeling is that it attempts to change behavior directly. Lecture-style training, for example, aims primarily at improving participants' knowledge. Its aim is to make people more expert. As a by-product, people may develop improved attitudes and behavior. Experiential training aims primarily at improving a participant's attitudes. This may lead to an increased desire for work-related knowledge. Like a lecture, however, experiential training gives no direct help in acting out new knowledge and attitudes. Behavior modeling, in contrast, comes at behavior directly. It concentrates neither on knowledge nor attitudes, but on new ways of behaving. A participant's ability and commitment to use the skills are integral to the training (motivation), but, initially at least, how that participant thinks or feels is secondary.

A final unique feature of behavior modeling is its widespread use and testing within business and industry. Because of its direct link to behavior and behavior change, many within business and industry find it to be an effective and practical method for delivering training. Organizations do not need employees who merely understand theory; they need employees who use a skill to achieve measurable results.

Measurable results can be described in five different ways. These include: (1) reactions to training; (2) knowledge gains; (3) changes in on-the-job performance; (4) changes in attitudes about the organization, management, and climate; and (5) bottom-line results or changes in organizational performance. Each of these types of results has been measured in studies of behavior modeling.

In the aggregate, the research on behavior modeling is impressive. Since many people are reluctant to read lengthy and detailed research studies, we present only the conclusions of the major studies, with citations, to allow the reader to investigate further any topic of interest. After a brief history of behavior modeling, we present a summary of current research on (1) the results of behavior modeling training, and (2) refinements in its delivery.

6.1 Overview

The first research on behavior modeling in industry, which was designed at General Electric and reported by Sorcher and Goldstein (1972) and Goldstein and Sorcher (1973, 1974), studied programs intended to reduce the turnover among "hardcore unemployed" employees. Firms needed unskilled labor, but these employees often left their new jobs after only a few weeks.

Sorcher and Goldstein felt that behavior modeling would be ideal. Such employees lacked good role models, for few of them knew other people who held steady jobs. GE foremen and supervisors also lacked role models who could demonstrate how to deal with these new employees. Therefore, parallel but separate programs were developed for the employees and their supervisors.

Six months after training, the turnover rate for those following the usual orientation procedures was almost three times higher than that for employees receiving the behavior modeling training. Further evaluation showed that during training, productivity increased among workers reporting to the trained supervisors as compared with workers reporting to the control group supervisors.

Because of its success, GE expanded this program to include all first-level supervisors (Burnaska, 1976). Later, other researchers reported on the effects of behavior modeling programs that taught communication and interpersonal skills and were developed for first-level supervisors in numerous organizational settings (Zenger and Hargis, 1982). Behavior modeling programs were also used for different levels of staff in a variety of business and industrial settings. Meyer and Raich (1983) described a behavior modeling program used to increase sales performance. Burke and Day (1986) summarized the results of several different approaches to managerial training and reported behavior modeling to be one of the more effective methods. Russ-Eft (1985b) reported on a series of studies of a supervisory training program conducted in a variety of settings; banking, insurance, public utilities, electronics, semiconductors, aerospace, pharmaceutical, hospital, federal agencies, manufacturing, mining, and higher education. Russ-Eft (1986) also reported on a series of studies of a nonsupervisory training program.

Recent efforts by a committee of the National Research Council included an examination of techniques for enhancing human performance (Druckman and Swets, 1988; Swets and Bjork, 1990). The committee reported that models of expert performance can serve as an effective foundation for training programs.

6.2 Results of Behavior Modeling Training

6.2.1 Reactions to Training

Behavior modeling effectively changes participants' attitudes about training. After attending a session of behavior modeling training, participants report measurably improved attitudes about participating in training. Other kinds of training programs have not reported these positive gains.

In 30 studies of a supervisory training program and 25 studies of a leadership program (11 of which contained control groups), we examined changes in opinions about training (Russ-Eft, 1985b, 1985c, and Research Summary: *Supervision* available from Zenger-Miller). Statistically significant higher ratings after training, when compared with pre-training ratings, were obtained for the following items:

> To what extent do you think training will improve your ability to be a better supervisor?; will increase productivity?; is a good use of your time? To what extent do you: think your fellow supervisors/first-level managers think training will help develop better supervisory skills?; think this training is a good use of their time?

Thus, behavior modeling training leads to improved attitudes about training and the benefits of training.

6.2.2 Knowledge Gains

Behavior modeling produces measurable improvements in participants' knowledge of the subject being trained. These results appear in paper-and-pencil tests as well as assessments conducted using role-playing situations.

Two studies reported on the differences between pre- and post-test results. Hards (1981) reported on a study using pre- and post-training knowledge and skills tests. These tests were designed to assess participants' understanding of the basic concepts of each training module. The tests consisted of twelve completion, multiple-choice, and true-false questions. There was an overall gain of 90 percent in supervisory skills and statistically significant differences in the average pre/post test scores.

A pharmaceutical company (Research Summary) assessed knowledge of good supervisors' practices, using a 35-item knowledge test for trained supervisors only. The average score before the course was 4, with scores ranging from -11 to 12. After training, scores ranged from 21 to 35, with a mean of 26 points. Training therefore resulted in significant pre/post differences, including a 64 percent increase in the number of items answered correctly.

A study of the effects of positive and negative models (Russ-Eft and Zucchelli, 1987) included measurement of knowledge gains. Each subject in the testing received both a behavioral and a written test. Subjects who, during training, viewed one or more positive models illustrating correct behaviors showed significant knowledge gains. Recently, some college seniors participated in leadership training as part of their academic course work. Both prior to and after the training, these students received written descriptions of four situations that they might encounter. The open-ended responses were scored independently by the course instructor and by graduate students who showed high inter-rater reliability. Raters observed significant improvements in the students' knowledge of how to handle these situations after training.

Together these studies indicate that behavior modeling training can lead to knowledge gains, particularly in terms of handling interpersonal situations. But the important question is whether such knowledge gains result in changes in behaviors on the job (Russ-Eft and Zenger, 1985).

6.2.3 Changes in On-the-Job Performance

Behavior modeling makes enduring changes in the on-the-job behavior of participants. Baldwin and Ford (1988) argue that such transfer of training depends on generalization of learning to contexts outside of training, as well as motivation and the opportunity to use such skills. The earliest studies of behavior modeling documented this transfer of training to the work setting (e.g., Burnaska, 1976; Byham, Adams and Kiggins, 1976). Also, Latham and Saari (1979) showed significant improvements in job performance for trained supervisors by using behavioral observation scales designed for the study, as well as the company's traditional performance appraisal instruments.

In a study of a behavior modeling program designed for nonsupervisory staff (Russ-Eft, 1985a), interviews were conducted with participants, their supervisors, and their co-workers. This program was designed to help workers learn interpersonal skills to cope with on-the-job problems. The interviews used the critical incident technique in interviews to collect reports of observations of human behavior (Flanagan, 1954, 1962, 1974). After the training program, reports from the participants' supervisors noted that employees seemed to be thinking before acting in certain interpersonal situations. One observer commented about an employee confronting the boss:

> [The employee] protested, but in a fashion that was unlike him in the past. He actually had thought about his case and presented it first to his own supervisor and then to me and in a very gentlemanly fashion.

Such studies provide evidence for the effectiveness of behavior modeling, but more rigorous information can also be presented to corroborate reactions and anecdotes.

During the past 10 years, Zenger-Miller, Inc., has encouraged research and evaluation studies of behavior modeling training systems. The separate research projects in table 6.1 were completed, some of which were done independently by client organizations or by external researchers.

All of these studies attempted to answer the question, "Do the participants in this training improve in their on-the-job behavior?" Thus, these studies included measures of behavior change, and all but two of the studies examined behavior change through ratings of on-the-job performance. The ratings were obtained from participants and from observers of participants their managers, peers, and subordinates. From the studies conducted on Zenger-Miller training programs, we have behavioral results from the groups in table 6.2.

Table 6.1 Studies of behavior modeling training systems.

Type of Training	*Number of Studies*
Group facilitation skills	5
Leadership skills	45
Supervisory skills	58
Nonsupervisory skills	16

All studies reported improvements from before training to after training, with most showing statistically significant improvements. Further, all studies with control groups reported statistically significant improvements for the trained group as compared with the control group. These results provide convincing evidence of the effectiveness of behavior modeling in improving performance on the job.

Depending on the specific training objectives, we see different changes in behavior. For example, studies of leadership training report gains in: displaying basic supervisory skills; communicating goals; focusing, preparing, and planning; involving employees (sharing responsibility); working with upper management; and working with groups or teams.

Table 6.2 Detail of study group respondents.

Type of Training	**Number of Respondents**			
	Participants	*Bosses*	*Peers*	*Subordinates*
Facilitation	326	----	114	------
Leadership	937	589	303	1262
Supervisory	1825	897	----	3508
Nonsupervisory	627	315	673	------
TOTAL	3715	1801	1090	4770

In contrast to the leadership training, supervisory training programs showed gains focused on the basic supervisory skills. Figure 6.1 summarizes for 30 companies the rating changes in basic supervisory skills from before to after supervisory training; changes are shown for the supervisors themselves, for their managers, and for their employees. Rating changes above the dashed line indicate positive improvements from before to after training, while those below the dashed line indicate decrements.

Figure 6.1 Change in supervisory skill.

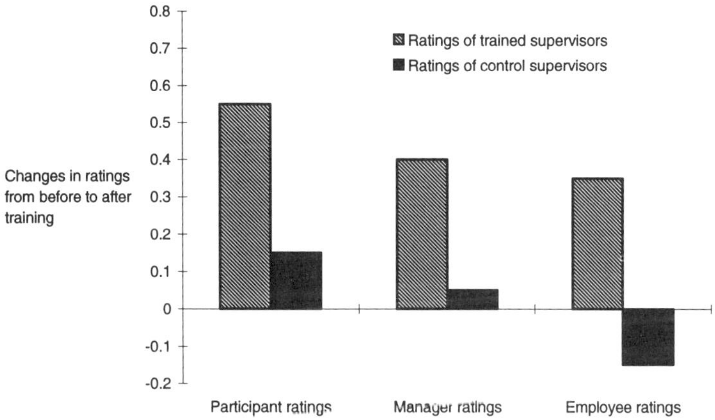

The figure shows that the trained supervisors and the managers and employees of the trained supervisors reported large improvements. Employees of control group supervisors reported declines in the skill of their supervisors. Such results show the effectiveness of behavior modeling in changing on-the-job performance.

Greater change over time

One of our most important findings is that positive behavior change not only lasts, but improves over time. Behavior modeling, the only kind of training we know that produces such continuing gains, disproves the common assumption that the effects of training must diminish over time.

Porras and Anderson (1981) noted continuing improvement in their study of a supervisory training program conducted in the manufacturing operation of a forest products company. They found large improvements in supervisory behavior during the intervention period when comparing the trained with the control group. Further, the behaviors maintained or increased their improvements through the six months following training.

McDaniels (1985) investigated the issue of increase in behavior change over time. Self-reported ratings of supervisory behavior were obtained immediately after training and again six months after training. Positive changes appeared in 25 of 26 behaviors being measured. Only one, "notice the good things subordinates do," remained at the same level over this period.

Russ-Eft (1986) examined the impact of nonsupervisory training over a period of one year. Skill ratings before training were compared with skill ratings midway through training and one month following training. Midway, overall gains in skills occurred, but they were about half as large as overall gains following training. Of greater interest was the finding that the behaviors covered early in training maintained a high level of proficiency from the midpoint to the end of training.

In a study examining behavior retention following training, Mazzarese (1984) obtained ratings of supervisory skills before training, and 30 and 60 days after training. Significantly greater gains appeared 60 days after training as compared with gains 30 days after training. This may be explained by subordinates having had more time and/or occasions to see the new behavior.

These findings might be surprising given that research on verbal learning and memory suggest a decline in performance over time. The present studies, however, concerned not participants' memory of the training but on-the-job performance. These studies suggest that behavior modeling training can lead to permanent changes in participants' behaviors.

Inequality of change

Behavior change is not reported at the same level by all rating groups. Further, within a rating group, gains are not equal across all dimensions or behaviors being trained. When evaluating behavioral change, we must not assume that all dimensions will change equally; we should be prepared for differences.

Overall, the largest gains appear in the ratings by the participants and their superiors. In contrast, the smallest gains appear in the ratings by the employees and peers of the participants. For supervisory training and for leadership training, the greatest gains occurred in basic supervisory skills. These skills consist of such behaviors as: asking for subordinates' ideas about how to solve a problem; setting a follow-up time to check on things a subordinate has agreed to do; making sure subordinates have clear goals to achieve; preparing and thinking through what to cover in a discussion with subordinates; and expressing appreciation for the work that subordinates do well.

In addition to the basic supervisory skills, leadership training participants and their managers report the greatest gains in communicating goals; preparing, focusing, and planning; and working with upper management. In contrast, employees report the greatest gains for their supervisors in working with groups and teams.

The results indicate that behavior modeling training is a very powerful agent in changing specific behaviors.

Attitudes about the organization, management, and climate

Behavior modeling produces some positive changes in participants' attitudes about the organization, management, and changes may appear unrelated to skills training; positive behavior change in participants' leadership abilities fosters a more positive view of the organization. The studies on leadership training showed statistically significant improvements in terms of behavioral factors. Improvements in factors describing job satisfaction and organizational climate, although observed, were not statistically significant.

Similar results can be seen in an overview of the supervisory training program. In 30 studies of a supervisory training program using behavior modeling (Russ-Eft, 1985c), supervisors and their employees rated items relating to organizational climate. Figure 6.2 displays the rating changes from before to after training for supervisors and employees. Positive changes are shown for the trained group of supervisors and their employees, while negative changes appear for the control groups.

Figure 6.2 Change in organizational climate.

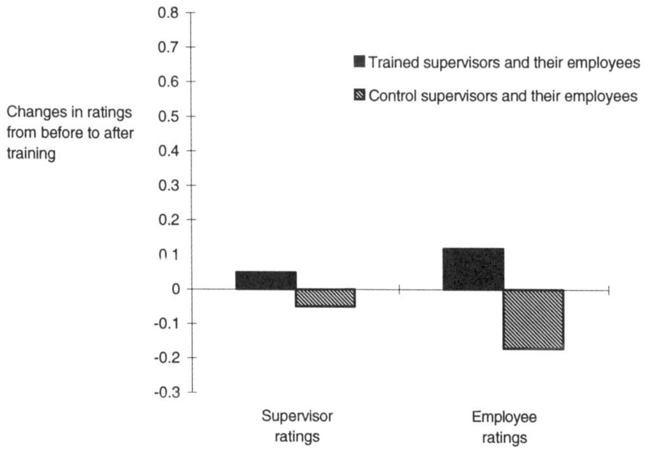

Bottom-line results

Training may result in behavior changes made on the job, but some decision makers question whether these changes translate into improved organizational performance and productivity. Results of behavioral modeling training do show up in bottom-line or hard measures of organizational performance. Some of these changes include higher productivity, reduced turnover, fewer labor grievances, reduced scrap rates, and lower absenteeism.

Porras and Anderson (1981) described a study examining the effects of behavior modeling supervisory training in a large manufacturing operation of a major forest products company. In addition to measuring changes in supervisory behavior, they assessed changes in organizational productivity and efficiency on the basis of three main indices of plant performance: total monthly production per direct labor worker hour, average daily plant production, and recovery rate (an index reflecting the degree to which a log is effectively converted to an end product). All three measures showed improvement from before to after training.

Meyer and Raich (1983) conducted an evaluation of a behavior modeling program used to increase sales performance. Sales representatives from 14 retail stores participated. The stores were matched in size, sales, and geographic area. Behavior modeling training was then introduced into one store in each of the seven pairs, and other kinds of sales training were provided to the control groups in the remaining seven stores. Sales performance was compared for the six months before and six months after training. Salespersons receiving behavior modeling training increased their sales by about 7 percent following training, while the sales of the control group salespersons decreased by about 3 percent. In addition, the turnover for the sales representatives trained using behavior modeling was only 7 percent compared to 22 percent for the control group.

One approach to measuring bottom-line impact is to examine improvements in the work activities of subordinates. If managers and supervisors improve their leadership skills, then employees should display increased efficiency and effectiveness. In our studies of leadership training, we find improvements in employees' behaviors on the job.

These gains appear in job areas that include: solving problems with other employees, rather than with the supervisor; understanding priorities and goals; and feeling commitment to the team.

Russ-Eft and Hurson (1987) determined the internal rate of return (IRR) on an investment in training for innovation skills. Benefits were determined based on the results of special projects undertaken by participants. Costs were calculated for the training materials, the trainers' salaries, and participants' time in the course, as well as project costs. At the end of training, discounted cash flow techniques were used, with the payback period set for ten weeks. Even with such a short payback period, the training showed a 36 percent return rate.

What skills improved from before to after training?

Mazzarese, Nyvelt and Russ-Eft (1990) undertook a cost-benefit analysis on worker training. In this case, the researchers asked the following questions:

> What skills have improved from before to after training?; How much are these skills worth?; How much does the training cost?; and, What was the net benefit of training?

Here are the answers to their questions: The researchers measured worker skill levels before and after training. Specific skills were grouped into the following competency areas: communicating with co-workers; working with superiors; dealing with problems; and improving work. Statistically significant improvements were observed in specific skills, as well as in all four competency areas.

How much are these skills worth?

The primary benefits from training involved changes in skill. These skill changes were transformed into dollar benefits to the organization by determining: the degree of skill change for specific work activities; and the amount of work time trainees spent on these areas. The results indicated that for a sample of 42 trainees out of the total population of 85 trainees, the return on investment (ROI) was approximately $305,000. If we assume a similar ROI for the remaining trainees, then the total ROI would be estimated at $610,000.

How much does the training cost?

Determining the costs for training is fairly straightforward. First, we must recognize two types of costs: (1) variable costs and (2) fixed costs. The variable costs consist of the costs for running each training session. These costs are incurred if and only if a session takes place. The fixed costs are those that have been or will be incurred even if a specific session never happens.

The variable costs include the following: trainees' time away from work; trainers' time for preparation and training; and actual materials used during the sessions. The fixed costs in-

Table 6.3 Net benefit.

Gross Benefits	$305,000
Gross Costs	$ 70,000
Net Benefits	*$235,000*

clude the following: time for designing the sessions; and certification costs. Costs incurred for the entire population of 85 trainees were estimated at approximately $70,000.

What was the net benefit of this training?
The final step in this cost-benefit analysis involved subtracting the costs from the benefits to arrive at a net benefit. The above amount somewhat underestimates the net benefits. As previously mentioned, the gross benefits were determined for about half of the population. If we assume total gross benefits of $610,000, then the net benefits would be $540,000.

A second reason for the underestimation involves some indirect benefits from the training. We observed the following changes in the percentage of time trainees spent in various activities (table 6.4):

Table 6.4 Indirect training benefits.

Category	*Percentage Before Training*	*Percentage After Training*
Communicating with co-workers	18%	26%
Working with superiors	19%	16%
Dealing with problems	26%	31%
Improving work	22%	22%
Other	15%	5%

After training, trainees spent more time communicating with co-workers and less time working with superiors. This can be viewed as a benefit since trainees are handling issues and problems directly with their co-workers. We have not, however, included any of these indirect benefits in our analysis.

6.3 Enhancing Delivery Methods

Having assured ourselves that behavior modeling produces measurable results, we now turn to how we can make those results even better or achieve the same results more economically.

6.3.1 Positive Versus Negative Models

Most behavior modeling training uses videotaped models who perform the key behaviors correctly. These are referred to as positive models. Diverse opinions exist on whether or not training programs should use negative models who perform the key behaviors incorrectly or not at all. Indeed, one of the authors contacted several leading researchers of behavior modeling on this question, only to find sharply diverse opinions. As a result, we encouraged several researchers to investigate this issue, supported their efforts, and also conducted our own pilot study.

Findings indicated that either positive models only or a mixture of positive and negative models result in the highest levels of behavior change and cognitive gain (Mills 1985; Newman and Fuqua, 1988; Russ-Eft and Zucchelli, 1987; Trimble, Decker and Nathan, 1985; Trimble, Decker and Nathan, 1991). For a given skill, seeing one negative model with positive models does not interfere with learning and performance and does lead to high subjective ratings on personal benefit and on believability. These benefits of a single negative model do not extend to viewing multiple negative models. Indeed, those who saw two negative models within the same training module experienced the least gain and provided the lowest ratings. In a more recent study, Baldwin (1992) found that a combination of positive and negative models led to a significant positive effect on generalization to situations outside of training. Further research is under way to determine whether viewing a mixture of positive and negative models can lead to (1) better ability to distinguish between positive and negative behaviors, and (2) better awareness of the critical behaviors.

6.3.2 One Model Versus Multiple Models

Research confirms the superiority of multiple examples of anything being taught in the behavior modeling process. Several examples seem to reinforce the skill and emphasize the concepts and substance of the behavior being taught rather than any specific style (Russ-Eft and Zucchelli, 1987; Trimble, Decker and Nathan, 1985).

Learning and memory researchers agree that repetition leads to better learning and memory, whether done gradually or in an all-or-none fashion (e.g., Estes, 1950, 1960, 1964; Guthrie, 1935, 1952; Hull, 1943; Postman, 1963). The studies on positive and negative models provided an opportunity to test whether the gains resulting from repetition also hold for behavior modeling. The results indicated that recall and recognition memory improved between the testing done after showing the first model and the testing done after showing the second model.

Further research on this issue can help to determine whether the effect actually results from repetition or from generalization (through the presentation of different models showing the same key behaviors).

6.3.3 Individual Feedback

Clearly the purpose of training is to change or improve the behaviors of the participants. Feedback on performance also can lead to improvements in performance (e.g., Ammons, 1956; Ashford and Cummings, 1983; Ilgen, Fisher and Taylor, 1979; Komaki, Barwick and Scott, 1978; Payne and Hauty, 1955). Much of this work showed improvements in production quantity. More recently, however, Ilgen and Moore (1987) successfully demonstrated performance improvements along the separate dimensions of quantity and quality.

Individual feedback falls within a theoretical framework set forth by Bowers and Franklin (1972). According to these authors, change occurs through the use of: a model of current behaviors; a goal, involving the selection of alternative future behaviors; an activity initiated to attain the goal; and feedback used to compare, confirm, adjust, and correct responses.

Thus, the use of individual feedback is completely consistent with social learning theory (Bandura and Cervone, 1983). Feedback provides information to the performer that allows a comparison of current behaviors and desired behaviors. This comparison creates the motivation to invest further effort to change his or her behavior or performance standard.

Recently, we examined the impact of individual feedback given to participants prior to training. As with our previous research, we undertook pre-training and post-training measurements of skills. First, we found significant differences in the ratings of participants' skills from before to after training. What was surprising was the magnitude of the improvements as reported by the subordinates. Typically we see small but significant improvements. For groups receiving individual feedback, we found that the greatest improvements in participants' skills were reported by subordinates. Thus, it appears that individual feedback heightens participants' awareness of strengths and areas for improvement. This information can be used by participants to focus their attention on areas needing the greatest improvement.

6.3.4 Massed Versus Spaced Training

Research over the past century confirms the general superiority of spacing the sessions of behavior modeling out over time (Dempster, 1988; Ebbinghaus, 1885, 1913, 1964; Hovland, 1940, Jost, 1897, Underwood, 1961, Underwood, Kapelak and Malmi, 1976). Although spacing may slow the rate of learning, it may be optimal for post-training effectiveness.

We undertook a study on spacing effects using a program that trains workers in the interpersonal skills needed to cope with on-the-job problems. One manufacturer implemented the program in sessions held during three full days off site. A second manufacturer implemented the same program in sessions held twice a week over five weeks. The research study included ratings of worker behaviors before and after training for both the trained group and a comparable group of control workers (who did not receive the training).

Statistically significant improvements in worker skills from before to after training were reported for the trained groups as compared with the control groups in both organizations. However, differences did appear in the ratings between organizations using spaced and massed training. Improvements in co-worker ratings were significantly greater for the trained workers in the organization using spaced or distributed training. Such highly significant differences were not observed in the co-worker ratings from the organization using massed training (Russ-Eft, 1985a). We also found that covering two topics in one day, with one-week intervals between these two topics, produced equally good results as covering one each day. This suggests that a moderate amount of massing is acceptable.

6.3.5 Video Technique

Video technique seems to have little impact on participants. Whether or not a hand-held camera is used or whether lighting is natural versus studio-lit seems of little significance. We tested participants' reactions to these differences. Such differences were not noticed by the participants (Russ-Eft, 1985c).

6.3.6 Participant Characteristics

Decker and Nathan (1985) point out some characteristics of the observer or participant that can affect the success of behavior modeling training. Important characteristics mentioned are those relating to attention and reinforcement. These include the individual's work load, capabilities, attention to the materials, and expectations for reinforcement.

Porras and Hargis (1982) investigated the effects of personal characteristics on changes in supervisory behavior as the result of a behavior modeling training program. Supervisors in both the trained group and control group received questionnaires before and after a ten-week training program. Role clarity, control over the job, feelings of competence on the job, self-actualization, and self-regard were positively correlated with behavioral change. Role conflict, overload, and job-generated stress negatively correlated with change. Demographic variables of education, number of years worked at the company, and number of years on the job failed to reach statistical significance.

One large utility company examined the issue of whether psychological characteristics influence training effectiveness (Mazzarese, 1984). The study included ratings of supervisory skills before training, and 30 and 60 days after training. Ratings by managers obtained 60 days after training showed that those participants with abstract learning styles improved more than those with concrete learning styles. Similarly, more improvement in scores 60 days after training appeared for those with an external as compared to internal locus of control.

Using data from the leadership training program, Russ-Eft and Mazzarese (1990) identified individuals who reported large positive skill gains and those who reported smaller gains. We compared these two groups in terms of before scores, after scores, and gain scores in the dimensions of employee performance, job satisfaction/organization climate, and opinions on training. We found the following (table 6.5):

Table 6.5 Comparison of results from leadership training program.

Dimension	*Results*
Employee Interpersonal Skills	Gainers rate employees' skills lower than non-gainers before training. After training, both groups rate employees at about the same level.
Employee Bottom-Line Performance	Both groups rate employee skills at about the same level before training. After training, gainers rate employees' performance higher than non-gainers
Job Satisfaction/ Organization Climate	Both groups rate this dimension at the same level before training. After training. gainers rate some improvement, while non-gainers rate some decline over time.
Opinions on Training	Both groups rate this at the same level before training. After training, gainers rate improvement, while non-gainers rate a small decline.

Such results indicate that the effects of behavior modeling spread beyond participant skill improvements.

Increased effort and improvement peformance seem to result directly from goal setting (Locke and Latham, 1990; Werner, O'Leary-Kelly, Baldwin and Wexley, 1994). Such behavioral improvements occur whether goals were assigned or set participatively (Wexley and Baldwin, 1986). In addition, having trainees monitor such goals after training through the use of checklists leads to better application of training (Wexley and Nemeroff, 1975).

However, goal setting can have a negative influence as well. Research by Kanfer and Ackerman (1989) shows that designating goals in the early stages of learning leads to lower performance when compared with assigning goals in the later stages. Complex, specific goals can impair performance, particularly for unique and complicated tasks (Earley, Connolly and Ekegren, 1989). Dweck (1986) contrasts learning goals and performance goals. This researcher reasons that learning goals motivate individuals to increase their efforts when encountering obstacles, which leads to improved performance. Conversely, performance goals lead to defensive strategies and to peceiving mistakes or failures as a lack of abilty. Although

Klein and Thoms (1995) provide some empirical evidence to support the use of learning goals, additional research is needed to clarify the most effective use of goal setting.

6.3.7 Management Involvement and Support

One of the most significant findings from recent research is that results differ when there are varying degrees of management support. One study in which two plants with the same technology underwent supervisory training showed dramatically different results for each plant. The only discernible difference was the level of management support. Another study done in a group of hospitals showed one hospital that produced behavior change far in excess of the others. Again, the only difference appeared to be the degree of line management involvement (Taylor, 1992). Taylor found immediate supervisors' support important in training success as defined by reactions, learning, and skill use. Top management suppot proved important in leading to positive reactions.

Russ-Eft and Mazzarese (1990) examined the impact of higher degrees of management support on the transfer of training to on-the-job performance. Participants, their managers, and their employees reported on participants' skill level before and after training. In addition, participants reported on their perceived level of management support. Participants reporting high levels of management support were compared with those reporting low levels of management support. Results showed the greatest improvements from before to after training among participants reporting high levels of management support.

6.4 Conclusion

The summary effect of all this research has been to validate the pioneering work in behavior modeling and to justify the wide acceptance of the method. Rather than showing behavior modeling to be a fad like so many other training methods, the research has demonstrated both a solid theoretical foundation and significant practical gains in the workplace. Certainly no other training methodology rests on anything approaching the broadly based research evidence that supports behavior modeling.

At present, sound research continues in a few university and industrial settings, but much more needs to be done in order to fully exploit the power of this methodology and to answer many gnawing questions, among them:

> Should participants develop the key behavioral steps for a given skill, or should the trainer provide them? What's the best way to highlight the key behaviors in the video-

tape model? What's the longevity of participants' changes in behavior? When do declines set in? When and how should follow-up training be conducted?

The surprises from the research have all been pleasant ones. The fact that on-the-job behavior continues to improve over time is frankly more than most practitioners had ever hoped for. Given the effectiveness of behavior modeling, applications have been surprisingly limited. Most have appeared in supervisory and management training, with a minor amount in selling skills and middle management training. Future efforts will likely be directed toward expanding the applications of this highly effective approach.

References

Ammons, R.B. (1956). Effects of knowledge of performance: A survey and tentative theoretical formulation. *Journal of General Psychology, 54*, 279-299.

Ashford, S.F. and Cummings, L.L. (1983). Feedback as an individual resource: Personal strategies for creating information. *Organizational Behavior and Human Performance*, 370-398.

Baldwin, T.T. (1992). Effects of alternative modeling strategies on outcomes of interpersonal skills training. *Journal of Applied Psychology, 77,* 147-154.

Baldwin, T.T. and Ford, J.K. (1988). Transfer of training: A review and directions for future research. *Personnel Psychology, 41,* 63-105.

Bandura, A. (1965). Vicarious processes: A case of no-trial learning. Berkowitz, L. (Eds) *Advances in experimental social psychology. Vol. II.* New York: Academic.

Bandura, A. (1977). *Social Learning Theory.* Englewood Cliffs, N.J.: Prentice Hall.

Bandura, A. and Cervone, D. (1983). Self-evaluative and self-efficacy mechanisms governing the motivational effects of goal systems. *Journal of Personality and Social Psychology, 45*, 1017-1028.

Baron, R.A. (1970). Attraction toward the model and model's competence as determinants of adult imitative behavior. *Journal of Personality and Social Psychology, 14*, 345-351.

Bowers, D.G. and Franklin, J.L. (1972). Survey-guided development: Using human resources measurement in organization change. *Journal of Contemporary Business, 1*, 43-55.

Burke, M.J. and Day, R.R. (1986). A cumulative study of the effectiveness of managerial training. *Journal of Applied Psychology, 71*, 232-245.

Burnaska, R.F. (1976). The effects of behavior modeling training upon managers' behaviors and employee perceptions. *Personnel Psychology, 29*, 329-335.

Byham, W.C., Adams, D. and Kiggins, A. (1976). Transfer of modeling training to the job. *Personnel Psychology, 29*, 345-349.

Decker, P.J. and Nathan, B.R. (1985). *Behavior Modeling Training: Principles and Applications.* New York: Praeger.

Dempster, F.N. (1988). The spacing effect: A case study in the failure to apply the results of psychological research. *American Psychologist, 43*, 627-634.

Dowling, T.H. and Frantz, T.T. (1975). The influence of facilitative relationship on initiative learning. *Journal of Counseling Psychology, 22*, 259-263.

Druckman, D. and Swets, J.A. (Eds.) (1988). *Enhancing Human Performance: Issues, Theories, and Techniques*. Washington D.C.: National Academy Press.

Dweck, C.S. (1986). Motivational processes affecting learning. *American Psychologist, 41,* 1040-1048.

Earley, P.C., Connolly, T. and Ekegren, G. (1989). Goals, strategy development and task performance: Some limits on the efficacy of goal setting. *Journal of Applied Psychology, 74,* 24-33.

Ebbinghaus, H. (1885). *Über das Gedächtnis.* Leipzig, Germany: Duncker and Humblot.

Ebbinghaus, H. (1913). *Memory.* (H.A. Ruger and C.E. Bussenius, Trans.) New York: Teachers College. (Original work published 1885)

Ebbinghaus, H. (1964). *Memory.* (H.A. Ruger and C.E. Bussenius, Trans.) New York: Dover. (Original work published in 1885)

Estes, W.K. (1950). Toward a statistical theory of learning. *Psychological Review, 57,* 94-107.

Estes, W.K. (1960). Learning theory and the new mental chemistry. *Psychological Review, 67,* 207-223.

Estes, W.K. (1964). All-or-none processes in learning and retention. *American Psychologist, 19,* 16-25.

Flanagan, J.C. (1954). The critical incident technique. *Psychological Bulletin, 51,* 327-358.

Flanagan, J.C. (1962). *Measuring Human Performance.* Palo Alto: American Institutes for Research.

Flanagan, J.C. (1974). *Measuring Human Performance.* Palo Alto: American Institutes for Research.

Goldstein, A.P. and Sorcher, M. (1973). Changing managerial behavior by applied learning techniques. *Training and Development Journal,* 36-39.

Goldstein, A.P. and Sorcher, M. (1974). *Changing Supervisor Behavior.* New York: Pergamon Press.

Guthrie, E.R. (1935). *The Psychology of Learning.* New York: Harper.

Guthrie, E.R. (1952). *The Psychology of Learning.* New York: Harper.

Hards, K.E. (1981). *Supervisory skill workshops: final report.* Stanford, California: Stanford University Hospital, Department of Human Resources Development.

Hovland, C.I. (1940). Experimental studies in rote learning theory. VI. Comparison of retention following learning to the same criterion by massed and distributed practice. *Journal of Experimental Psychology, 26,* 568-587.

Hull, C.L. (1943). *Principles of Behavior.* New York: Appleton-Century-Crofts.

Ilgen, D.R., Fisher, C.D. and Taylor, M.S. (1979). Consequences of individual feedback on behavior in organizations. *Journal of Applied Psychology, 64,* 349-371.

Ilgen, D.R. and Moore, C.F. (1987). Types and choices of performance feedback. *Journal of Applied Psychology, 72,* 401-406.

Jost, A. (1897). Die Assoziationsfestigkeit in ihrer Abhngigkeit von der Verteilung der Wiederholungen. *Zeitschrift der Psychologie, 14,* 436-472.

Kanfer, R. and Ackerman, P.L. (1989). Motivation and cognitive abilities: An integrative/aptitude-treatment interaction approach to skill acquisition [Monograph]. *Journal of Applied Psychology, 74,* 657-690.

Kazdin, A. (1974) Effects of covert modeling and model reinforcement on assertive behavior. *Journal of Abnormal Psychology, 83,* 240-252

Kazdin, A. (1975). Covert modeling, imagery assessment, and assertive behavior. *Journal of Consulting and Clinical Psychology, 43,* 716-724.

Klein, H.J. and Thoms, P. (1995). The settings of goals for skill acquisition. Holton, III, E.F. (Ed.) *Proceedings from the Annual Meeting of The Academy of Human Resource Development.*

Kloba, J.A., Jr. (1975). The effects of model status and participant dependency-independency on adolescent learning of a helping skill using the micro-counseling training paradigm. *Dissertation Abstracts International, 36*, 2027A. San Francisco: University Microfilms. (No. 797, 75-22)

Kloba, J.A., Jr. and Zimpfer, D. (1976). Status and independence as variables in micro-counseling training of adolescents. *Journal of Counseling Psychology, 23*, 458-463.

Komaki, J., Barwick, K.D. and Scott, L.R. (1978). A behavioral approach to occupational safety: Pinpointing and reinforcing safe performance in a food manufacturing plant. *Journal of Applied Psychology, 63*, 434-445.

Latham, G.P. and Saari, L.M. (1979). Application of social-learning theory to training supervisors through behavior modeling. *Journal of Applied Psychology, 64*, 239-246.

Locke, E. and Latham, G.P. (1990). *A theory of goal setting and task performance.* Englewood Cliffs, NJ: Prentice-Hall.

Mazzarese, M. (1984). *Supervision research report.* Somerset, N.J.: A.T. & T. Communication.

Mazzarese, M., Nyvelt, R. and Russ-Eft, D. (1990). *Cost-benefit analysis of worker training.* Unpublished manuscript.

McDaniels, R.N. (1985). *Effectiveness of a supervisory training program using behavior modeling.* Unpublished master's thesis, Pepperdine University, Malibu, CA.

Meyer, H.H., and Raich, M.S. (1983). An objective evaluation of a behavior modeling training. *Personnel Psychology, 36*, 755-761.

Mills, G. (1985). *The effects of positive and negative models in learning and displaying basic communication skills.* Provo, Utah: Brigham Young University, Department of Communications.

Moses, J.L. and Ritchie, R.J. (1976). Supervisory relationships training: A behavioral evaluation of a behavior modeling program. *Personnel Psychology, 29*, 337-343.

Newman, J.L. and Fuqua, D.R. (1988). A comparative study of positive and negative modeling in counselor training. *Counselor Education and Supervision, 28,* 121-129.

Payne, R.B. and Hauty, G.T. (1955). The effect of psychological feedback on work decrement. *Journal of Experimental Psychology, 50*, 343-351.

Porras, J.L. and Anderson, B. (1981). Improving managerial effectiveness through modeling-based training. *Organizational Dynamics*, 60-77.

Porras, J.L. and Hargis, K. (1982). Precursors of individual change: Responses to a social learning theory based on organization intervention. *Human Relations, 35,* 973-990.

Postman, L. (1963). One-trial learning. Cofer C.N. and Musgrave B.S. (Eds.) *Verbal Behavior and Learning*. New York: McGraw-Hill.

Russ-Eft, D. (1985a). *Preview Client No. 2: Working training*. Cupertino, California: Zenger-Miller.

Russ-Eft, D. (1985b). *Research Summary: Supervision*. Cupertino, California: Zenger-Miller.

Russ-Eft, D. (1985c). *Seven years of evaluating supervisory training: What have we learned?* Paper presented at the Annual Meeting of the American Society for Training and Development in Anaheim, CA.

Russ-Eft, D. (1986). *Evaluating worker training: what can we learn?* Paper presented at the Annual Meeting of the American Psychological Association, Washington, D.C.

Russ-Eft, D. and Hurson, K. (1987). *Transforming supervisors into innovators: one way to get bottom-line results from training*. Paper presented at the Special Interest Group in Training and Business and Industry Meeting of the American Educational Research Association in Washington, D.C.

Russ-Eft, D., Ravishankar, L.P. and Krishnamurthi, S. (1994). Evaluating Return on Investment: A Case Study. Phillips, J. (Ed.) *In action: Measuring Return on Investment Volume I.* Alexandria, Virginia: ASTD, 199-213.

Russ-Eft, D. and Mazzarese, M. (1990). *Management support: is it worth it?* Unpublished manuscript.

Russ-Eft, D. and Zenger, J.H. (1985). Common mistakes in evaluating training effectiveness. *Personnel Administrator, 30.*

Russ-Eft, D. and Zucchelli, L. (1987). When wrong is alright. *Training and Development Journal*, 78-79.

Schoening, J.M. (1981). *Effectiveness of a behavior modeling training program on management trainees.* Unpublished master's thesis, Pepperdine University, Malibu, CA.

Sevy, B.A. and Olson, R.D. (1982, September). *Assessment of knowledge and skills acquired in the Supervision training program.* Minneapolis, MN: Personnel Decisions, Inc.

Sorcher, M. and Goldstein, A.P. (1972). A behavior modeling approach in training. *Personnel Administration, 35*, 35-41.

Sorcher, M. and Spence, R. (1982). The interface project: behavior modeling as social technology in South Africa. *Personnel Psychology, 35*, 557-581.

Swets, J.A. and Bjork, R.A. (1990). Enhancing human performance: An evaluation of New Age techniques considered by the U.S. Army. *Psychological Science, 1*, 85-96.

Taylor, P. (1992). Training directors' perceptions about the successful implementation of supervisory training. *Human Resource Development Quarterly, 3,* 243-259.

Trimble, S.K., Decker, P.J. and Nathan, B.R. (1985). *Effect of positive and negative models on learning: A report to Zenger-Miller.* St. Louis, MO: University of Missouri- St. Louis, School of Business Administration.

Trimble, S.K., Decker, P.J. and Nathan, B.R. (1991). Effect of positive and negative models on learning: Testing for proactive and retroactive interference. *Journal of Human Behavior and Learning, 7(2),* 1-12.

Underwood, B.J. (1961). Ten years of massed practice on distributed practice. *Psychological Review, 68*, 229-247.

Underwood, B.J., Kapelak, S.M. and Malmi, R.A. (1976). The spacing effect: additions to the theoretical and empirical puzzles. *Memory and Cognition, 4*, 391-400.

Werner, J.M., O'Leary-Kelly, A.M., Baldwin, T.T. and Wexley, K.N. (1994). Augmenting behavior-modeling training; Testing the effects of pre- and post-training interventions. *Human Resource Development Quarterly, 5,* 169-183.

Wexley, K.N. and Baldwin, T.T. (1986). Post-training strategies for facilitating positive transfer: An empirical exploration. *Academy of Management Journal, 29,* 503-520.

Wexley, K.N. and Nemeroff, W.F. (1975). Effectiveness of positive reinforcement and goal settings as methods of management development. *Journal of Applied Psychology, 60,* 446-450.

Zenger, J.H. and Hargis, K. (1982, January). Assessing training results: It's time to take the plunge. *Training and Development Journal*, 10-16.

Notes

1 The overview of studies conducted in the field of behavior modeling training is added as an appendix at the end of this book

7 Changing Leadership Style: a Training Model for Lasting Effects

Nico L. Krijger and Silvia M. Pol

In this chapter, we will describe the design of an external training program for managers whose goal is to change the ineffective aspects of their leadership style and interpersonal behavior. Earlier research on this program has shown that lasting effects can be achieved. We will report the results of follow-up research on design variables and trainer interventions which, according to the participants, contributed most to the desired changes. These are specifically the variables which enhance the transfer of training and learning and which are mentioned in research literature as deserving more attention. In addition, the essentials of these variables are given.[1]

7.1 Introduction

7.1.1 Leadership

Leadership and how it is most effectively practiced has always been of interest to managers, theorists and researchers. Each decade had its own line of approach. In the 1970s the concentration was on human relations; the 1980s were characterized by a goal-orientated, no-nonsense approach; in the 1990s we see a synthesis of both these approaches. Currently there is a greater focus on the quality of leadership than ever before (Bennis, 1989; Morgan, 1988; Van der Vlist, 1991). This is due particularly to the growing interest in company cultures and in changing these cultures. Leadership plays an important role in this area (Schein, 1985).

7.1.2 The Field of Management Development

Within organizations, interest in the effectiveness of managers has increased considerably, over the last decades. This certainly has to do with economic changes and their effects on the competition potential and the innovative capabilities of organizations. In addition, restructuring and reorganization lead to many questions about performance and social problems, which in turn appeal to the potential of managers (Taylor, 1984). The success of each change in the field of leadership and personnel management depends on the extent to which the individual manager succeeds in bridging the gaps in his style and in making permanent changes in specific ineffective approaches.

At the present time we can distinguish roughly between three methods of developing management skills. There are courses in which participants become acquainted with a certain theoretical model. These are models which are found in authoritative literature on leadership (for instance, Bass, 1985; Fiedler and Chemners, 1984; Hersey and Blanchard, 1969; Vroom, 1973). These models organize the complex reality into clear cognitive constructs. The participants are expected to use this knowledge to structure their environment in a clear, meaningful way and to gain insight into the relationship between certain factors. Despite the fact that a number of these models are very useful, they merely provide the practicing manager with a cognitive change rather than a behavioral one (Burke and Day, 1986; Swieringa and Wierdsma, 1990). For one thing, little attention is paid to factors that enhance transfer of behavior after the course. Den Ouden (1992) in her study found that not only behavior intentions, social norms and social support, but also the role of the observable mastery of specific behavior on the part of the participants is of importance in order for transfer to take place. These necessary conditions for a concrete change of behavior are virtually never part of the above mentioned management courses.

Skill training programs are also offered with a theoretical model as their basis. The skills to be learned here are considered to be of general use to all managers. Besides trying to achieve cognitive changes through the transfer of knowledge there is an attempt to achieve behavioral changes through practice. A limitation of these often open training courses is their general character, so that the learned behavior does not necessarily coincide with the skills each particular manager needs for his specific work situation.

The third method of learning about leadership is, in our point of view, a perfection of the two. The skills to be learned are not predetermined by the external training institute. The desired skills are determined by an analysis of the participant's work situation and his personal strength-weakness analysis. The manager is offered skills which he can use immediately in his work situation. The importance of this is recognized by Mumford, for one, who says the following: "I believe that one of the causes of relative ineffectiveness in this area within organizations has been the over-emphasis on developing managers for the future instead of working current requirements. This argument almost certainly applies even more strongly to training and education institutions which offer taught experiences outside the organization." (Mumford, 1989).

We can distinguish between three important movements within the third method:

- action-learning (Pedler, 1983; Revans, 1980);
- behavioral role modeling (Bandura, 1977; Goldstein, 1986);
- experiential based learning (Kolb, Rubin and McIntyre, 1984; Roskin, 1986).

The training program which we will describe in this chapter can be considered to be one of the last approach.

In our view there are two problems to deal with in training programs which attempt to change or influence leadership styles. The first problem is the transfer of learning (Michalak, 1981). The second problem is the relationship between the personality structure of the person involved and his ability to learn to control skills in order to give effective leadership. Various books and articles have drawn attention to this relationship (Benfari, 1991; Kets de Vries and Miller, 1984; Spector, 1978). We are convinced of the need to examine personal needs and emotional blocks for the effective learning of skills.

7.1.3 Research in the Field of Management Development

At around the time an article was published in which Harrison (1971) made a plea for research on the processes which take place in training courses, studies were done which compared the results of various training designs and various trainer characteristics. For design research the reader is referred to Byrd, 1967; Kinder and Kilmann, 1976; Lieberman, Yalom and Miles, 1973; Van der Vegt, 1974; Ware and Barr, 1977 and for trainers' characteristics to Cooper, 1969; Culbert, 1968; Lieberman et al, 1973; Lundgren and Knight, 1977; O'Day, 1976; Russell, 1978. It is remarkable that although relevant variables were studied, the process of training and learning as such was not studied. An explanation for this is given by Hartman in his review, in which he states that "There is probably no area in psychology where such research is more difficult and controversial, more fraught with philosophical and methodological conundrums" (Hartman, 1979). One year later Smith reviewed the research in the area of management training and behavior change, and he concluded that the group-dynamic and process-oriented method led to various demonstrable results. In the months following the training program, however, the effects fell away. It was time for more specific questions, particularly about how a design works, why changes do, or do not, take place and what to do to improve the transfer of learning in order to achieve more lasting effects (Smith, 1980). Baldwin and Ford (1988) comment on transfer of training in their review: "While researchers have similarly concluded that much of the training conducted in organizations fails to transfer to the work setting (e.g., Goldstein, 1986; Mosel, 1957; Wexley, 1984; Wexley and Latham,

1981) a comprehensive review and critique of the empirical research on transfer has not appeared." With their extensive review they set right this shortcoming.

7.1.4 A Management Development Program

Confronted with the learning needs of managers to cope with the increasingly greater demands on managers and on teamwork, we have been experimenting for the past several years with various other approaches and methods.

We developed a coaching and training program which incorporates various approaches in behavior change. It corresponds with what is now known as experiential based learning (Roskin, 1986). The learning principles are described in, among others, Walter and Marks (1981). The actual design is an entity in itself which is characterized by its explicit attention to the learning of skills based on personal objectives, causes of ineffective behavior and attention to the transfer of learning. This leads to lasting behavioral change in a majority of the participants as demonstrated by research carried out one to two years after the training. The results of this research project were published in 1986 (Van de Vliert, Huismans, Krijger and Van der Leeuw, 1986). In this chapter we will mainly go into the results of continued research on those aspects, program activities and trainer interventions which, in the opinion of the participants, contributed most to successful effects.

In the following sections we will describe the goals and the design of the management development program. Then we will go into the research design and report on the results of the first part of a broader study of the variables that contribute most to lasting behavioral changes. Finally, we will give a description of these variables c.q. program activities and interventions.

7.2 The Goal of the Management Development Program

The main goal of the management development program is to promote lasting behavioral change in leadership style and in interpersonal interaction during daily work in the organization. To achieve this we work on three main points:

a. obtaining more knowledge about the effects of their behavior on others;
b. obtaining more insight into their personal style of leadership and interaction with others;
c. practicing with alternatives for those aspects of behavior which prove to be inadequate and ineffective.

The insight mentioned in (a) and (b) is related to the manner of leadership in the participant's own work situation as well as to insight into the participant's own personality. It provides answers to questions like: What do I do? and Why do I do it that way and not differently? The behavioral changes (c) are comprised of concrete overt behavioral changes and the knowledge of why one type of behavior is more effective in a certain situation than another type.

Although the program was designed ultimately to promote lasting changes in attitude and behavior, the program leaders do not claim that this can be achieved by the end of the first part (one full week) or even after the follow-up. The participant's own initiative, attention and practice (based on an individual action plan) in the work situation are essential conditions for the quality of the long-term results. We do believe, however, that we are able to create important conditions for long-term results. For some participants support within the organization is desirable in order to maintain and develop what was learned.

7.3 A Description of the Training Design

In order to put the research results into their proper perspective, we will give a short description of the training design. The training design consists of a preliminary interview, a one-week residential training program (including the evenings), an application period of three months and a two-day follow-up. During both the application period and the period after the follow-up, the participants implement their individual action plans. The program is led principally by one trainer: an organizational psychologist, first author of this article. A second trainer, a qualified therapist, is responsible for a specific part of the program, psychodrama, which appears later in the program. The participants are upper middle and higher managers all of different organizations. A maximum of ten participants ensures individual attention.

7.3.1 The Preliminary Interview

The preliminary interview is held with each participant approximately three weeks before the start of the program. In this interview the individual learning goals are decided on after they have been discussed and described as concretely as possible. How these learning objectives can be incorporated into the program is also discussed at this time. The following topics are also discussed: the reason for enrollment, the expectation of the organization with regard to the learning objectives, the method of working during the training program and examples of situations in which the desired skills are to be applied after training. In consultation with the participant, additional information is requested from the manager and the management development team in order to attain as complete and exact a description of the individual learning objectives as possible. Huczynski and Lewis (1980) found that management training that included pre-course discussion with one's boss and subsequent boss sponsorship contributed most to the transfer of skills.

7.3.2 The Main Parts of the Program

The training week is composed of the following elements:

- *work sessions*, in which the participants work on case studies of organization problems. These sessions generate behavioral experience on an intra-, interpersonal and group level;
- *analysis sessions*, in which the effects of behavior and the method of dealing with issues are studied and pointers for change are given;
- *skill training* with the help of simulations of social situations in the organization, whereby certain skills must be applied when back in the work situation;
- *psychodrama techniques* for intensive awareness, particularly of the emotional background of behavior or blocks;
- *theory*: very short lectures on themes which come up during the program, regarding specific events;
- *action planning*: designing a plan of approach for each desired situation. This plan is to be applied in the period after the first week.

The work sessions and analysis sessions take place on the first three days of the week and alternate with each other. The former last about one hour and, as the participants increase their experience with each other, the length of time spent on the latter increases. In this way the attention given to each participant's learning goals also increases. The first three days are led by one trainer.

The simulation games and psychodrama sessions take place on the fourth day and first half of the fifth day. During that time a second trainer was present (who entered the program on the third day) and observed the participants at work. This second trainer is familiar with the personal learning goals of the participants.

The sections of the program *simulation game* and *psychodrama* take place simultaneously, in subgroups. Each participant has a turn at being the main player in a special setting for him which is based on personal learning goals and on what has been achieved during the first three days. The other participants also have a role or task in these sessions. They can join a different subgroup per session according to how much the learning goals coincide with, or are related to their own. In this way there is continuity in the learning process of each participant and the possibility to support each other. The first week concludes with the abovementioned action planning.

7.3.3 The Follow-up

Two subgroup meetings take place before the start of the follow-up. The participants meet, without the trainers, in order to stimulate the execution of the plans. During the follow-up the participants assess each other's results. On the basis of the progress of each individual participant, a program is devised which consists primarily of skill training in a simulated organization setting, the application of psychodrama techniques and counseling. The follow-up finishes once again with action planning. The accent of the planning is on what the participants need to do in order to continue along in the right direction.

7.4 Participants and Their Goals

The program is designed for upper-middle and top management from profit and non-profit organizations: both males and females of ages varying from 30 to about 50. The participants have made a career for themselves on the basis of their professional capacities. Although many have taken general management courses, some area of their style of managing has proved to be no longer satisfactory.

If this inadequate or inefficient area is related to personality structure, experienced management development officers in the organization know that the desired changes in style and behavior cannot be achieved by participating in a training program in which the emphasis is on skills only, or in which there is too little individual attention for the personal goals to be achieved. Apart from this, the question is whether there is a training program available whose goal sufficiently coincides with that of the person in question.

Managers are better aided and have a better chance to change successfully when coached individually over a period of time (Krijger, 1988, 1992; Yeager, 1983). During this time attention must not only be paid to the desired skills, but also to the organizational circumstances within which the person operates, as well as to the personal needs, standards, values, motives and possibly emotional aspects which are related to the non-effective part of the work behavior. Each participant has personal learning goals which (can) differ from those of others.

The program design discussed and studied in this chapter was developed on the basis of notions on the coaching of individual managers, team-building and various forms of skill training (Krijger, 1987, 1988). The design has developed over the years into its present form. Participants have made a major contribution by constantly stimulating reflection and change with their comments. Particularly important was the information about their progress, given during the follow-ups.

Of course, not all participants face difficulties in their management task. Some people participate in the sessions primarily because they want more knowledge about the effects of their style, and want to learn about interactions between people in a short and intensive course.

Examples of personal learning goals are:
influencing others more effectively, standing up for your own interests and for those of your department, being more aware of other people's feelings, being less in the forefront and less dominating, being able to motivate, stimulating a better work atmosphere, dealing with irritation and tension, being able to confront.

In addition to the above-mentioned skills, attention is paid to the emotions which go along with such skills, both in the positive as in the negative sense. How such diversity can be fitted into the framework of one program will come up in the discussion of the research results.

7.5 Method of Research

Objective of the Research Project
Earlier research on the effects of the program shows that for a majority of the participants, the described design leads to lasting behavioral changes (Van der Leeuw and Huismans, 1986; Van de Vliert, Huismans, Krijger and Van der Leeuw, 1986).

The present study is aimed at the factors that contribute most to these changes. The entire research project is concentrated on design variables, trainer interventions and approach, training conditions and the applied learning principles. In this chapter the first results of the part concerning the design variables and the trainer interventions are reported. The opinion and perception of the participants are pivotal in this study. We believe that their opinions are at least as important as those of the researchers or program leaders. This is especially true with regard to their perception of the strengths and weaknesses of the program in order to improve it ultimately. At the same time this approach informs us about how participants think they learn from the program, which is one of the primary goals of the entire research project.

Participants
All participants in the four training programs were asked to cooperate in the research project. All programs followed the same design. There were differences in the processes because the course of the program is based on personal learning goals. In our opinion, however, this was not important for the interpretation of the results and the conclusions. Ultimately, data was provided by 36 of the 40 participants (4 training programs of 10 people each). Two partici-

pants were on holiday, one was ill and one reacted after the data had been processed. By the time this book is published, data will have been received from an additional 40 participants.

Research Instrument

Data was collected with a questionnaire of 38 design variables and 20 intervention variables. Design variables refer to (sub-parts of) program activities which contain a learning opportunity, for example: observation of one's own behavior by way of video recordings (simulation game), getting concrete behavioral pointers (analysis sessions) and experiences as the main-player in a psychodrama. Intervention variables refer to how learning takes place. The trainer is usually responsible for this, for example he concentrates on concrete behavior which is observed by each participant, the trainer intervenes when insufficient or inaccurate feedback is given and the trainer sees inadequate behavior as being more a habit rather than a problem. The participants gave their opinion about the value of each of the program components and trainer interventions mentioned, for three effects:

- concrete behavioral changes;
- acquired insights into their personality and social situation;
- changes in self-image about the effects of behavior and way of interacting with others in the organization.

They were asked to give the absolute value of the variables on a five-point scale ranging from *very little* (1) to *very much* (5). The questionnaire was compiled on the basis of the professional experience of the trainers and research co-worker and of extensive interviews with former participants.

The questionnaire contained questions about the degree of the effects of the program and satisfaction with its quality. We used the concept of change described by Golembiewsky, Billingsley and Yeager (1976). A change can take place on three levels, so-called alpha, beta and gamma types of changes, respectively: changes which are related to concrete overt behavior (alpha), realistic self image (beta) and new insights in terms of reconceptualization of social situations and one's own behavior (gamma) (Golembiewsky et al, 1976). Although the above-mentioned article caused quite a stir, little research based on its findings has been done. It is, however, clear that it is very important to make a distinction between these effects in research on training and organizational development interventions and effect studies (Van de Vliert, Huismans and Stok, 1985). For this reason we made use of this distinction when measuring the effects in this research project.

Research Design and Processing of the Data

Both the design variables and the intervention variables were related to the effects by use of the Pearson correlation. In addition, the average scale values of these two sets of variables were compared with each other and tested.

Figure 7.1 Research design.

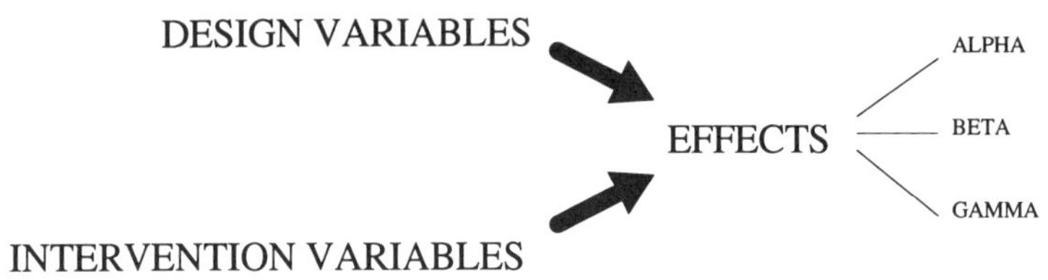

7.6 Results

In this section we describe the results found; this includes respectively, the results of the reliability calculations, the correlations between the design variables and the effects, the correlations between the intervention variables and the effects, and the average scale values for the effects of the design variables and the intervention variables.

7.6.1 Reliability of the Scale Values

When calculating the correlations or average scale values, reliability coefficients are used to make sure that the questions supplement each other and do not overlap. The alpha's of the reliability coefficients of the scales of the design variables and the effects of the program are high (.75 to .80). This means the participants make a distinction between various aspects of a particular part of the program (design variable) and between the diverse interventions (intervention variable). They also made a distinction between the three effects.

7.6.2 Correlations between Design Variables and the Effects of the Program

Correlations indicate the relationship between two types of variables. The calculated Pearson correlations between the design variables and the effects of the program point to a positive relationship between the extent to which someone has achieved his learning goals and the importance attached to the variable concerned. With regard to the effects, the correlations are calculated for alpha, beta and gamma changes.

It appears, however, that the correlations provide insufficient information on the question of which specific variables contribute to lasting changes, since some design variables found to be very important do not correlate with the effects. This occurs because virtually all participants attach a high value to them and there is practically no difference in response. A number of design variables show a clear relationship with a behavioral change. These are given in table 7.1.

Table 7.1 Correlations between design variables and behavior change (alpha).

	Variable	No.	Corr.
a	behavioral effect search	15	.50*
b	learning objectives	4	.36*
c	getting concrete behavioral clues	16	.24
d	parallel between training processes and work situations	18	.30*
e	the follow-up as a whole	32	.39*
f	application of pointers and subsequent behavioral effect investigation	7	.41**
g	observation of training of skills by others	24	.28

*Correlations with ** , and * have a respective significance level of .01 and .05. The other correlations are significant at level .10, and indicate trends.*

There is a positive relationship between lasting behavior change and the behavioral effect search after the work sessions (a). The clearer the subjects' objectives are, specifically as a result of the pretraining session (b), the greater is the effect achieved. The same applies to receiving concrete pointers during the analysis sessions (c), looking for the parallels between what happens in the training session and in the work situation (d) and the follow-up as support during the application period (e). We should like to stress the link between positive effects and regular explanation by the trainers (during the program) about the way the program is structured (f). The better people understand this, the better they can make use of the opportunities. Finally, observations of training skills by others (g) also show a positive relationship to behavioral change.

7.6.3 Correlations between the Intervention Variables and the Effects of the Program

The calculated Pearson correlations between the intervention variables and the effects of the program indicate a positive relationship between the extent to which one has achieved his objectives and the importance attached to the intervention variable concerned. When calculating these correlations there appeared to be little difference between the various scores given by the participants. Table 7.2 shows the intervention variables which are clearly related to effects.

Table 7.2 Correlations between intervention variables and effects.

	Variable	No.	Alpha	Beta	Gamma
a	the trainer gives pointers during work sessions	11	.42**	.47**	.42**
b	the trainer considers inadequate behavior as a habit which can be changed	10	.39*	.43**	.30*
c	the trainer makes use of information from the participants about their work situation	9	.35*	.33*	.28*
d	the trainer explains a method of working several times	3	.43**	.35*	-
e	the trainer checks the accuracy of his observations	8	-	.43**	-
f	the trainer indicates parallels with work situations	7	.33*	-	-

*Correlations with **, and * have a respective significance level of .01 and .05.*

It appears that giving individual pointers during work sessions (a) is closely related to all three levels of change; change in behavior, change in judging one's own behavior and an increase in insight. The same holds true for the trainer who sees inadequate behavior as something which can be changed rather than as a problem (b), and the trainer has information from the participants and makes use of this when giving pointers (c). The intervention; the trainer explains a method of working several times (d), shows a connection between behavioral change and another assessment of one's own behavior. This finding is consistent with the strong correlation found for the design variable concerned (section 7.6.2). The intervention; the trainer checks the accuracy of his observations with the participants (e), shows a close connection with another assessment of one's own behavior. The close connection shown by the design variable concerned indicates that it is important for the trainer to draw parallels with the work situation in order to effect a change (f).

7.6.4 Average Values of the Effects, the Design Variables and the Intervention Variables

The average values for both the achieved objectives and the contributing design variables are high. On the one hand, it is interesting for a trainer-researcher to observe that participants are consistent in attributing a high effect value to the design. On the other hand, after years of experimenting with design, techniques, interventions and approaches, this is not so surprising. It is more important to find out what the essence is of a component which leads the participant to experience it as an important contribution and how these variables are interrelated.

Looking at the results one can conclude that the following activities in the program are perceived as being the most influential for changing behavior or gaining insights: (the numbers

Table 7.3 Design variables (mean and standard deviation).

Variable	No.	Mean	S.D.
getting concrete behavioral pointers (analysis sessions)	16	4.3	.84
effects on others (psychodrama techniques)	26	4.3	.89
behavioral effect research (analysis-sessions)	15	4.2	.74
personal experience as the main player (simulation game)	19	4.1	.70
training of specific skills (simulation game)	20	4.0	.76
effects on others and behavioral clues (simulation game)	21	4.0	.84
personal experiences as the main player (psychodrama techniques)	25	4.0	1.21
observation of one's own behavior (video-simulation game)	22	4.0	.64
the follow-up as a whole	32	3.9	.67
learning from others (psychodrama techniques)	28	3.9	.94
application of clues and subsequent behavioral effect investigation (work sessions)	17	3.8	.91
learning from others (psychodrama techniques and follow-up)	36	3.8	.82
observation of training of skills by others (simulation game)	24	3.7	.76
getting concrete behavioral pointers (work session)	14	3.6	.69
learning objectives (specification in pre-training session)	5	3.6	.80
parallel between training processes and work situations (during every session)	18	3.5	.85
experiences as role-player in game of others (simulation game)	23	3.5	.85
action planning (plan for the application period between the end of the first week and follow-up)	30	3.5	.88
experiences as role-player in game of others (simulation game - follow-up)	35	3.5	.79

in parentheses represent the average scale value) the analysis sessions (4.3), psychodrama techniques (4.3), simulation games (4.1), the follow-up (3.9), the work sessions (3.8), the specification of learning objectives (3.6), experiencing parallels between inter-personal processes during the program and those in the daily work situation (3.5), and action planning (3.5).

These then are the components with a high average rating ranging from 4.3 to 3.5. The ratings of all sub-components with a mean rating above 3.5 are given in table 7.3. We would like to point out once more that the range of the answers is low to very low, which means that many participants assign the same high value to the stated variables.

Statistically speaking a mean rating of 4.3 does not differ from a mean of 4.2 or 4.0. The boundary appears to lie at 3.9 ($p=.05$). If the mean ratings are classified on the basis of the significant boundaries, then the most important factors for achieved effects can be put into the following three groups, in which the first group contains the highest averages.

category 1: analysis sessions, psychodrama and simulation games.

category 2: learning from others during psychodrama and simulation games, the use of behavioral pointers during the work sessions and the two-day follow-up.

category 3: action-planning, specification of learning objectives in the pre-training sessions with the consultant/trainer, and drawing parallels between processes during training and those in the work situation.

The intervention variables which are perceived as being most influential for changing behavior and gaining insights (those with an average of 3.8 or higher), are given in table 7.4.

A number of these variables concern the professionalism of the trainer and need no explanation. The following variables appear to be very important for the method of approach (the numbers in parentheses represent the mean values): the trainer gives pointers during work sessions (4.2); he concentrates on concrete behavior (4.0); he appeals to the participant's own sense of responsibility (3.9); he sees inadequate behavior as a habit which can be changed (3.9); he checks the accuracy of his observations (3.8). Four of these five variables also belong to the group of important variables for the correlations (see section 7.6.3).

Now that we have reported the results, the question remains as to what is the essence of the components which lead participants to experience them as important contributions to their learning. In the following three sections we will try to describe this for the most important design variables and intervention variables.

7.7 Getting Information from Others about Oneself

Searching for and obtaining information from others is the central activity in six of the eight most valued design variables (section 7.6.4). During this activity, information is obtained which concerns the effects of the behavior on the one hand (the individual approach) and information which contributes to a greater awareness of one's own feelings and thoughts during interactions, on the other. We will discuss two methods in which getting information from others is of primary importance.

Table 7.4 Intervention variables (mean and standard deviation).

Variable	*No.*	*Mean*	*S.D.*
the trainer gives pointers during the discussions	20	4.2	.61
the trainer knows what he is doing and what he is talking about	1	4.1	.75
the trainer concentrates on concrete behavior	13	4.0	.77
the trainer intervenes when insufficient or inaccurate feedback is given	2	4.0	.86
the trainer pays attention to whether a person can cope with feedback	6	3.9	.82
the trainer appeals to your own sense of responsibility	18	3.9	.80
the trainer sees inadequate behavior as a habit which can be changed rather than as a problem	10	3.9	.76
the trainer is calm and maintains an overview	4	3.8	.65
the trainer checks the accuracy of his observations with the participants	8	3.8	.81
the trainer takes on a confrontation when necessary	19	3.8	.96

7.7.1 Behavioral Effect Search

Behavioral effect search, as it is called during the program, is based on the experiences undergone during the work sessions and worked out in the analysis sessions. It is during these sessions that most of the information about the effects of one's own behavior is obtained. The applied feedback cycle consists of six elements:

- one's own formulation of the presumed effects in terms of the thoughts and feelings of others;
- the actual feelings and thoughts of others;
- determining the similarities and differences;

- linking similarities and differences with the concrete behavior of the person concerned, both by the trainer and by the other participants;
- one's own formulation of concrete behavior which leads to the desired effects, aided by pointers from participants and trainers;
- naming the behavioral signs of others to which one reacts and the kind of behavioral reactions these actually are, including the accompanying feelings and thoughts.

In this way, a behavioral feedback system develops which can stimulate behavioral changes and which is much more influential and informative than those reported in a review of the literature (Wing, 1991).

Looking at the intervention variables with the highest averages and correlations (see sections 7.6.4 and 7.6.3) it appears that participants consider it very important that the trainers ensure the high quality of this information-seeking and awareness process. This is true for the carefulness (safety) as well as for the precision and concreteness of the information and pointers. These three characteristics are part of the five aspects of the trainer interventions which were considered to have the greatest influence as far as behavioral changes and gaining insight are concerned (section 7.6.4, table 7.4).

On the basis of the results and interviews with participants, we conclude that it is very important for an individual to build up a valid picture of his own behavior and the effects it has on others. In most cases, the subjects' communication with other people in his organization about their behavior, had been extremely limited, or of poor quality. Apart from this, some people are not even aware of certain events, although they did arouse comment. The trainer and other participants are seen as *the objective outsiders*, against which people can check what is *actually* true and not true, and what they should and should not take to heart. This conclusion is strengthened by the importance attached to the precision with which the trainer leads the effect survey, and the score given to the overall impression of competence (section 7.6.4). This relates on the one hand to learning under the familiar condition of security, and on the other hand to the reliability and precision of the information about the effects of an individual's own behavior. The latter is not only very useful for participants in deciding which alternative behavior or attitude is more satisfactory, but is above all a condition for motivated practice with indications and alternative behavioral approaches to a situation.

7.7.2 The Use of Psychodrama Techniques

For information which contributes to a greater awareness of one's own feelings and thoughts during interactions, we designed a special type of psychodrama which was originally used as a therapeutic technique. Our version of this is experienced by managers as being safe and yet intensive. Psychodrama is used for the exploration of feelings and attitudes. The "voice-dialogue" approach, in particular, has a very enlightening effect on managers (Stone and Winkelman, 1985). Adapted and applied at the right level (non-therapeutic), they make a major contribution to insight into the background to, and the causes of, inadequate behavior. The interviews clearly reveal that this insight is indispensable and is an essential complement to the approach based more on behavior modeling that is also incorporated in the program.

7.8 The Work Sessions

The work sessions consisted of all participants carrying out assignments as a team. These assignments were simulations of processes which occur in organizations and call for various task-oriented and social-emotional behavior. In the work sessions the following skills were called for because they are important in the work situation for team functioning and managing people: formulating ideas, influencing each other, making collective decisions for which team members take responsibility, dealing with the possible resistance of some team members, monitoring progress, appealing to adequate behavior patterns, stimulating or curbing team members and diagnosing differences of opinions.

The work sessions lasted approximately one hour during which time the task should be completed. The group was not allowed to appoint anyone as formal leader or chairperson, nor will the trainer play this role. During the work sessions demands are made on the group regarding the quantity of production and quality of the work atmosphere. How the team deals with these demands was determined by the members of the group. This led to a certain amount of task stress which is familiar to the participants in their regular work. The sessions were structured on the basis of the assigned task but remained unstructured in the sense that there was no formal leader. The unstructured aspect caused each participant to *fall back* on his own strong and weak behavioral characteristics. For example, a participant who tends to dominate discussions will very quickly do just that; a participant who finds it very difficult to stand up for his interests will withdraw; a participant who needs clarity and structure will attempt to introduce these (in excess) or will become frustrated. In other words, personal motives, drives, needs and defense mechanisms become visible very quickly. This is an undesirable situation from the point of view of efficient team functioning, but desirable from that of the learning goals of the participants.

The trainer observes the behavior of each participant in terms of his learning goals and from this line of approach leads the analysis sessions in which the behavioral effect search plays a key role. At the beginning of the program, the analysis sessions are primarily about non-adequate and inefficient behavior and its effects. In later analysis sessions positive feedback (reinforcement) plays a major role through the pointers and the efforts of the participants to apply these in later work sessions.

It is important that the participants know each other's learning goals well so that they can give specific information so helping each other with concrete behavior. The latter is usually also an exercise for the participant during the work sessions. In the work and analysis sessions a combination of the structured and unstructured approach took place. An interesting study about the learning possibilities of this combination is described by Mezoff (1982).

In view of the intervention variables which score highest (see section 7.6.4, table 7.4), we should point out that participants consider the following elements important about the interventions of the trainer during the work and analysis sessions: the extent to which the trainer is concerned with how much a person can cope with; and the extent to which the trainer appeals to the participant's sense of responsibility and efforts to continue working on the learning goals. In this connection we mention one aspect of the trainer's style which scores highly. Namely, his vision of behavioral change that views inadequate behavior as a habit rather than as a negative characteristic or problem, as such behavior is often viewed within organizations. Inadequate habits are learned and can be replaced by more adequate habits.

7.9 Attention to the Transfer of Learning

The results confirm that attention to the transfer of insights and skills is essential in achieving lasting effects. The possibility of transferring learning and adopting other behavioral habits is achieved by practicing with the aid of pointers. It is evident that participants find this very important. These possibilities have already been implicitly and explicitly described. Practice, however, is not sufficient. On the basis of the results we will mention five design variables which strengthen the transfer process and the development of permanence: the application of the simulation technique, the support of a follow-up, work and organization related learning objectives, the so-called *parallels* and the action planning (section 7.6.3, table 7.3). These variables parallel the transfer-fostering factors which are mentioned by Baldwin and Ford (1988) and Den Ouden (1992).

7.9.1 Simulation Games

In the second half of the week a situation was set up which could occur in the organizations of the participants. Each of them practices a skill important to his own functioning with the other participants playing the role of boss, colleagues or subordinates. The participant concerned remains himself and is not assigned any other role. Practising specific skills leads to the recognition by participants of observable mastery of the skills through which the transfer of new behavior to the organizational setting is fostered (Den Ouden, 1992). In this form of simulation technique practising of specific skills plays a central role.

7.9.2 The Follow-up

Besides being able to get additional practice, the follow-up is important in obtaining practical, interim support for working out the action plan. The follow-up takes place approximately three months after the first week of instruction. From experience we know that this is the ideal time lag. From interviews with participants it also appears that the social control aspect of the follow-up has a positive influence. When people know that their achievements and efforts will be addressed later, they pay more attention to applying what they have learned. Two subgroup meetings were planned in the period between the training week and the follow-up in which the participants keep each other informed about their progress. The participants discuss their attempts, both successful and unsuccessful to cope more effectively with certain situations. The goal of these meetings is to provide support and to maintain the focus on the process of change in order to prevent a waning of interest.

Experience has taught us that this contributes to the lasting effect of what was learned and stimulates the continuation of experimentation with the new behavior. The importance of this contact for transfer is found in a study by Karol and Richards (1978). They found that a group in a *buddy system* condition, which involves two trainees being paired to reinforce each other in order to maintain learning, exhibited substantially less relapse to old behavior than did a group in a control condition.

7.9.3 Work and Organization-related Learning Objectives

Learning objectives in training programs are always based on what people lack and want to learn when carrying out the assignment. They are in this sense work-related. Here we mean, however, that the learning goals are determined by each person independently in a pre-training interview. The reason for participation is also discussed at this interview, as well as possible incidents at work and the specific culture of the organization. If necessary the trainer modifies the learning objectives with the aid of the manager and others in the organization. According to the participants, the specification of the learning objectives also increases the goal-orientedness of working during the program and thereby the chance of a lasting effect.

7.9.4 Parallels between Training and Organization

A criticism often heard of behavioral training programs is that they are *cultural islands* isolated from the organization. This is partially corrected if the work sessions are simulations of the processes which occur in every organization. In addition, the participants attribute change value to the so-called parallel assignment. This refers to the constantly returning assignment to determine the similarities between what happens during the work and analysis sessions and what is experienced and observed in the organization. This can be different for each person. The trainer supports the awareness of similarities by making use of the information from the pre-training interview and his experience with processes and interactions in organizations. He is constantly on the alert for parallel situations from which a specific participant can learn. For example: the learning goal *addressing someone critically* is a perfect example of something which can be realistically practiced in the analysis sessions when someone is giving negative feedback.

7.9.5 Action Planning

On the last day of the first week each participant writes down what he himself intends to do in the organization according to his learning goals and what he has learned. The emphasis here is specifically on what he intends to do and how he intends to do this, and not on what he must not do. This is one of the learning and changing principles behind the approach. The action plan is discussed with other participants and the results are evaluated in the subgroups and again in the follow-up. In addition to this, the continuation of the talks with the manager is included in the planning. Our research findings completely correspond with those of Wexley and Nemeroff (1975) and those of Wallice (1984) regarding the importance of goal-setting and feedback for transfer of learning.

7.10 Final Conclusions

Through an external coaching and training program it is possible to achieve lasting changes in the leadership style and interpersonal behavior of managers. The lasting effects of the changes have been demonstrated in earlier research. The results of the study presented in this chapter indicate which design variables stimulate attitudinal and behavioral change in the opinion of the participants involved. Influential variables are: intensive information about the effects of the behavior on others with the accompanying pointers for more adequate and more efficient behavior; the possibility to practice in situations which are as similar as possible to those in the organization; the combination of skill training with insights into the emotional processes which can cause a reduction in good functioning, precise and concrete formulation of learning objectives which are derived from daily interactions in the organization, and follow-up activities during the first months in which the participants apply what they have learned. These design variables should be combined with certain trainer interventions. These variables coincide with those which are named in the research literature as being important for actual change, but which are too often lacking (Goldstein, 1986).

References

Baldwin, T.T. and Ford, J.K. (1988). Transfer of Training: A Review and Directions for Future Research. *Personnel Psychology, 41,* 63-105.

Bandura, A. (1977). *Social Learning Theory.* Englewood Cliffs. New Yersey: Prentice Hall.

Bass, B.M. (1985). *Leadership and Performance: Beyond the Expectations.* New York: The Free Press.

Benfari, R. (1991). *Understanding your Management Style: Beyond the Myers-Briggs Type Indicator.* Lexington Books.

Bennis, W.G. (1989). *On Becoming a Leader.* New York: Addison-Wesley.

Burke, M.J. and Day, R.R. (1986) A Cumulative Study of the Effectiveness of Management Training. *Journal of Applied Psychology, 71,* 232-245.

Byrd, R.E. (1967). Training in a Non-Group. *Journal of Humanistic Psychology, 7,* 18-27.

Cooper, C.L. (1969). The Influence of the Trainer on Participant Change in T-Groups. *Human Relations, 22,* 518-530.

Culbert, S.A. (1968). Trainer Self-disclosure and Member Growth in Two T-Groups. *Journal of Applied Science, 4,* 47-74.

Den Ouden, M. (1992). *Transfer na Bedrijfsopleidingen. Een Veldonderzoek naar de Rol van Voornemens, Sociale Norm, Beheersing en Sociale Steun bij Opleidingstransfer.* Utrecht University, Amsterdam: Thesis Publishers. A Study on Transfer after Management Courses.

Fiedler, F.E. and Chemners, M.M. (1984). *Improving Leadership Effectiveness : The Leader Match Concept,* 2nd edition. New York: John Wiley.

Goldstein, I.L. (1986). *Training in Organizations: Needs Assessment, Development and Evaluation.* C.A. Monterey: Brooks/Cole, 2nd. ed.

Golembiewsky, R.T., Billingsley, K.R. and Yeager, S. (1976). Measuring Change and Persistence in Human Affairs: Types of Change Generated by OD Designs. *Journal of Applied Behavioral Science, 12,* 133-157.

Harrison, R. (1971). Research on Human Relations Training: Design and Interpretation. *Journal of Applied Behavioral Science, 7,* 71-85.

Hartman, J.J. (1979). Small Group Methods of Personal Change. *Annual Review of Psychology, 30,* 453-76.

Hersey, P. and Blanchard, K.H. (1969). *Management of Organizational Behavior.* Prentice Hall, Englewood Cliffs: New Jersey.

Huczynski, A.A. and Lewis, J.W. (1980). An Empirical Study into the Learning Transfer Process in Management Training. *Journal of Management Studies, 17,* 227-240.

Karol, R.L. and Richards, C.S. (1978). *Making Treatment Effects Last: An Investigation of Maintenance Strategie for Smoking Reduction.* Presented at the meeting of the Association for Advancement of Behavior Therapy, Chicago.

Kets de Vries, M.F.R. and Miller, D. (1984). *The Neurotic Organization.* San Francisco: Jossey-Bass.

Kinder, B.N. and Kilmann, P.R. (1976). The Impact of Differential Shifts in Leader Structureon the Outcome of Internal and External Group Participants. *Journal of Clinical Psychology, 32,* 857-863.

Kolb, D.A., Rubin, I.M. and McIntyre, J.M. (1984). *Organizational Psychology: An Experiental Approach to Organizational Behavior,* 4th edition. New Yersey; Prentice-Hall, Englewood Cliffs.

Krijger, N.L. (1987). *Social Effectiveness for Managers: Effects, Design and Interventions.* Third West European Congress on the Psychology of Work and Organization. Antwerp, Belgium. Kryger Consulting, Loenen a/d Vecht, The Netherlands.

Krijger, N.L. (1988). Persoonlijke Management Coaching: een Practische Benadering van Gedragsverandering. Krijger, N.L. (Ed.), Persoonlijke Management Coaching. *Praktisch Personeelsbeleid,* Capita Selecta, 25. Personal Management Coaching.

Krijger, N.L. (1992). Management Coaching. Kampermann, A. and Gerrichhausen, J. (Eds.) *Interventiestrategieën in Organisaties.* Open universiteit, Heerlen, 139-152.

Krijger, N.L. and Pol, S.M. (1993). *Het verbeteren van de stijl van leidinggeven - resultaten van een onderzoek naar manieren waarop managers veranderen.* Kryger Consulting, Loenen a/d Vecht.

Lieberman, M.A., Yalom, I.D. and Miles, M.B. (1973). *Encounter Groups: First Facts.* New York: Basic Books.

Lundgren, D.C. and Knight, D.J. (1977). Trainer Style and Member Attitudes Toward Trainer and Group in T-Groups. *Small Group Behavior, 8,* 47-64.

Mezoff, B. (1982). Cognitive Style and Interpersonal Behavior: a Review with Implications for Human Relations Training. *Group and Organization Studies, 7,* 13-34.

Michalak, D.F. (1981). The Neglected Half of Training. *Training and Development Journal, 35, (5),* 22-28.

Morgan, G. (1988). *Riding the Waves Of Changes.* Jossey-Bass.

Mosel, J.N. (1957). Why Training Programs Fail to Carry Over. *Personnel, 4,* 56-64.

Mumford, A. (1989). Effectiveness in Management Development. *Handbook of Management Development,* 2nd edition, 20-38.

O'Day, R. (1976). Individual Training Styles: An Empirically derived Typology. *Small Group Behavior, 7,* 147-182.

Pedler, M. (1983) (Ed.). *Action Learning in Practice.* England: Gower.

Revans, R.W. (1980). *Action Learning: New Techniques for Management.* Blond & Briggs.

Roskin, R. (1986). Experiental Based Learning. Mumford, A. (Ed.) *Handbook of Management Development.* London: Gower, 281-284.

Russell, E. (1978). The Facts about 'Encounter Groups: First Facts.' *Journal of Clinical Psychology, 34,* 130-137.

Schein, E.H. (1985). *Organizational Culture and Leadership.* San Francisco: Jossy-Bass.

Smith, P.B. (1980). *Group Processes and Personal Change.* London: Harper and Row.

Spector, P. (1978). Organizational Frustration: A Model and Review of the Literature. *Personnel Psychology, 31,* 815-829.

Stone, H. and Winkelman, S. (1985). *Embracing Ourselves.* Marina Del Rey: Devorse & Company.

Swieringa, J. and Wierdsma, A.F.M. (1990). *Op Weg naar een Lerende Organisatie.* Groningen: Wolters-Noordhoff. To the Way to a Learning Organization.

Taylor, B. (1984). Management Training and Development in the 1980's. Taylor, B. and Lippit, G. (Eds.) *Management Development and Training Handbook.* New York: McGraw-Hill, 3-35.

Van der Leeuw, J.R. and Huismans, S.E. (1986). *Een Managementtraining heeft Effect. Samenvatting van de Resultaten van een Effectonderzoek.* University of Amsterdam and Kryger Consulting, Loenen a/d Vecht, The Netherlands. A Study on the Effectiveness of a Management Program.

Van der Vegt, R. (1974). *Opleiden en Evalueren: Een Veldexperimentele Studie naar de Uitkomsten van een Bedrijfsopleiding.* Meppel, The Netherlands: Boom. A Study on the Outcomes of an Incompany Training.

Van de Vliert, E., Huismans, S.E. and Stok, J.J.L. (1985). The Criterion Approach to Unraveling Beta and Alpha change. *Academy of Management Review, 10,* 269-274.

Van de Vliert, E., Huismans, S.E., Krijger, N.L. and Van der Leeuw, J.R. (1986). Evaluatieonderzoek naar Veranderingen in Denkkader. Von Grumbkow, J., Van Kreveld, D. and Stringer P. (Eds.) *Toegepaste Sociale Psychologie,* 2, Swets & Zeitlinger, Lisse, The Netherlands. An Evaluation Study on Shifts in Thinking.

Van der Vlist, R. (1991). *Leiderschap in Organisaties: Kernvraagstuk voor de Jaren '90.* Utrecht: Lemma, B.V. Leadership in Organizations.

Vroom, V.H. and Yetton, P.W. (1973). *Leadership and Decisionmaking.* Pittsburgh: University Of Pittsburgh Press.

Wallice, S.R. (1984). Criteria for What? *American Psychologist, 20,* 411-417.

Walter, G.A. and Marks, S.E. (1981). *Experiental Learning and Change.* New York: Wiley.

Ware, J.R. and Barr, J.E. (1977). Effects of a Nine-Week Structured and Unstructured Group Experience on Measures of Self-Concept and Self-Actualization. *Small Group Behavior, 8,* 93-100.

Wexley, K.N. (1984). Personnel Training. *Annual Review of Psychology, 35,* 519-551.

Wexley, K.N. and Latham, G.P. (1981). *Developing and Training Human Resources in Organizations.* Glenview, I.L.: Scott Foresman.

Wexley, K.N. and Nemeroff, W.F. (1975). Effectiveness of Positive Reinforcement and Goal-setting as Methods of Management Development. *Journal of Applied Psychology, 64,* 239-246.

Wing, K.T. (1991). Implications of Feedbackresearch for Group Facilitation and the Design of Experiental Learning. *Small Group Research, 21,* 113-127.

Yeager, I. (1983). A Model for Executive Performance Coaching. In: *Occupational Clinical Psychology.* New York: Preager.

Notes

1 We would like to thank Marjolein Houps, coworker at Kryger Consulting for her valuable comments.

8 Human Resources Development and On-the-job Learning

Jeroen H.A.M. Onstenk

Changes in technology, organizational renewal, optimization of the quality of production (efficiency, flexibility, product quality) and orientation to changing consumer demands require higher standards of skills and flexibility in the work force. In order to meet these standards, it is necessary to deliver more training to the work force and define training in terms of investment rather than costs. It also means dealing with people who are learning in learning organizations (Engeström, 1994; Marsick and Watkins, 1990). Training of employees in general, and learning in the workplace can be regarded as a major challenge for Human Resources Development. Informal and integrated on-the-job learning – at all levels of the organization – is an important characteristic of the new organizational paradigm which must be developed to make use of the opportunities and challenges of information technology (Arbetsmiljöfonden, 1991; Kochan and Osterman, 1991; Stahl, Nyhan and D'Aloja, 1993). On-the-job learning is not structured by specific pedagogical activities, but by the structural characteristics of the work activity itself. It takes place if and when the work situation (task, task management and work organization) constitutes a learning environment. It should be distinguished from on-the-job training, which is characterized by explicit pedagogic structuring: explicit training objectives and plans, printed course material, computerized job guides or active involvement of a trainer (Jacobs and McGiffin, 1987; De Jong, 1991; Onstenk, 1994). This chapter deals mainly with on-the-job learning.

The chapter is based on comparative research, carried out in 1991/1992 and commissioned by the Dutch Ministry of Education (Onstenk, 1994). The project included a survey of on-the-job learning and on-the-job training in six industrial countries: the Netherlands, Sweden, Germany, Great Britain, Japan and the United States.

In an extensive study of professional literature, the concepts of on-the-job learning and (structured) on-the-job training were explored. A theoretical framework, based on activity psychology, cognitive science and socialization theory, was developed for defining and analyzing on-the-job learning (section 8.1). More specifically, a model of the learning potential of jobs was developed (section 8.2). This model states that learning processes result from the interplay of the learner, work characteristics and the organization as a learning environment. Learning effects and characteristics of the employment situation as a learning environment were considered. On-the-job learning contributes not only to the acquisition of task-specific skills, but also of key-qualifications and broad competence (section 8.3).

In the second and major part of the research figures, policies and projects with regard to learning and training on the job were described and analyzed, based on a literature survey, document analysis and expert interviews. *Good practices* were noted in the six countries and different approaches adopted to increase the learning potential of jobs were analyzed. Two main groups of strategies can be distinguished. The first group is aiming to enhance the willingness and ability of workers to learn (section 8.4). The second group has as a major objective: the establishment of work and the organization as a learning environment, by the creation of learning possibilities and the removal of learning barriers. These strategies aim to both offer opportunities and stimulate motivation (section 8.5). Specific attention was directed at attempts to promote on-the-job learning beyond the level of managers and professionals to a growing number of employees, including *rank and file* production workers. The chapter concludes with some notes on the learning organization and learning on the shop floor as a challenge for Human Resources Development (section 8.6).

8.1 On-the-job Learning: Looking for Concepts

Almost any handbook on Human Resources Development includes recommendations on training and learning; for example, attempts to strive for cultural change and to encourage feedback or double-loop learning (Marsick and Watkins, 1990). Learning activities and processes themselves receive much less attention, although it is recognized that, in order to design effective policies to promote informal on-the-job learning, a more thorough understanding of how such actual learning occurs is required (Stern, 1990). Recently, a set of useful concepts to analyze informal and integrated learning has been developed. Both activity psychology and modern cognitive science stress contextual learning in practice and real-life situations based on a growing amount of research. This was the point of departure for developing a theoretical framework for analyzing on-the-job learning. On-the-job learning takes place where the work situation (task, task management and work organization) constitutes the learning environment. Learning is structured by the working practices in which employees learn.

On-the-job learning is a multi-dimensional process, which can be differentiated according to the dimensions of work activities and the work situation. Many different approaches are used to conceptualize on-the-job learning. On closer examination, it appears that these differ, not so much with respect to the underlying learning theory, which often consists of some form of action or activity theory, but with respect to the emphasis placed on the particular aspects of the work situation to which learning is related. Four types of approach can be distinguished (Onstenk, 1994): immanent learning, situational learning, critical-reflective learning and socialization (table 8.1).

Table 8.1 On-the-job learning.

Approach	*Learning from:*
Immanent learning	Performing the activity Solving job problems
Situated learning	Work environment Managers, colleagues Culture of the occupational group
Critical-reflective learning	Innovation, design Reflection on professional practice Decision-making
Work socialization	Company and occupational culture Hierarchy, power relations

The first two approaches are primarily concerned with learning to master the task or activities to be performed (acquiring the necessary competence, in the strict sense). The social organization of the labor process is considered to play an important supporting and enabling role in this process. The third type of approach focuses chiefly on reflective learning, while the fourth group emphasizes the socialization processes in the working organization.

The first group of approaches draws on critical activity-psychology and is summarized here under the heading "immanent learning." Immanent learning regards work itself as a learning process. Competence is acquired by the actual performance of work operations, actions and activities and by solving problems on the job (Frei, Duell and Baitsch, 1984). Learning by performing work activities is coupled with the development of the work activity itself (Engeström, 1987, 1994). Skills, knowledge, work motives and goals are all integrated in the work activity.

The second, related group of approaches, which has been particularly developed in the United States, may be classified as "situated learning" (Lave and Wenger, 1991; Raizen, 1989; Scribner, 1986). This approach emphasizes cognitive apprenticeship (Brown, Collins and Duquid, 1989), which implies learning in and from the physical, symbolic and social working environment, resources and social contacts with colleagues and superiors. Learning occurs in the course of performing tasks, but draws mainly on the specific physical or symbolic (work) environment. The social environment at work also plays an important role. This refers particularly to the transfer of specialized knowledge via communication with colleagues and superiors. This entails a process of gradually becoming a member of the community of practice by legitimate peripheral participation (Lave and Wenger, 1991).

A third type of approach may be labeled as "critical-reflective learning." The focus here is on learning in relation to reflection on one's own professoinal practice, to decision-making and objectives (Marsick, 1987, 1988). This is often associated with the learning process of managers and professionals, but is also expected to become more important for employees on the shopfloor (Nyhan, 1991). In broader terms, critical-reflective learning refers to learning about work performance – backgrounds, assumptions and action objectives – with a view to improving it. This approach stresses the enhancement of learning capacity and receptiveness via reflection and feedback, double-loop learning, mastering particular methods and learning to learn. The focus is on problem solving, seeking improvements, making decisions and making choices.

For want of a better term, the last group of approaches may be summarized under the heading "work socialization." The concern here is no longer primarily with the performance of tasks, but with learning how to operate in an organization (Windolf, 1981). This includes, initially, acquiring the "habitus" required by the company or occupation, that is, learning the culture, norms and values of the occupation and organization (Bourdieu, 1977). A closely related aspect is learning to deal with the various groups in the organization, that is, with the hierarchy and the balance of power. This type of learning plays an important part not only when first entering an organization (or the world of work, in the case of initial vocational training), but also at times of fundamental change in jobs or in the organization as a whole.

There is an obvious overlap between situated learning and socialization approaches. The social dimension of situated learning in many cases presupposes and reinforces socialization. These two approaches overlap, particularly in their emphasis on the cultural values of the occupational group. This in turn stresses the fact that the approaches distinguished here are not regarded as mutually exclusive, but as complementary viewpoints.

8.2 Learning Potential of Jobs

On-the-job learning requires that the workplace fulfills certain conditions in order to qualify as a strong learning environment (Onstenk, 1994). Adopting the terminology of Baitsch and Frei (1980), these can be summarized as the learning potential of jobs (see table 8.2).

The learning potential refers to the likelihood of learning processes occurring in a particular job situation. Learning processes and the development of competence result from the specific combination of the workers skills and qualifications, (formal education, work experience, learning skills), their ability and willingness to learn and develop competence, and the learning possibilities on the shop-floor (for instance, tasks, cooperation, control, autonomy, training policies and organizational change). Learning occurs in an interaction between employees and the opportunities for learning presented by the job, mediated by skills and receptiveness to

Table 8.2 The learning potential of jobs.

A. Employee's skill base:
- Training
- Experience
- Learning skills

B. Employee's receptiveness to learning
- Motivation
- Active or passive receptiveness
- Resistance to learning

C. Opportunities for learning at the workplace
- Job characteristics:
  - Broad content and comprehensiveness
  - New problems, methods, technology, material
  - Opportunities for self- and external regulation
  - Adequate opportunities for social contacts
  - Scope of action and decisions
- Work environment
  - Social contacts (colleagues, bosses)
  - Material environment (information, job aid)

D. On-the-job Training
- Structuring learning opportunities at the workplace
- Participation in innovation
- Structured on-the-job training

learning of employees. Learning opportunities on the job can be subdivided into the characteristics of the job and the working environment itself as an element of the learning process, (or the job as an environment for on-the-job learning) and on-the-job training. Measures and projects to foster on-the-job learning should focus directly on shaping and changing the subjective (employees' willingness and ability to learn) and objective (supply of learning opportunities; factors which either promote or impede learning) dimensions of learning potential, in order to qualify the workplace as a strong learning environment.

It is impossible to establish simple correlations between the particular features of a job, the learning processes and the intended learning effects, although obvious connections can be made. Immanent learning, for example, is particularly related to characteristics of the job and work environment. Learning opportunities are particularly dependent on the content and complexity of the work and on the extent to which the person is free to operate and take decisions autonomously and the scope for social contact. Situated and immanent learning processes may be reinforced by providing support and feedback, by emphasizing reflection and allowing room for personal experimentation and problem-solving, including the opportunity to make mistakes.

8.3 Acquiring skills and developing competence

Traditionally learning on-the-job is regarded as a not very efficient way of acquiring skills (Jacobs and McGiffin, 1987). It is expected to have only a limited learning effect, as it is supposed to be restricted to task specific skills as well as to jobs which have a strong physical and dexterity component (Zuboff, 1988). It could be argued, however, that if the learning potential fulfills certain conditions, on-the-job learning can have recognizable and important learning effects in terms of the acquisition of both practical knowledge (Scribner, 1986) and broad vocational competence. On-the-job learning can be important for the whole range of required skills in the workplace (Onstenk, 1992a), which includes knowledge of systems and procedures (Scribner and Sachs, 1990) and more general problem-solving and broadly applicable key-qualifications (Nijhof and Streumer, 1994). On-the-job learning is essential in developing competency (Frei, Duell and Baitsch, 1984) and expertise as a direct, "holographic" capacity to act (Dreyfus and Dreyfus, 1986).

Competence can be regarded as a set of "action programs which are objectively and subjectively necessary or desirable for accomplishing tasks and solving problems on the job" (Frei, Duell and Baitsch, 1984). These action programs enable experts to act quickly and adequately by recognizing complex problem situations. Practical competency combines declarative and procedural knowledge, a specific domain of knowledge with a specific organization of knowledge. It includes using the attributes of the particular environment in performing the task, such as tools, physical environment, other actors (supervisors, co-workers, clients) and conceptual tools. A seductive description of a competent, effective worker, based on extensive cognitive and ethnographic research, is given by Raizen (1989). Effective workers simplify tasks by developing strategies for using the least amount of effort, which means they make short cuts. They redefine, when necessary, externally-defined problems into personally-constituted problems. They use flexible strategies when they depart from a literal framework and reorganize the assigned task to *fit* the available social, symbolic, technical and material resources, and develop tentative *gap-closing* or intermediate solutions. To achieve this they co-operate with colleagues to develop situated solutions, examine contradictions, explore procedural possibilities and discuss alternative solutions; the end result being the production of accurate task-completion solutions. In addition and significantly, they continue to develop competence. In this *thick description* of effective workers, we recognize task-oriented as well as social-communicative and learning aspects.

As the *one best solution* approach of classic Taylorism loses its dominance in the shop-floor, this type of effective worker is increasingly in demand. Such an effective worker not only must have declarative and procedural task related knowledge, but also must be able to handle the material, symbolic, cultural and social context in which these skills and knowledge are used (Onstenk, 1992a; Onstenk, Moerkamp and Dronkers, 1990). Learning processes imply acquiring competence, including changes in the motives and goals of work activities (Engeström, 1987, 1994; Marsick and Watkins, 1990). Development of competence is intricately connected to the structure and development of an activity and its social-organizational context. Not only do managers and professionals have to make choices, solve problems and make decisions, so too do a growing number of rank and file workers in production, administration and services. They must contribute to continuous improvement and solve malfunction and regulation problems in order to secure the continuation of production (De Sitter, 1986; Projectgroep WEBA, 1989). The degree to which they have to make effective decisions and choices, and deliberately apply knowledge and skills to an appropriate set of action alternatives determines the expertise needed.

Competence includes the capacity to solve occupational "core problems" (Onstenk, 1992a; Onstenk, Moerkamp, Voncken and Van den Dool, 1990). Core problems refer to occupational situations in which 1) complex problems are solved, dealing with 2) the specific characteristics of the situation, and 3) the social context. This implies uncertainty and the need to balance different, sometimes contradictory considerations and interests against each other. These "core problems" occur regularly as a part of occupational practice and are characteristic of the profession. Experienced workers are expected to find efficient and effective approaches and solutions for the core problems of their job. A distinction must be made between the level of complexity and the situational dimension of core problems. Complexity refers to the complexity of job activities: simultaneous handling different kinds of information, recognizing different dimensions and possible contradictions of a problem, the degrees of importance, and the need for deliberate reasoning and choices as part of the job or task itself (Engeström, 1994). Cognitive theory and research on generic and transfer skills (Nijhof and Streumer, 1994; Salomon and Perkins, 1989; Simons, 1990) concentrates on the transition of partial observation and concrete training to more abstract and complex insights, and procedural and schematic knowledge.

In this line of thought only marginal reference is made to social and communicative skills or learning to handle conflicts. Yet these are of central importance in the *situational* dimension of labor activities in *real life* situations. Actual occupational practice in real working situations is characterized by a strategic and social dimension (Buck, 1989). Strategic action relates to task management and the structure of regulation, in so far as these are characterized by a certain amount of internal and/or external regulation autonomy (De Sitter, 1986) and action latitude (Frei, Duell and Baitsch, 1984). Each task and work environment is characterized by a degree of uncertainty, uniqueness or conflict (Buck, 1989), however small. Social (people oriented) activity is also characterized by a large amount of uncertainty and informality. This is especially true in areas where social activity is a part of occupational practice itself, as it involves *working with people*, such as the caring and service professions. Social, communicative and strategic skills rank highly among the basic skills that employers require (Carnevale, Gainer and Meltzer, 1990a). In Germany, new occupational profiles in engineering and electro-technical occupations are broadened and refer not only to technical competencies, but also to social and methodical competencies (Laur-Ernst, 1990).

Competency is also acquired by using the environment. This is true for so called *unskilled work*, for example in a warehouse (Scribner, 1984), but also for learning processes in automation (Scribner and Sachs, 1990) and complicated repair jobs (Raizen, 1989). Work place or professional culture contributes to learning to cope with the key problems of daily working life. Handling core problems is not only central to competence development, it is also a decisive element in learning. Learning to learn is not an *empty* process, which can be analyzed independently from the actual contexts of jobs, occupations or industries. General concepts of learning to learn (Simons, 1992; Smith, 1992), transfer skills (Nijhof and Remmers, 1989) or "people's ability to learn" (Nyhan, 1991) seem to have only limited value with regard to vocational learning. In earlier research we argued that learning and transfer skills of workers are best developed by handling the core problems of occupations (Onstenk, Moerkamp and Dronkers, 1990; Onstenk et al, 1990). Core problem-solving activities such as making decisions, considering different action possibilities, weighing up alternatives and discussing possibilities with others, seem to be important mechanisms of learning. Learning how to handle core problems is a way of developing more general learning, problem-solving and meta-cognitive skills. People learn by solving specific and concrete core problems how to handle complexities, contradictions and uncertainties (De Jong, Moerkamp, Onstenk and Babeliowsky, 1990). Learning through core problems contributes to the development of transfer skills, and it is therefore suggested that learning through the work process itself is the best way to acquire this kind of work-related knowledge and key qualifications.

8.4 The Worker as Learner

The challenge for a management strategy which aims to develop competencies and to create a learning organization is to enlarge the learning potential. To accomplish this, all dimensions must be taken into account. In fact, however, many companies endeavor to change only the first dimension, in the hope that the other two dimensions may change *by themselves*. Human Resources Management that concentrates on formal task-related training with respect to the supply of skills is, in fact, choosing a qualification strategy which aims at only the first dimension of the learning potential. Having read some books on HRD and recognizing the need for the modern worker to be a learner (Engeström, 1994; Marsick and Watkins, 1990; Stahl, Nyhan and D'Aloja, 1993), many companies decide they need (some) learning workers. They prefer a hiring strategy to get workers who are both able and willing to learn and consequently stress that generic, basic skills should be acquired in education (Carnevale et al, 1990a; Nijhof and Streumer, 1994). Companies try to screen new employees for their ability and willingness to learn, using school achievement records and the educational level attained as indicators. It is assumed that more learning, communicative or problem solving skills are acquired (only) by more education. Japanese success in this area would appear to validate this argument. The level of general education in Japan has risen very steeply and has resulted in the highest ever percentage of students attending college or university (Dore and Sako, 1988). These students merge easily into companies and are considered to be one of the secrets of Japanese success (OTA, 1990). It must be stressed, however, that this high level intake is only a precondition for a very active on-the-job learning and training policy (Dore and Sako, 1988; Sako, 1990). Contrary to their European or American counterparts, Japanese firms do not expect their new employees to be directly productive, but are prepared to give them extensive learning and training opportunities by job rotation, coaching and policies of continuous improvement.

Problems can be expected when skill formation strategies concentrate solely on (new) employees who are educated to a higher level. Better educated people require higher salaries and place more emphasis on job quality. They may simply be unavailable. Most importantly, there still exists the problem of upgrading present employees.

The worker as an active learner is a rather new phenomenon in organizational literature. The radical change in demands on the worker could be formulated as a transition from the Taylorist viewpoint, whereby a company (or an engineer) thinks for the worker, as opposed to the HRD-viewpoint that a worker should think for the company (Onstenk, 1992a). A great deal of HRD-literature shows a tendency to switch from description to prescription or from an analysis of learning opportunities to an emphasis on learning obligations. The European action program, Eurotecnet, proposes a strongly prescriptive concept of "Self Learning Competency" (Nyhan, 1991) and stresses the responsibility of the worker/learner to the learning process (as opposed to the trainer). According to this concept, the modern worker is expected to possess transfer skills ("know how to apply knowledge gained in one situation, dealing with a particular industrial/commercial process, to other situations") and endurance ("to puzzle out problems without giving up, or becoming too frustrated"). Learning competency is conceptualized as an individual and moral obligation, and is based on "three pillars – self motivation, self awareness and self control" (Nyhan, 1991). A conceptualization like this tends to underplay the importance of the work environment as a learning environment, since it is not clear how workers should acquire this self-learning competency or how labor should be organized and managed, in order to be able to actually utilize this competency. Significantly, most examples given deal with changing training strategies and not with redesigning jobs, or major changes in hierarchical structures or cultures. The program tries, however, to popularize the concept and to make *good practices* available by establishing a network of companies who are experimenting in this area (Stahl et al, 1993).

It should be stressed that the employer's interest in occupational learning or in learning to learn is not automatically the same as that of his employee. This is arguable of more importance to a country like Japan, which is characterized by the strong mutual commitment of employees and company (at least in large corporations), than to the U.S.A., Sweden or Holland, where vocational learning is much more oriented toward individual careers and the labor market, which may imply change of employer. Also, because individualism and industrial democracy are more rooted in western countries, it is quite possible that when workers are requested to be flexible, willing to learn, more motivated to continuous improvement, they may desire to learn more than is expected of them, for instance on designing the labor process or changing power structures.

The subjective dimension of the learning potential of a job is influenced both by learning ability, and the motivation and willingness to learn. A potential learning situation arises when the "knowledge and/or self-image of an actor do not correspond to the situation in which experiences occur" (Jarvis, 1987). But actual learning takes place only when there is a willingness and a capacity to learn. Willingness to learn relates to confidence, identification with the job, the company or the profession, and a positive attitude towards learning. Companies try to stimulate and motivate people to learn by promises of promotion or increased pay. They can also attempt to remove (subjective) learning barriers (i.e., anxiety about learning) or to influence learning attitudes. Many attempts to create a learning organization or a learning culture are aimed at this dimension.

Fear and uncertainty with respect to learning, change, new tasks or new technology can be very powerful barriers. An employee may experience a lack of confidence in his/her ability to learn and do the job properly, because previous knowledge and experience is no longer applicable. "Learned helplessness" (Leymann and Kornbluh, 1989) can also stand in the way of an active and change-oriented attitude. Research (Onstenk, 1992b) shows that acquiring positive experiences in this respect is vital and the learning climate of the organization can influence this.

"Concentration of experience" (Thijssen, 1992) can be another barrier. Learning outside one's own field of experience can be very difficult particularly if extensive experience (and confidence) has been acquired over a period of time, but in a restricted field. Learning styles are related to both the learning history and the learning environment. The learning style of less-educated adults is characterized by *learning by doing*. In general, they have had negative experiences with school-based learning, have not received much training during their working life and are often in work environments which actively discourage learning. The great challenge for developing the learning abilities and willingness of older and less-educated workers is to counter processes of concentration of experience by developing learning experiences (Onstenk, 1992b). A considerable proportion of training is aimed at acquiring social or learning skills. Positive experiences can diminish anxiety. Carnevale, Gainer and Villet (1990b) stress the importance of increasing an awareness of informal learning strategies among employees. These strategies include: "identifying the assumptions for underlying interpretations, testing assumptions for validity, generating and testing of alternative interpretations, developing an orientation that decreases the likelihood of error." These strategies presuppose opportunities and maneuver-room for employees to actually develop different concepts or solutions. There must be made room for real learning activities, enabling employees to foray into the zone of proximal development (Engeström, 1994).

"Subjective development of competencies" (Frei, Duell and Baitsch, 1984) can be a strong incentive to learn. People attain a commitment to the profession or the job. They want to do their job better and to learn how to handle more difficult (and more rewarding) tasks and problems. There seem to be cultural disparities in this respect between different countries. In countries with a strong system of vocational education like Germany, this commitment to an occupation is indeed a strong incentive to learn, whereas in countries like Japan, where the system of vocational education is weak, there is little if any commitment to a specific occupation, but a considerable amount to the company (related to lifetime employment). In the U.S.A. a willingness to learn is strongly connected to career possibilities (Carnevale et al, 1990a) and until quite recently, this was also the case in the Netherlands.

Subjective commitment to competence development can be stimulated by recognition of work experience through assessment and certification (Klarus, 1993; Koike, 1989), which also means self-recognition of work experience as a learning process. The lack of certification possibilities is seen as a major reason for lack of achievement in on-the-job learning by workers, as employees have no way to certify to prospective employers, the general knowledge and skills they have acquired from previous employment (Bishop, 1990; Stern, 1990). It is of paramount importance to stimulate, recognize, and reward acquired skills with appropriate certification, increased pay or better job prospects in order to stimulate informal learning (Grootings, 1987; Koike, 1989). Dutch research on the implementation of autonomous work groups in Dutch industry shows that lack of appropriate reward structures, which reflect changes in responsibility, complexity and extension of tasks, can be one of the main obstructions to successful innovation (COB/SER, 1990). In a research project, consequences of pay systems and function classification of new work organizational structures are studied. Some companies are experimenting in this area (Bilderbeek and Buitelaar, 1990; Huiskamp and Jetten, 1993). The Japanese reward experiential learning and growing expertise by a slow-but-steady long-term promotion system (Dore and Sako, 1988; Koike, 1989). One of the main objectives of establishing a system of New Vocational Qualifications in Britain is offering employees and employers a tailor-made opportunity to assess skills acquired at work. In the project on Core Skills and Work Based Learning (Levy, 1987), recognition of experience based knowledge and skills was enhanced by developing an experience chart constructed from a core skills list. Levy and her colleagues identify a set of 113 core skills, divided into four types of skills: number, communication, problem-solving and practical skills. These skills are formulated on an intermediate abstracted level, in order to function as a "common language" in the comparison of concrete skills from different fields. As cognitive science recognizes arithmetic or problem-solving skills in daily work routines of warehouse workers, shopping housewives or copier-repairmen (Raizen, 1989), the Core Skills Project tries to identify skills in all kinds of experience and translate them into required skills.

8.5 Work and Organization as a Learning Environment

The job environment is the most important dimensions of the learning potential. On examination of the literature and the analyzed programs and projects in this area, we can identify two dimensions when assessing the shop floor as a learning site. Some approaches emphasize work itself as a learning process (i.e., theories on development of competence), whereas others emphasize the organizational context as a learning environment. At times they concentrate on the organization itself as a prerequisite for learning (offering learning possibilities). More recently the organization rather than the work or activity has been stressed in the learning process, for instance, by theorists of the learning organization (Harrison, 1993; Stahl et al, 1993; Wood, 1988), who concentrate on decision-making and goal-setting in organizations. It seems more beneficial to take into account both dimensions. In all six countries, programs and projects were found that promoted new organizational methods, by regulating the quality of labor and developing models or organizational concepts.

8.5.1 Quality of labor

In Sweden, Holland and Germany, learning and personal development as a dimension in the quality of labor is a very important subject. After "autonomy and industrial democracy" and "health and ergonomics", "learning and development" is becoming the third most important element in the quality of labor (Leymann and Kornbluh, 1989). In Holland, labor protection regulation has been extended in line with learning and development in relation to socio-technical approaches in the 1980s. To execute this regulation the WEBA-methodology (Projectgroep WEBA, 1989) has been developed. It measures learning opportunities as part of the quality of labor by using the following dimensions of the job and job-context: occupational unity and completeness of the job; simple and difficult tasks in the job; internal and external steering possibilities and adequate possibilities for social contact. The most important dimension is the fine tuning of steering necessities (to solve production problems) and steering opportunities (both in terms of autonomy and qualification). This approach is based on a convergence of socio-technical principles, the design of the labor process (De Sitter, 1986), and a pedagogic approach aimed at stimulating (immanent) learning on the shop floor (Grootings, 1987). In Germany a comparison of the "Humanisierung der Arbeit"-program with the follow-up program of "Technik und Arbeit" also shows an increased attentiveness to learning in addition to more traditional topics on the quality of labor (Onstenk, 1994).

8.5.2 Organizational context

Although the learning organization is theoretically a predominantly American idea, in practice it seems to be most broadly developed in Sweden, Germany and Japan. In the American model, it is primarily managers and professionals who learn by changing and adapting their theories-in-action (Marsick and Watkins, 1987, 1990), whereas in Sweden, Germany and Japan the entire workforce is expected to participate in the learning organization. This does not mean that the whole spectrum of possible learning incentives on the shopfloor is developed evenly in these countries.

In Sweden, programs and projects initiated by the Work Environment Fund aim to introduce new technology with reference to industrial democracy and the development of competence for all members of the organization. This includes not only formal training, but also the planned, systematic growth of experience through on-the-job learning (Docherty, 1989). In successive action programs, learning has become increasingly important. The Development

Program (1982-1987) concentrated on new technology and its consequences for management and working life, which are neatly summarized in the title of the final report "Towards a learning organization" (Development Program, 1989). The MDA-program (People, Computers and Work, 1987-1992) concentrated on the impact of computerization on people and work, including the use of computers as a support for learning. The Swedish case indicates how difficult organizational renewal is with respect to developing learning opportunities. After two decades of development programs it still seems very difficult to implement and diffuse good practices (Docherty, 1989; Markin, 1991).

In 1990 a program, referred to in Swedish as the Learning Organization, and in English as "Learning on the job" started, in order to stress the difference with the concept of the learning organization as a management device. It is stressed that "yesterday's models for the transfer of knowledge are no longer sufficient. These days you need to learn on the job, while doing your job." The program aims to "stimulate new thinking regarding skills development in working life; support the development of on-the job-learning; explore factors and conditions supporting or obstructing on-the-job learning; further employees development at work; enlarge awareness of the importance of tactic knowledge; facilitate utilization of knowledge skills and experience of the workforce; spread available knowledge and experience regarding learning processes" (Arbetsmiljöfonden, 1991). In the best Swedish tradition this program intends to concentrate on supporting experiments and diffusing experience. To a certain extent, by following this program, Sweden is trying to create a kind of Japanese learning culture in companies. But while the labor market is not predominantly internal and so job security is not to be ensured at a company level, as is the case in Japan, but rather at a national level, there arises a serious problem with regard to recognition and marketable value of learning results. In this respect, there is a very significant dispute between employers and unions. Contrary to the Swedish tradition of joint-decision making, a conflict situation is apparent with regard to informal on-the-job learning. Unions prefer formal to informal training, because it gives workers more of an advantage on the market. In Sweden there seems to be no initiative in the development of a system of experience-based qualifications (like the National Vocational Qualifications in Britain).

In Japan and the Anglo-Saxon countries, which lack a well-developed system of vocational education, learning and training on-the-job has major importance, even for acquiring primary skills. We can distinguish two models: a company-oriented model (Japan) and a market-oriented model (Great Britain, U.S.A.).

In Japan training is more extensively integrated into company policy as a whole. Whereas formal training statistics are not very impressive (and training consists mainly of mail-ordered individual courses), there is a great deal of training on the job, integrated into organizational policies (Dore and Sako, 1988). Japanese labor relations are characterized by a strong emphasis on managing human resources in support of a strategy of continuous quality improvement (Carnevale et al, 1990b; Sako, 1990). This includes lateral job rotation, dual promotion systems, work groups, consultative decision making and a strong learning culture. A general prerequisite for the successful application of such learning strategies is the promise of life-long job security for the core workers in the economy, a strong commitment to the company and a high general education level of workers. Life-long employment in reality only includes some 20 to 30% of workers, most of whom are employed in large firms, although some small firms are also trying to achieve this ideal (Dore and Sako, 1988). To a large extent Japanese policies do not include the improvement of the quality of labor in the German or Swedish sense. External motivational factors seem to be more significant than intrinsic motivation for job performance or learning attitudes (Bishop, 1990; Dore and Sako, 1988). In Japan learning by job content is determined by job rotation, rather than by job enrichment. A strongly hierarchical managerial style is combined with an openness to learning in which every experienced employee and manager expects requests for help and explanation, and is evaluated on his accomplishments in this field by his superior (Sako, 1990). Continuous learning to improve the quality and efficiency of the production process combines with an intensification of the working day. Incentives to learn and continuous improvement of performance (Kaizen) can easily lead to heavy work pressure and are often combined with very tight and autocratic control (Delbridge, Turnbull and Wilkinson, 1991; Sierksma, 1991). For the majority of Japanese workers with temporary contracts or employed by subcontractors, labor conditions and learning possibilities are more inferior (Kamata, 1986).

In the U.S.A. projects and models are more dependent on the initiatives of individual private firms and the activities of professional organizations like the Quality Circles movement (Cole, 1989) or the American Society for Training and Development ASTD (Carnevale et al, 1990b). In many respects there are still only isolated examples of good practices and there is no indication of a changing organizational culture in general (Bishop, 1990; Carnevale et al, 1990b; OTA, 1990). Stern (1990) gives examples of a number of Californian companies which stimulate the conditions for learning-intensive production, such as doing by learning, using slack time for informal training, delivering embedded training (i.e., making use of tutoring or help functions in computers), sustaining motivation by collaborative employment relationships (work teams, quality circles, flexibility in allocation and classification), concentrating on smaller plants/units, introducing new compensation systems (skill-based pay) and employment security. Interestingly enough, we encounter here both training and organizational dimensions, but not learning on-the-job itself. Very significantly, work teams are considered as a motivational factor, not as a learning environment.

Interest in on-the-job learning seems more prominent in the area of training rather than in organizational or job related issues. Only 55% of Americans acquire any qualifying education or training at all and half of this is informal training (Carnevale et al, 1990b). Most critics and researchers in this area agree that training both on and off the job should be expanded and that training should be considered more as an investment. In literature on on-the-job training coaching, tutorship and supportive feedback contexts are getting renewed interest (Jacobs, 1991; Onstenk, 1994). Employers should use applied pedagogy to ensure that learning will be embedded in work processes and training should receive more emphasis through being connected to performance-based selection, appraisal and rewards (Bishop, 1990; Carnevale et al, 1990b; OTA, 1990).

The situation in Britain is comparable to that of the United States. Very good examples of organizational renewal and on-the-job learning can be found, but they are still largely isolated phenomena, and in many cases occur in foreign owned companies (Sako, 1990; Wood, 1988). To improve this, the British Institute for Personnel Management launched its program on Continuous Development (Wood, 1988). The government tries to stimulate companies by awarding outstanding companies as Investors in People (Harrison, 1993).

Also a system of vocational qualifications (NVQ) is developed, which includes on-the-job learning. Since the decline of the apprenticeship system, Great Britain lacked a system of vocational education, resulting in employees receiving very little training (TIB, 1989). Recently new emphasis has been placed on the need for better qualified workers to improve the competitive strength of the national economy. It is surprising to note that there is not so much emphasis on improving the learning potential of jobs, but on stimulating learning by individuals through the assessment of prior learning. Several projects have been launched for assessing skills that are acquired through experiential learning. The system of National Vocational Qualifications explicitly recognizes learning by experience as an alternative to formal training. The previously mentioned project on Work Based Learning (Levy, 1987) is not only aiming at recognizing skills, but also at "linking learning to the work role". The development of job competence on three levels (tasks, task management and role/job environment) can be fostered by a mix of learning opportunities provided by structuring learning opportunities at the workplace, by on-job training and learning opportunities and by relevant off-job learning opportunities (Levy, 1991). Structuring learning opportunities at the workplace means allocated work activities, which are productive and at the same time provide an opportunity for learning. Strategies must take into account the worker/learner's location in the organization, the allocation of activities and learning opportunities, the scope of learner activities and worker/learner awareness of skill and performance (Matthews, Oates, Levy and Work Based Learning Project Team, 1992).

In Holland sometimes the learning paradigm is restricted to professionals (Van der Krogt, 1990), as distinguished from traditional jobs in machine bureaucracies. Occasionally an integral policy is advocated, stressing the need to integrate learning and socio-technical redesign of jobs (Van Terwisga and Van Sluijs, 1990). It is stated that growing learning opportunities exist on the job for social-communicative and organizational skills, as a consequence of technological and organizational renewal (Kessels and Smit, 1989; Van Terwisga and Van Sluijs, 1990). The Dutch TAO-program (Technology, Labor and Organization) emphasizes both organizational and individual learning as important themes, however most projects still concentrate on organizational problems or professional groups (Den Hertog and Ramondt, 1994). The Center of New Technology of Dutch trade unions supports trade union representatives and works councils in innovation projects. One of their goals is to develop learning opportunities for less-educated workers, for instance by simulation or providing them with experience (Haffmans and Sombroek, 1990). Some good examples of integrated courses for less-educated workers can be found in Holland (Onstenk, 1992b), where training courses are developed which combine on-the-job learning and training, a certification system and formal, classroom learning.

We are in agreement with Carnevale et al (1990b), who stress the learning organization as a two way learning system: a training structure which teaches employees the required new skills and a system that allows employers to learn from their employees ways of reducing costs and improving quality (the learning organization in the broad sense). Japanese Kaizen policy is an example of this, but only to a limited extent. Better examples can be found in the Swedish Development Program. A good example is of a paper factory where production workers were involved in developing and adapting new technology. They discussed the new machinery with engineers and construction workers, thereby learning a great deal about the production of paper. They also visited the company's principal customer and discussed the specific demands with regard to quality and features of the product. They then translated these into new specifications which led to a better product, produced in a more efficient manner (Docherty, 1989; Development Program, 1989). In a Dutch paint producing firm personnel from the Research and Development department participated in the training of production workers, and by so doing learned a great deal about daily problems in the production process (Onstenk, 1992b).

8.6 On-the-job Learning as a Challenge to the Learning Organization

Work and organization as strong learning environments presuppose a specific set of characteristics with respect to the content of the job, degree of autonomy, social context, support and feedback structure, and possible rewards for learning. Learning possibilities depend on the content and complexity of a task, and on the amount of actual autonomy and room for decisions and the possibilities for social contacts. Informal and immanent learning processes can be reinforced by giving feedback; by support from colleagues, supervisors or computer systems; by stressing reflection in action; by allowing workers to solve problems that are encountered on the job, including flexibility for experimentation and the making of mistakes. Some preconditions are also stressed. There must be some sort of guarantee that new skills can actually be used in the near future, either through increased job security or marketability (recognition, assessment and certification).

An integrated HRD approach should be aiming at all dimensions of the learning potential. The analysis of the state of affairs in six industrial countries indicates that there is still a long way to go in this direction. We did indeed find programs and projects which concentrate on the willingness of workers to learn. There is evidence that a growing number of companies attempt to stimulate and motivate people to learn by promising either better jobs or better pay. They also try to remove (subjective) learning barriers (i.e., fear of learning) and influence learning attitudes. In many cases, an attempt to create a learning organization or a learning culture concentrates on this point. We also found projects and examples of strategies which endeavored to create greater possibilities for learning and remove learning barriers, and observed different forms of organizational culture which offer possibilities for autonomy, participation and career development, and which characterize by a positive learning climate. But according to most experts these examples are still the exception, not the rule.

We found organizational concepts and practices which are in many respects compatible with the findings on cognitive and activity psychology and learning theory. Further development should be enlightened by these findings. The development of a learning organization should not concentrate solely on management and the developing feedback structures or cultural involvement of workers. The chances for personal development should be increased (quality of labor) and explicit training strategies, including informal and integrated learning, should be developed. The challenge to HRD is the development of integrated strategies and policies which aim to stimulate motivation and provide strong learning opportunities, backed up by training (instead of being restricted to training aimed at *skills for new technology*).

If a dimension is missing counter-effects may be expected. As the Japanese case shows, a strong incentive for learning and improving performance, without emphasis on quality of labor leads to strong work pressure, stress and even death. Emphasis on the learning organization, without the development of appropriate training strategies can lead to a very limited range of people who actually learn within the learning organization, as the case of the U.S.A. shows (Carnevale et al, 1990a). International comparison can be very helpful in looking for solutions to specific problems. But it can never lead to the simple adoption of specific strategies or solutions without reflecting on necessary preconditions or unwanted consequences.

Striving for multi-skilled and quality conscious workers intimates that on-the-job learning at the lower levels of the organization implies more than (initial) training on the job. It means a break with established Taylorism, where learning is neglected or restricted to specific movements prescribed in great detail which dissuade workers from learning on the job. It remains to be seen, however, if the change to a learning society means a break with a power structure based on the control of the labor process or a tightening up of it (Delbridge, Turnbull and Wilkinson, 1991; Sierksma, 1991). Skill formation by job rotation, learning in task groups and developing learning competencies can be analyzed in terms of more effective work performance, but should also be evaluated in terms of human development. This should not be measured in terms of an optimistic portrait of the *knowledge*-worker of tomorrow, but in terms of consequences for rank and file workers in factories, offices and services, for women, for older and less-educated workers and other groups of *marginal* workers.

References

Arbetsmiljöfonden (1991). *The Learning Programme.* Stockholm: Arbetsmiljöfonden.

Baitsch, C. and Frei, F. (1980). *Qualifizierung in der Arbeitstätigkeit.* Bern: Verlag Hans Huber.

Bilderbeek, R. and Buitelaar, W. (1990). *Informatisering en organisatie-strategie in de bankensector.* Apeldoorn/Rotterdam: TNO/STB/RISBO.

Bishop, J. (1990). *The Skills Shortage and the Payoff to Vocational Education?* Working paper # 90-07. New York: Cornell University.

Bourdieu, P. (1977). *Outline for a Theory of Practice.* Cambridge: Cambridge University Press.

Brown, J.S., Collins, A. and Duquid, P. (1989). Situated Cognition and the Culture of Learning. *Educational Researcher, 18* (1), 32-42.

Buck, B. (1989). Technologie oder Praxis? Berufsbildungsverständnis und seine Auswirkungen auf Vermittlungsformen. *Neue Entwicklungen in den Kaufmännische Berufen.* Berlin: BIBB.

Carnevale, A.P., Gainer, L.J. and Meltzer, A.S. (1990a). *Workplace Basics. The essential skills employers want.* San Francisco: Jossey Bass.

Carnevale, A.P., Gainer, L.J. and Villet, J. (1990b). *Training in America. The organization and strategic role of training.* San Francisco: Jossey Bass.

COB/SER (1990). *Zelfstandig samenwerken in autonome taakgroepen.* Den Haag: COB/SER.

Cole, R.E. (1989). *Strategies for Learning. Small group activities in American, Japanese and Swedish industry.* Berkeley: University of California Press.

De Jong, J.A. (1991). Opleiden op de werkplek. Theoretische benaderingen. Kruijd, D. (Ed.) *Opleiden op de werkplek.* Capita selecta. Handboek Opleiders in Organisaties. Deventer: Kluwer.

De Jong, M., Moerkamp, T., Onstenk, J.H.A.M. and Babeliowsky, M. (1990). *Breed toepasbare beroepskwalificaties in leerplan en beroepspraktijk.* Amsterdam: SCO.

De Sitter, U. (1986). *Het flexibele bedrijf.* Deventer: Kluwer.

Delbridge, R., Turnbull, P. and Wilkinson, B. (1991). *Pushing Back the Frontiers: Management Control and Work Intensification under JIT Factory Regimes.* Paper for the 9th Labour Process Conference. Manchester.

Den Hertog, J.F. and Ramondt, J.J. (1994). *Competente Vernieuwers. Een proeve uit het TAO-programma.* Maastricht: MERIT.

Development Program (1989). *Towards a Learning Organization.* Stockholm: Arbetsmiljöfonden.

Docherty, P. (1989). *Skill Development in Working Life: Swedish Experiences.* Paper to the Eurotecnet Conference on Self Learning Competency. Essen, 19-21 April.

Dore, R. and Sako, M. (1988). *How the Japanese Learn to Work.* London: Routledge.

Dreyfus, H.L. and Dreyfus, S.E. (1986). *Mind over Machine.* New York: The Free Press.

Engeström, Y. (1987). *Learning by Expanding. An activity-theoretical approach to developmental research.* Helsinki: Orienta-Konsultit Oy.

Engeström, Y. (1994). *Learning for change: new approach to learning and training in companies.* Geneva: ILO.

Frei, F., Duell, W. and Baitsch, C. (1984). *Arbeit und Kompetenzentwicklung. Theoretische Konzepte zur Psychologie arbeitsimmanenter Qualifizierung.* Bern: Verlag Hans Huber.

Grootings, P. (1987) (Ed.). *Work and Learning.* Maastricht: Presses Interuniversitaires Européennes.

Haffmans, J. and Sombroek, C. (1990). *Kwalificatie voor de toekomst. Bedrijfsopleidingen en nieuwe technologie.* Amsterdam: FNV Steunpunt Technologie.

Harrison, R. (1993) (Ed.). *Human Resource Management. Issues and Strategies.* Wokingham (etc.): Addison Wesley.

Huiskamp, M.J. and Jetten, B. (1993). *Vernieuwing van functies en beloning.* Rotterdam: RISBO.

Jacobs, R.L. (1991). *Forecasting the Financial Benefits of Unstructured and Structured OJT.* Paper to the International Conference on Research on Corporate Training and Development, University of Twente, Enschede. Ohio: Ohio University.

Jacobs, R.L. and McGiffin, T.D. (1987). A Human Performance System Using a Structured On-the-Job Training Approach. *Performance & Instruction,* 25.

Jarvis, P. (1987). *Adult Learning; the Social Context.* London: Croom Helm.

Kamata, S. (1986). *Japan aan de lopende band.* Amsterdam: Jan Mets.

Kessels, J.W.M. and Smit, C.A. (1989) (Eds.). *Handboek opleiders in organisaties.* Deventer: Kluwer.

Klarus, R. (1993). *Ervaring telt.* Den Bosch: CIBB.

Kochan, T.A. and Osterman, P. (1991). *Human Resource Development and Utilization: is there too little in the US?* MIT/Sloan School of Management. Paper for the Time Horizons Project of the Council on Competitiveness.

Koike, K. (1989). *Human Resource Development on the Shop Floor in Contemporary Japan.* Contribution to the OECD-conference on 'Japanese employment in the context of a changing economy and society.' Paris: OECD.

Laur-Ernst, U. (1990) (Ed.). *Neue Fabriksstrukturen und veränderte Qualifikationen.* Berlin: BIBB.

Lave, J. and Wenger, E. (1991). *Situated Learning. Legitimate peripheral participation.* Cambridge: Cambridge University Press.

Leymann, H. and Kornbluh, H. (1989). *Socialization and the World of Work.* Aldershot: Gower.

Levy, M. (1987). *The Core Skills Project and Work Based Learning.* London/Bristol/Sheffield: FESC/MSC.

Levy, M. (1991). *Work Based Learning: a Good Practice Model.* Bristol: The Staff College.

Markin, C. (1991). *Quality of Working Life in Sweden.* Stockholm: Governmental Commission for the Development of Competence and Skill in Working Life.

Marsick, V.J. (1987) (Ed.). *Learning in the Workplace.* London: Croon Helm.

Marsick, V.J. (1988). Learning in the Workplace: the Case for Reflectivity and Critical Reflectivity. *Adult Education Quarterly, volume 38, number 4,* 187-198.

Marsick, V.J. and Watkins, K. (1990). *Informal and Incidental Learning on the Workplace.* London/New York: Routledge.

Matthews, D., Oates, T., Levy, M. and Work Based Learning Project Team (1992). *Work based learning - Strategies for structuring learning opportunities in the workplace and implementing work based learning.* Bristol: The Staff College.

Nyhan, B. (1991). *Developing People's Ability to Learn.* Brussels: Eurotecnet/EIP.

Nijhof, W.J. and Remmers, J.L.M. (1989). *Basisvaardigheden nader bekeken.* Enschede: OCTO.

Nijhof, W.J. and Streumer, J. (1994). *Verbreed Beroepsonderwijs.* Enschede: Universiteit Twente.

Onstenk, J.H.A.M. (1992a). Skills needed in the workplace. Tuijnman, A. and Van de Kamp, M. (1992) (Eds.) *Learning across the Lifespan. Theories, research, policies.* London: Pergamon Press, 137-156.

Onstenk, J.H.A.M. (1992b). *Deelname aan scholing door laag opgeleide werknemers.* Bunnik: A&O-Beleidsstudies.

Onstenk, J.H.A.M. (1994). *Leren en opleiden op de werkplek.* Een verkenning in zes landen. Bunnik: MGK/A&O.

Onstenk, J.H.A.M., Moerkamp, T., Voncken, E. and Van den Dool, P.C. (1990). *Leerprocessen in stages.* SCO-rapport 209. Amsterdam: SCO.

Onstenk, J.H.A.M., Moerkamp, T. and Dronkers, J. (1990). *Broadly Applicable Vocational Qualifications: a Challenge for Vocational Education.* Paper for the international experts conference on vocational education and training, Boekelo. Amsterdam: SCO.

OTA - Office of Technology Assessment (1990). *Worker Training. Competing in the new International Economy.* Washington: Library U.S. Congress.

Projectgroep WEBA (1989). *Functieverbetering en organisatie van de arbeid.* Den Haag: DGA/Ministerie SoZaWe.

Raizen, S. (1989). *Reforming Education for Work: a Cognitive Science Perspective.* Berkeley, National Center for Research in Vocational Education.

Sako, M. (1990). *Enterprise Training in a Comparative Perspective: West Germany, Japan and Britain.* London: London School of Economics.

Salomon, G. and Perkins, D.N. (1989). Rocky roads to transfer: rethinking mechanisms of a neglected phenomenon. *Educational Psychologist, 24,* 113-142.

Scribner, S. (1984). Studying working intelligence. Rogoff, B. and Lave, J. (1984) (Eds.). *Everyday Cognition. Its Development in Social Context.* Cambridge, MA: Harvard University Press, 9 - 40.

Scribner, S. (1986). Thinking in action: some characteristics of practical thought. Sternberg, R. and Wagner, R.K. (Eds.) *Practical Intelligence: Nature and Origins of Competence in the Everyday World.* Cambridge: Cambridge University Press, 13 - 30.

Scribner, S. and Sachs, P. (1990). *A Study of On-the-job Training.* Technical Paper 13. Laboratory for Cognitive Studies of Work, City University of New York.

Sierksma, R. (1991). *Toezicht en taak. Pragmatisme, taylorisme en het beheer van arbeid.* Amsterdam: SUA.

Simons, P.R.J. (1990). *Transfervermogen.* Oratie. Nijmegen: KUN.

Simons, P.R.J. (1992). Theories and principles of learning to learn. Tuijnman, A. and Kamp, M. van de (Eds.) *Learning Across the Lifespan. Theories, Research, Policies.* London: Pergamon Press, 159-171.

Smith, R.M. (1992). Implementing the learning to learn concept. Tuijnman, A. and Kamp, M. van de (Eds.) *Learning Across the Lifespan. Theories, Research, Policies.* London: Pergamon Press, 173-188.

Stahl, T., Nyhan, B. and D'Aloja, P. (1993). *The learning Organisation. A Vision for Human Resource Development.* Brussels: Eurotecnet Technical Assistance Office.

Stern, D. (1990). *U.S. Employers' Investment in Human Resources.* Contribution to the conference on Investing in Human Resources, Amsterdam.

Thijssen, J. (1992). A model for adult training in flexible organizations: Towards an Experience Concentration Theory. *Journal of European Industrial Training, 16*, 9, 5-15.

TIB (1989). *Training in Britain. The Main Report.* London: HMSO 1989.

Van der Krogt, F.J. (1990). De leerfunctie in verschillende organisaties. *Opleiding en Ontwikkeling 3-11.*

Van Terwisga, H.B. and Van Sluijs, E. (1990). *Opleiden voor de toekomst, onderdeel van bedrijfsbeleid.* Alphen a.d. Rijn: Samson/STT.

Windolf, P. (1981). *Berufliche Sozialisation. Zur Produktion des beruflichen Habitus.* Stuttgart: F. Enke Verlag.

Wood, S. (1988). *Continuous Development.* London: Institute for Personnel Management.

Zuboff, S. (1988). *In the Age of the Smart Machine. The Future of Work and Power.* New York: Basic Books.

9 Effectiveness of Seminars as a Training Tool in International Companies

Martin Mulder, Wim J. Nijhof and Afina C. Steinvoort

The training and development of employees in international organizations is often organized by a seminar model. Apart from the fact that this model facilitates the formation of employee skills, it enhances the establishment of a common corporate culture. In the seminar model, employees are invited to attend a training or seminar center for some days or weeks to study certain topics or to learn specific skills. This model is often used in technologically advanced industrial environments. For instance, when companies have a central research and development branch, expertise on particular systems, products and processes is centralized. Dissemination of this expertise to the foreign subsidiaries often follows the seminar approach. Representatives from the companies in the host countries travel to the technological training center in the home country. These recipients get an introduction to the new technologies, and after a short period of time they return to their countries, preferably having acquired the necessary competencies and background documentation to disseminate their newfound knowledge and skills. Although this model is frequently used, little is known about the effectiveness of international seminars. What are the obstacles to the success of international seminars? What about the learning results and subsequent knowledge transfer to the job performance of the participants? What about the ultimate goal of this approach, and the dissemination of the expertise in the foreign subsidiaries? Do the participants share their information with colleagues in their organizations?

A study into these issues has been carried out by the Department of Curriculum Studies of the Faculty of Educational Science and Technology of the University of Twente. The Research & Development Center (R & D Center), which is a department of an international company in the Netherlands, commissioned the department to study the effectiveness of the seminar approach during the period September 1989 to August 1990. This R & D Center produces new detergent technologies for business, industry and large public organizations such as health care institutions. These technologies are being marketed and maintained by several European subsidiaries of this international organization (in the remainder of this chapter the company will be referred to as *Detergent Technologies*, abbreviated as DT).

The study was aimed at determining the effectiveness of international seminars organized by the R & D Center for DT-companies by focusing on the dissemination of expertise which is necessary to market, install, and maintain new detergent technologies.

The seminar approach employed by the R & D Center is characterized by the fact that participants of a seminar have to further disseminate the provided knowledge and skills throughout their companies to sales and service professionals. Furthermore, these professionals are expected to transfer this knowledge to the customers of their national DT-companies.

9.1 Objectives and Research Questions

The primary objective of the study was rather practical. Within the framework of a project on Total Quality Improvement, the quality of the training and development function had to be assessed. This context is rather common in several industries, as many organizations are implementing total quality management systems, and training and development is being envisaged as a dedicated tool for quality improvement. With respect to the study of the seminar approach, this culminated in the the following questions: (1) what are the effects of the international seminars provided by the R & D center of DT?, and (2), can the quality of these international seminars be enhanced, and if so, how?

The R & D Center was particularly interested in these questions as the only evaluation strategy employed before this study was a post seminar satisfaction evaluation. These evaluations did not reveal substantial information about the effectiveness of the international seminars, as these superficial satisfaction evaluations are unable to yield decisive conclusions as to the impact, if any, these seminars had on performance, and on the solving of expertise problems in the subsidiaries in the home countries.

Based on an analysis of the evaluation literature, the general questions mentioned above were re-interpreted and translated into five evaluation questions.

The first question relates to the training needs assessment stage in the instructional design process. Effective training and development processes should only be provided if there is a need for skills and knowledge formation. If neither the organization nor the individual has a need for learning, little learning will take place. The general need for learning was quite obvious in this situation, because the R & D center of DT produces extensive knowledge on detergent technology, and the DT subsidiaries in their home countries have a requirement for this information. Not all aspects of the new technologies are relevant to these subsidiaries. Sales and service procedures may vary between and within different countries, therefore it is necessary to evaluate the specific needs of each DT-company individual. Accordingly, the first research question is:

1 To what extent is there a training need among DT companies regarding the new technologies that are developed by the R & D Center?

DT-companies may identify a training need with respect to the technologies that are at the core of the seminars, select their representatives, and send them to the seminar. There is no guarantee, however, that these participants indeed acquire the knowledge and skills offered by the seminar. Motivation, cultural preferences, and language proficiency may impede the learning process and prevent the acquisition of the required expertise. Therefore the second research question is:

2 Did the participants learn from the knowledge and skills presented in the seminars?

When learning has taken place and the participants have acquired the necessary expertise, many obstacles can prevent them from disseminating their expertise in their own DT-company. These obstacles can be related to personal characteristics, such as the competitive advantage of an individual's expertise, a shortage of dissemination technique (such as tutorials, work groups, briefing sessions), or only partial retention of the acquired expertise. But the work environment may also be destructive with respect to the expertise dissemination. Management may create conditions that foil dissemination, such as creating (or allowing) work overload, task divisions, or competitiveness among employees. Of course, the training and development departments in organizations do not have control over personal characteristics and the conditions in the work environment of the seminar's participants. However, seminar programs can be designed in such a way as to facilitate the future dissemination of the acquired expertise. This may be accomplished by several approaches, such as providing information packages for the company in the home country, or the stressing of the *transmitter* role of the participants by giving them suggestions as to how the information of the seminars can be shared with others in their organization. Participants may even be encouraged to develop a dissemination plan for use on their return to their own country. If seminar designers want to take into account this future function of sharing expertise, the next question is:

3 Do the international seminars provide the necessary conditions for the dissemination of expertise in the national organization?

Even if the necessary conditions for the dissemination of information within the seminars are met, this is still no guarantee that the information will reach the right people in the national organizations. Again, personal characteristics, and characteristics in the working environment may impede this. Therefore, the next research question is:

4 To whom and how is the information, which is presented in the seminars, transferred?

And finally, if all prior conditions are met and the seminar information reaches the intended professionals, do they use the information? For that is the ultimate goal of the seminars. To check this goal, the last research question is formulated as follows:

5 Do the targeted professionals use the information in their job?

To summarize these research questions, the objective of the study was to accomplish a complete picture of the dissemination process in the DT organizations. On examining this study, strong and weak points in the dissemination process can be detected. The study had to be concluded with recommendations for improving the quality of the seminar approach.

9.2 Conceptual Framework

Much has been written about the dissemination of innovations (Hall and Hord, 1987; Havelock, 1973). The early work of Rogers and Shoemaker (1971) was aimed at analyzing the formal and informal domain of organizations, at classifying these organizations according to their readiness for change and at planning a series of interventions to enhance adoption of the innovation. The work of Fullan (1982) on the implementation of educational innovations took into consideration the concerns of the various groups that are affected by the innovation. Leithwood (1986) emphasized the configuration of the innovation itself as an important precondition of the dissemination of an educational innovation.

Little systematic knowledge is available, however, on the benefits of international seminars with regard to the dissemination of expertise via the seminar model, or on the processes of expertise dissemination from R & D Centers in industry to remote users (Ogranovich, 1993). Many publications on seminars consist of procedural guidelines for their organization them, such as the checklists presented by Reith (1987). Apart from that, an abundance of literature has appeared on the intercultural component of international training and development programs (Kohls, 1993).

Because of the lack of information about the expertise dissemination by seminars, this process is conceptualized in such a way as to suit the practical situation that was faced within company DT. Expertise dissemination, in the context of this study, is conceived of as the process by which the necessary and meaningful information for handling new technologies, which is developed by the R & D Center, is passed on to the intended professionals who operate these new technologies. Expertise dissemination in this sense is related to the concept of technology transfer, which is the process by which technology is disseminated to the candidate users of that technology. It will be clear that technology dissemination in general, requires more than training and development. In the specific case of DT company, large and complex detergent systems need to be available.

Figure 9.1 A model for information dissemination.

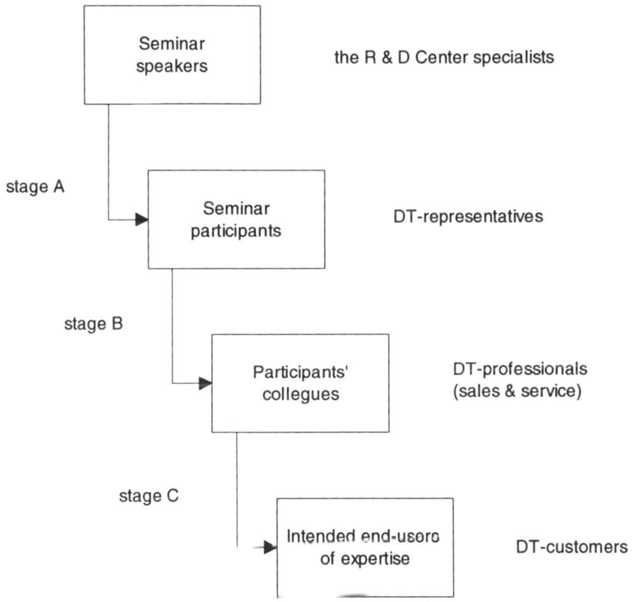

The DT-companies use a relatively simple three stage dissemination process:

Stage A: Dissemination of expertise from the R & D Center professionals to the participants of seminars, who are representatives of the several DT-companies.

Stage B: Dissemination of expertise from the participants of the seminar to the relevant target employees in the several DT-companies, in general the Sales and Service Professionals in this case.

Stage C: Dissemination of expertise from the regional DT-professionals to the customers of the DT-companies, who are the potential end-users of the R & D Center technologies.

The R & D seminar organizers exercise limited control over the whole dissemination process. In fact, they can only directly influence the dissemination in stage A. DT-companies decide whether, and to what extent, the presented information will be disseminated and used by themselves. As the R & D center is financially dependent on the DT-companies, it is rather difficult for the center to put pressure on the DT-companies to purchase and use the newly developed technologies.

9.3 Research Design

The five evaluation questions called for a descriptive-explorative research design, in which the subsequent dissemination processes were tracked down and analyzed. A mere effect evaluation was not sufficient in this context, as the R & D Center wanted to improve the quality of their seminars. Therefore, an effect, context and process evaluation was implemented. The effect evaluation is carried out at the level of learning results and job performance.

Further operationalization of the research questions has taken place. According to a transfer model of Baldwin and Ford (1988), variables were defined and classified into three different groups, which were comprised of personal, training design and contextual factors. The research questions implied that data should be collected immediately after the seminars, and a further examination of the concrete effects of seminars should be undertaken after a period of time.

Six seminars were available for analysis: four seminars, organized in the period of the data collection, and two seminars, which took place in the year prior to the study. The data were collected into the following groups:

- 93 participants of the seminars;
- 75 DT-professionals, who need the seminar information in their work with DT-customers;
- 21 supervisors of these DT-professionals;
- 7 seminar organizers at the R & D center.

Because of the constraints on the evaluation study (time, budget and geographical dispersion of the DT-companies), a choice had to be made with respect to the data collection plan. It was impossible to collect sufficient data to provide the optimum result from the study's point of view. The collected data, however, could be compared by employing at least two different data sources for each research question.

As described, six seminars were evaluated. Four of these took place in 1989, and the other two in 1990. There were 93 participants in these seminars, 35 in 1989 and 58 in 1990 (see table 9.1).

Table 9.1 Response table.

SEMINARS	INSTRUMENTS	INTENDED RESPONSE	ACTUAL RESPONSE	USEFUL RESPONSE
1989-seminars	Questionnaire to participants	35	32 (91%)	28 (80%)
	Questionnaire to DT-employees	75	35 (47%)	29 (39%)
	Questionnaire to supervisors	21	18 (86%)	15 (71%)
1990-seminars	Questionnaire to participants	58	58 (100%)	58 (100%)
	Test for participants	58	44 (76%)	44 (76%)

Questionnaires were sent both to all the participants of the 1989 seminars, and to 75 DT-employees and their supervisors. Furthermore, the achievements of all 58 participants in the 1990 seminars were assessed. Part of the actual response was useful and was higher than 71%. The questionnaires sent to the DT-employees, however, had a response rate of 39%. This low response rate can be explained by taking into account the difficulties experienced by some respondents with the English language and the mobile nature of their occupations. They spend most of their working time visiting customers. The response rate was perceived as being relatively high even in the eyes of the seminar organizers, who were used to far lower response rates.

Six instruments have been used in data collection:

- a questionnaire for participants which had to be completed immediately following the seminar;
- a test for the participants, to be taken immediately following the seminar;
- a questionnaire for participants after the seminar (to take along and send back);
- a questionnaire for DT-professionals from several DT-companies;
- a questionnaire for the supervisors of the DT-professionals;
- a structured interview with the seminar organizers.

All instruments were formatively evaluated by three experts. They analyzed the instruments both from the perspective of the research questions and from their experience with the different target groups in the seminars. This resulted in some revisions, but it did not change the basic structure and content of the research instruments. The face validity of the instruments appeared to be satisfactory.

9.4 Results

In this section, the results of the study will be presented with respect to the three dissemination stages (A, B and C), from the R & D Center to DT-companies and their clients. The section will be concluded with a synthesis of the correlations that were found between several variables that were identified according to the model of Baldwin and Ford (1988). But initially the response to the questionnaire will be described.

9.4.1 Stage A

The average satisfaction score of the participants on the 1989 and 1990 seminars is relatively high, 3.2 (on a four-point scale with a maximum satisfaction score of 4.0). However, the appraisal of the participants with respect to the amount of time available to practice new material is relatively low: 42% of the participants stated that the opportunity for practice was moderate to poor (see table 9.2 for further details).

Table 9.2 Satisfaction of participants on evaluation criteria for the seminars (in percentages).

	Scale[1]				
Evaluation criteria	++	+	+/-	-	*missing*
Seminar overall	38	52	2	-	9
Quality content	29	59	4	-	9
Quality presentation	38	43	10	-	9
Time to practice	12	33	33	9	14
Quality feedback	7	69	10	4	10
Quality environment	33	50	9	-	9
Organization	66	24	2	-	9
Length	17	55	14	5	9

[1] ++ = very good, + = good, +/- = moderate, - = poor.

The scores on the tests for the 1990 participants were relatively high; the total mean of the scores was 8.2 (on a scale with a maximum score of 10). But in more than one third of the cases, seminar information did not meet with the expectations of the participants. Most participants felt, however, that they could disseminate the information within their companies. About 70% of the participants stated that more than half of the presented seminar information was useful for their job performance and their organization.

9.4.2 Stage B

The majority of the participants disseminated less than 50% of the seminar information to the DT-professionals; 18.5% disseminated no information at all. The most important reason for not disseminating more than 50% of the information was: "the information was already widely known in the company" (50%). This indicates a major needs assessment and design problem within the organization.

In most cases (73%) the seminar information was disseminated by the passing on of the seminar documentation (see table 9.3). Table 9.3 shows that informal and less complex dissemination strategies are preferred to the other strategies. Formal courses were the least employed strategy (23%).

Table 9.3 Percentages of dissemination types employed by DT-companies for the seminars.

DISSEMINATION TYPES	%
Providing seminar documentation	73
Informal contacts	64
Training-on-the-job	55
Incidental instructions	32
Courses	23

DT-professionals, however, appreciated the way in which they received this information, and they were satisfied with the quality of the information. Two thirds of the DT-professionals also stated that they were also satisfied with the amount of information. More than 40% of the DT-professionals, however, stated that up to half of the information disseminated in their organization appeared to be inapplicable in their local situation. This is also a major issue in this case.

9.4.3 Stage C

Most DT-professionals use less than 50% of the received information in their jobs. The most important reasons for this lack of use of information were that it was too superfluous, or that it did not fit in with the current developments of their company.

A significant proportion of the DT-professionals faced problems while using the information they received in the field, as the information was not always practical.

According to their supervisors, however, more DT-professionals should make use of the seminar information in their jobs. More than one third of the supervisors stated that there were no differences in the job performance of DT-professionals, with respect to the seminar topic, since the seminar. Problems with respect to the use of the seminar information were predominantly attributed to insufficient ongoing (practical) training and information.

9.5 An Exploration of the Correlations within the Model

The study as described is rather practical and is a reminder for systematic program development and implementation. From a theoretical perspective, it is interesting to discover whether elements in the dissemination model are interrelated, and to what extent the model components are related to the characteristics of participants. Seminar designers could benefit from this.

Therefore an additional correlation analysis was carried out. In this analysis, the correlations between the model components A, B and C, on the one hand, and between individual characteristics and the model components, on the other hand, were computed. It is expected that learning results are a necessary condition for appropriate dissemination, but not as a stand alone condition. Dissemination will also be influenced by corporate strategy, structure, culture. The working conditions of the seminar participants whose responsibility is to disseminate the information may be suboptimal. In this case, where the learning results were satisfying, one essential condition for dissemination was met, but the lack of others may have hindered the actual dissemination.

Furthermore, it is expected that dissemination of information by seminar participants is a necessary precondition for the appropriate use of the information by the professionals in the organizations. Again, dissemination is not a sufficient variable for usage; other conditions may also influence the use of the information (Havelock, 1973).

While seminar organizers do not control organizational processes and variables such as corporate strategy, purchasing policy, corporate structure, and working climate, they can more or less control the target population characteristics, by the setting of matriculation requirements. They can, furthermore, develop adaptive (instructional) strategies that manage the differences between groups of participants.

In this additional analysis the relations between the statistically significant variables are presented. Figure 9.2 shows that model component A (learning results) does not correlate significantly with factor B (information dissemination). This means that whereas the learning results were rather positive, there indeed were other factors that influenced the dissemination of the information. Satisfaction with the seminar as a whole is the most important intervening variable in this respect (r = .43). The more satisfied the participants are, the more they tend to disseminate the information to the local professionals. Expectations of the participants as regards the seminar (r = .40) and its relevance (r = .34) also vary systematically with the dissemination of the information.

Figure 9.2 Significant correlations between different factors and learning results, amount of dissemination and use of information.

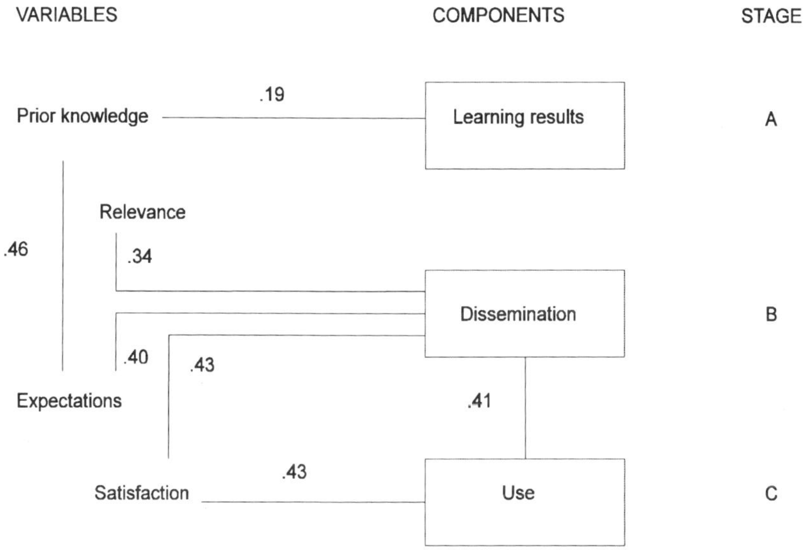

Factor B correlates significantly (r = .41) with factor C (information use) and the satisfaction of the participants with the seminar as a whole (r = .43). The satisfaction of the participants with the whole seminar seems to be the essential variable in the achievement of the ultimate objective of the seminar approach, which is the use of the information by the professionals in the local organizations who were not attending the international seminar. This result underlines the special attention that has been widely given to the satisfaction of attendees. This study reveals that the meeting of customer satisfaction is critical in achieving the ultimate objective of international seminars.

Learning results (r = .19) and expectations (r = .46) appeared to vary with respect to prior knowledge. This is obvious in this particular case, as both needs assessment and program design showed some important flaws. Whereas expectations generally are influenced by prior knowledge, if the seminar program does not take prior knowledge into account (because for some participants much of the information is already known), there will be only a limited correlation between prior knowledge and learning results.

9.6 Conclusions

If the data are interpreted in the light of the research, the following conclusions can be drawn.

First of all, DT subsidiaries do have a training need regarding the new technologies that are developed by the R & D Center. The programs as exercised, however, did not fully correspond with the needs of the potential users of the information. Many participants stated that their companies already had the information. If this is really the case, dissemination conditions in the local companies, which have the information, should be evaluated further. It would be helpful if the subpopulations, who influence the actual use of the information for job performance, were identified to determine the sections of information required by these subpopulations. It can be concluded that the heterogeneity of the clients of the R & D Center could have been integrated more fully in the seminar program design methodology, to facilitate the identification of the different uses, different clients have for information.

Second, the participants of the seminars appeared to have mastered the objectives of the seminars. The data shows that their test scores were rather high. But further analyses showed no significant relation between the test scores and the amount of disseminated information, which suggests that subject matter expertise is not in sufficient condition for disseminating information to the intended users. Personal characteristics and characteristics of the work environment also determine dissemination.

Third, the seminars only partly met the necessary conditions for expertise dissemination to the ultimate users. Of course, seminar staff do not have control over the intended use of the information in the remote workplace of DT-professionals or their clients. But there could be more attention paid to the actual practices of expertise dissemination in stages B and C. To achieve the intended use of the information needed in remote workplaces, the information must be needed and the information has to be disseminated. In order to accomplish this, those who are expected to disseminate the information should have acquired the necessary knowledge and skills for doing so. There are also other factors influencing the use of information, which were not included in this study. These factors, however, fall outside the scope of the training and development function. Factors, such as motivation, resource management, working conditions, and incentive systems, have to be taken into account when the actual use of information in the workplace is ultimately required.

Fourth, the data show that the more informal and extensive dissemination strategies are being employed by the participants. Further study has to reveal whether the seminar staff should encourage this practice and even support it by providing work aids for such dissemination strategies, or whether, on the contrary, they should advocate a somewhat different dissemination strategy in DT-companies. If the latter option is chosen, the seminar staff should incorporate skills training on the organization and management of more formal and intensive dissemination strategies.

Fifth, we may conclude that the actual use of the information, that is disseminated in stage A, is limited, due to the processes in stages B and C. There is much more information provided than is eventually used. It is not clear, however, whether this limited information use causes problems in the DT-companies or their client organizations. Perhaps part of the information provided by the seminars is redundant, and intended users only select necessary information and find this sufficient for solving their working problems, or they compensate for the lack of information by consulting other resources. Supervisors of the DT-professionals, however, think that they should use more of the information that is provided by the seminar organizers, which may indicate that the information has more potential than is actually being used, or that there is a lack of agreement on needs and strategy.

The main conclusion of the study is that the ultimate effectiveness of the dissemination model is limited. This is caused by dissonance between the seminar objectives and content on the one hand, and the needs of the DT-companies on the other hand. Seminar information was partly redundant, superfluous or insufficient, while in some cases the information did not fit in with practice, or it lacked relevance for the markets of the DT-companies. These problems may be solved by using an in-depth needs analysis of the end-users.

Quality improvement of the dissemination model can be achieved by enhancing the program validity of the seminars (Goldstein, 1987) for new technologies, related to the information needs of the intended expertise users in DT-companies and their customer organizations. This implies that the skills and knowledge of the intended users are to be analyzed to determine the training need. The results of such an analysis might be discussed in a nominal group comprising a select number of stakeholders, to accomplish a platform for the content of the seminars (Mulder, 1992).

Apart from this, the seminars themselves may be re-structured, allowing more time to put into practice the knowledge and skills learned during the seminar. Special attention directed at expertise dissemination may also enhance the actual transfer of information. One can even think of modifying the profile of participants in seminars. In the seminars under study, technical professionals were invited, who then have a training and development role after the seminar. To solve any possible tensions between these roles, seminar participants from the technological field may be instructed to take an additional role in their job, or training and development professionals may be invited as participants of the seminar. This may be a preferable strategy, especially in those cases where dissemination of expertise does not or does to a small extent depend on achievement (as is the case in this study). This strategy is related to the performance technology approach (Stolovitch and Keeps, 1992). The essence of this approach is that human performance can be supported by several systems. Training and development is only one of these systems. Seminar organizers may be biased by this system, as the short-term objective of many seminars is to teach the participants a given amount of knowledge and skills. But, as the actual use of this information by distant professionals is the long-term objective of the dissemination of new technologies, other options as to how to reach these professionals may have to be considered. Constant monitoring of the seminar quality, by using data from all intended users of the expertise, may enhance the effectiveness of the approach significantly.

The last option of course would be to cancel the seminar approach completely, and to choose other strategies of expertise dissemination. Distance training systems, in which the final users receive their information directly from the R & D center, supported by direct consultation with the DT subsidiaries, might be a cost-effective alternative. Distance training systems, however, may be more cost-effective in the cognitive domain. In the interactive, affective and psycho-motor domain, other approaches may be more attractive. Organizations may want to choose a seminar approach for acculturation, climate-building, cohesive corporate identity development, and international and intercultural team-building purposes. And it is also possible, as in this case, that the seminar providers have marketing purposes, in the sense that information provision may influence attitudes towards the technology provider, and may eventually increase the market share of the provider. A further analysis of the non-training motives of the seminar provider, the participants, the local professionals and their supervisors is recommended. This might reveal a more complete explanation of the suboptimal dissemination and use of the information.

References

Baldwin, T.T. and Ford, J.K. (1988). Transfer of Training: A Review and Directions for Future Research. *Personnel Psychology, 41,* 63-106.

Fullan, M. (1982). *The Meaning of Educational Change.* New York: Teachers College.

Goldstein, I.L. (1987). Content Validity as an Evaluation Strategy for Examining Training Programs. May, L.S., Moore, C.A. and Zammit, S.J. (Eds.) *Evaluating Business and Industry Training.* Boston: Kluwer Academic Publishers, 139-153.

Hall, G.E. and Hord, S.M. (1987). *Change in Schools: Facilitating the Process.* Albany: State University of New York Press.

Havelock, R.G. (1973). *Planning for Innovation through Dissemination and Utilization of Knowledge.* Ann Arbor: University of Michigan Institute for Social Research. Center for Research on Utilization of Scientific Knowledge.

Kohls, L.R. (1993). Preparing Yourself for Working Overseas. Reynolds, A. and Nadler, L. (Eds.) *The Global HRD Consultant's & Practitioner's Handbook.* Amherst: Human Resource Development Press, 35-56.

Leithwood, K. (1986). *Planned Educational Change: A Manual of Curriculum Review, Development, and Implementation (CRDI). Concepts and Procedures.* Toronto: OISE.

Mulder, M. (1992). *The Curriculum Conference.* Enschede: University of Twente, Department of Educational Science and Technology.

Ogranovich, S. (1993). Bringing Learners to the Technology-Source Country. Reynolds, A. and Nadler, L. (Eds.) *The Global HRD Consultant's & Practitioner's Handbook.* Amherst: Human Resource Development Press, 475-484.

Reith, J.L. (1987). Meetings, Conferences, Workshops, and Seminars. Craig, R.L. (Ed.) *Training and Development Handbook. A Guide to Human Resource Development.* New York: McGraw-Hill.

Rogers, E.M. and Shoemaker, F.F. (1971). *Communication of Innovations: A Cross-Cultural Approach.* New york: The Free Press.

Stolovitch, H.D. and Keeps, E.J. (1992) (Eds.). *Handbook of Performance Technology.* San Francisco: Jossey-Bass.

PART III

New Training and Development Devices

Introduction to Part III

Martin Mulder

The field of corporate training and development faces profound changes as to the delivery systems that are emerging due to the tremendously expanding power of electronic media. The new communications technology enables us to reduce distance problems, as we can communicate on-line with colleagues, friends, teachers and students on a global scale. The distance reduction is of course not of a physical nature, but psychologically spoken, we perceive our fellow human beings at the other end of the (e-mail or videophone) line as our neighbors. At least, the psychological distance is reduced significantly.

Physical distance is an important problem in corporate training and development. As learning is often connected to the interaction between teachers or instructors and learners or trainees, the recipients of training or the trainers needed to travel a lot. This costs a lot of time, energy and money. Think of the many international meetings, courses and seminars that are organized for training and development purposes. A substantial proportion of resources can be saved when the participants needed no or hardly any transportation. Telecommunication provides this opportunity.

Therefore, many new projects have been initiated to study the various features of new training and development devices, that are either cost effective solutions to distance problems or more efficient and effective instruments for learning.

In this third and last part of the book, several authors write about such new devices for training and development. In the literature, a host of such devices like computer-based-training, computer-aided-instruction, electronic tutorials, hypertext applications, computer mediated conferencing and computer simulations are described. This chapter part will not treat all possible new training and development technologies superficially, but rather highlights some new devices.

The first chapter in this part, chapter 10, will set the scene for various technological applications in the training and development context. It goes into the new dynamics of learning in a changing professional environment, and addresses the theme of the learning organization from a technological perspective. Asselborn and Jans take a critical stance as to the costs of traditional training approaches, and contend that training should be perceived as being integrated in the context of the whole organization. Organizations themselves, according to the authors, can be perceived as self-aware meta-systems with self-learning competence. They draw from various disciplines to make the argument that the key to corporate self-learning is the availability of a so-called corporate knowledge base. This corporate knowledge base should allow all members in an organization to learn from one another. Computer technology enables organizations to incorporate the knowledge base in computer systems that are accessible by all members of the organization. Access can be facilitated by so-called automatic agents, being interfaces between the corporate knowledge base and its user. The authors present and discuss three intelligent tools that serve as automatic agents: assistance agents, simulation agents, and training agents. The authors conclude that although elements of the corporate knowledge base can be implemented in computer systems and accesses through automatic agents, full implementation would need more advanced systems of artificial intelligence techniques in general, and knowledge representation techniques in particular.

In the next chapter Breuer and Streufert go into higher-order cognitive processes that can be stimulated by simulation-based assessment and training. They focus on training decision-making processes, and hence discuss issues at a more specific instructional level of detail. They agree with Asselborn and Jans that many changes have taken place in professional environments, pointing at changes from rather static and stable conditions in work situations towards dynamic and fluent ones, and that computer technology can make a difference in creating more effective learning processes. They stress the advantage of computer-based simulations: giving executives opportunities to experience situations that are characterized by levels of complexity that are comparable to reality, especially concerning unpredicted side-effects, exponential growth or load of information. The advantage of computer-based simulations is that the training situation does not include personal risks, losses of resources, or disruptions of staff that go along with many work situations in business and industry. Breuer and Streufert point at the limitations of many of the existing simulations and games, and describe the development of two so-called strategic management simulations. Next they describe a validation study done in Germany. The conclusion of the study is that the strategic management simulations showed a valid discrimination of measures between participants of different decision-making ability, which of course is of critical importance for assessing candidates who will be involved in complex dynamic decision-making situations. The simulations can be used in studies analyzing the effectiveness of management training and development programs that focus on the enhancement of decision-making competence.

In the next chapter, Van Schaick Zillesen, Min, Gmelich Meijling and Reimerink give another example of computer technology use in a training and development context. As Breuer and Streufert, they also go into the use of computer simulations. Their argument is that instructional feedback is critical during computer simulation sessions, and that this instructional feedback can be provided by another computer tool: hypermedia-based computer aided learning. The authors developed a prototype of such a learning environment, including a computer simulation component and a computer aided learning component. The simulation component was constructed with MacThesis, and the computer aided learning component with HyperCard. The training environment was developed for training process operators. The authors describe the development and the formative evaluation of the training environment.

Finally, Romiszowski goes into the opportunities of electronic networks and human resource development. His chapter focuses on the effective implementation of group discussion methodologies on electronic telecommunications networks. He observes that this line of inquiry is very important as much is known of self-instruction by telecommunications systems, but only little of the way in which to converse effectively on these electronic networks. He shows that seminars and case studies in a hypertext environment have great potential. Effectiveness research has shown that this approach is superior to traditional classroom sessions with respect to the volume of commentary of students, the number of different student-generated comments, and the quality of student-generated discussions. Furthermore, the acceptability of the approach was found to be high, both from the students and the discussion leader perspective.

As we stated, there is a host of new devices for human resource development. Computer support systems in various modes of course are the latest leave on the ever growing tree of modern media for learning in organizations. It is important to note that these media should not be viewed from the solutions' perspective. On the contrary, we think that human performance problems should be at the core of interest of the HRD professional. Attention to these problems, analysis of these problems, defining the HRD component to solving these problems, and from this perspective, determining the use of modern media in the support of human performance, is far more preferred. It creates the opportunity to view human resource development as an integrating factor in the performance of an organization, in that learning can be linked to corporate strategy, human resource management, and individual needs.

We think that this approach is much more appropriate to the needs of the HRD professional. If not carefully selected and designed according to the performance requirements, and the learning needs in the organization, applications of modern media can easily seduce designers and users to stroll with all kinds of uninteresting features, thus causing an enormous increase of the costs that go along with implementing modern media. So the adoption and implementation of new training and development devices should be preceded by thorough analysis of the performance problems in the organization, including a forecast of the cost-effectiveness of these media.

More case studies such as the ones presented in part III of this book need to be done to evaluate the full potential of new training and development devices. The studies in this part, however, show that there is such potential. It is interesting to note that the case study format is the one most frequently used in these studies. Breuer and Streufert used the case study methodology to validate the computer simulations they adapted. Van Schaick Zillesen et al used an expert appraisal within a case study of their simulation environment. Within this case study observation techniques and computer registered interactions were used amongst others in this case study. And Romiszowski set up a computer conference as a case study in which about 100 students participated.

It is also interesting to note that such studies tend to answer questions as to whether new training and development devices work. The studies serve as practical tests of the tools as it were. But the tools are embedded in theoretical notions about creating learning environments in corporate settings. Therefore, the case studies also serve theory building, in the sense that prototypes are developed, that they are tested, and the analysis of the tests result in better understanding of the potential of the particular tool in a given context. And, as more such case studies and tests of particular technological tools are conducted, they form a growing base of research on which studies of the underlying theories can be built.

10 The Self-learning Organization in a Changing Professional Environment

Jean-Claude Asselborn and Jean-Marie Jans

In a professional environment, traditional training approaches are of doubtful value and very cost-intensive; training must therefore be seen in the global context of the whole organization.

We use the Maturana and Varela approach to describe organizations as self-aware meta-systems with self-learning competence.

The key to corporate self-learning is the availability of a *corporate knowledge base*, allowing the whole organization and its member units to learn from each other.

Today, the corporate knowledge base is implemented in computer systems and accessed through *automatic agents*; we present in more detail *assistance agents, simulation agents* and *training agents*.

10.1 Introduction: the Limits of School Learning in a Professional Environment

The socio-economic and technical environment of companies is changing so quickly that the educational system of most countries is unable to provide companies with a skilled work-force who are aware of the latest developments and techniques for the narrow field of activity of a determined company. Therefore, there is a tendency to split professional training into two separate parts: the more general skills and basic subjects remain in the field of public education, whereas the more specific, context-sensitive skills and associated knowledge are assumed more and more by companies themselves or by organized groups of companies. A good example of these developments is provided by the Luxembourg Bankers' Association, which is organizing a training institute for its member banks providing two types of training (Krier 1991): a) *insertion training*, providing new bank employees with the basic banking skills, and b) *continuous training*, aimed at informing banking professionals of the latest developments in their field.

It is interesting to note that very often companies try to imitate the school model of goal-oriented learning (*guided learning*), which has been developed over centuries in a school context. A teaching agent (*tutor*) uses various channels of information and subtle ways of influencing a learner in order to modify his behavior with respect to a planned goal (*curriculum* or corporate model). The system is completed by some feed-back mechanism (*monitoring* or examination), which estimates the distance to the planned goal and proposes recovery measures in order to reduce this distance. Finally, the training system certifies that the distance to the planned goal is less than a given threshold. This very general model is slightly adapted in the professional environment, by replacing classroom activities with more individual channels, referred to as *self-studying*: computer-based training (CBT), distance learning, self-studying courses. Sometimes these individual channels are supported by group activities: seminars, group tutoring and tests (Ant and De Cillia, 1991).

This model, applied to a professional context, can be criticized in many respects:

- Very often one observes little if *any long-term effect* in goal-oriented learning. If the planned goal of training is not very close to the personal goals of the learner and if the acquired skills are not used frequently after the training phase, the benefit of training is lost very quickly. As an example, consider the effects of word-processing training: the majority of trainees never uses the advanced skills acquired during training, even if these advanced possibilities could increase productivity considerably. The effort of reviewing the subject is often greater than the estimated gain in productivity and a problem can very often be solved in a more cumbersome way, using simpler means.
- Goal-oriented learning is generally organized into separate subject areas; teachers observe a *partitioning* of knowledge in the skills of their students and it is very difficult to apply the result of one knowledge compartment to an activity related to another knowledge compartment. The same phenomenon is observed during the transfer of learned knowledge to practical work in the everyday professional environment.
- There are *other, more efficient learning mechanisms*, observable in all situations outside school: children learning before going to school and subsequently learning a lot outside school. In a professional environment workers and employees learn every day at their jobs: they learn how to make a correct diagnosis of the breakdown of a technical device; they acquire problem-solving skills by solving everyday problems; they recognize familiar situations and see where the problems lie. These learning mechanisms are often referred to as "self-learning competence" (Nyhan 1991).
- Goal oriented learning, organized in a professional environment, is a *cost-intensive* function and it is difficult to assess whether this activity is a profit or a loss factor. This is an important question because it is not clear if traditional goal-oriented learning is the

right way of proceeding in a professional environment; therefore, many evaluation techniques are proposed, in an effort to monitor the training process as a whole and to measure a lot of factors:

- the reactions of the students;
- the acquired knowledge, skills and changes in attitudes;
- the applicability of the training to a professional context;
- the effect on business results (Rueda, 1991).

"Training effectiveness" is evaluated in the context of the achievement of business goals as one of the factors influencing employee performance. Training should be exactly in accordance with these business goals, and the aim should be to provide the training that is needed, at the right moment, at a minimum cost.

The new element in this global approach is that it no longer focuses on a single training activity but considers the organization as a system, interacting dynamically with a changing environment. The enterprise is becoming an organism, trying to survive in changing environmental conditions. Such a view enables us to examine training from a new perspective, with a more general theoretical background and to deduce some interesting practical consequences.

10.2 Theoretical Background: the Self-learning Organization

Our considerations are based on the work of Maturana and Varela (1975, 1987), who studied the fundamental biological principles of living systems in a very general way, defining so-called *autopoïetic units* with self-organizing properties. Such systems are continuously adapting their internal structure in order to maintain their operational unity in a changing envi-

Figure 10.1 Diagram of a first order autopoïetic unit and its interactions with the environment.

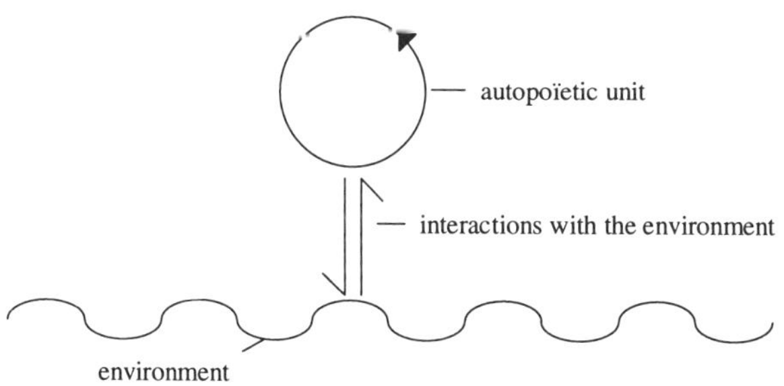

ronment, thus provoking new changes in the environment (*first order autopoïetic units*). Maintaining the self-organizing process and the adaptation-process are the necessary conditions for the survival of the system (see figure 10.1).

This model can be applied to unicellular organisms, but can also be generalized to multicellular organisms, considering that single autopoïetic units could be linked in their adaptation process by a structural coupling (see figure 10.2), maintaining a common autopoïetic structure (*second order autopoïetic units*).

Figure 10.2 Diagram of a second order autopoïetic unit and its interactions with the environment (formalism of Maturana and Varela (1987)).

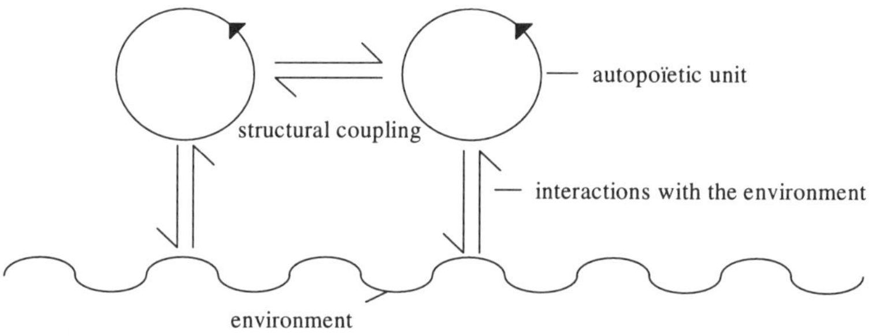

The human being can be described as a very sophisticated instance of this model, with a senso-motoric correlation made possible by a neural network (see figure 10.3).

Figure 10.3 Diagram of an autopoïetic unit with a nervous system.

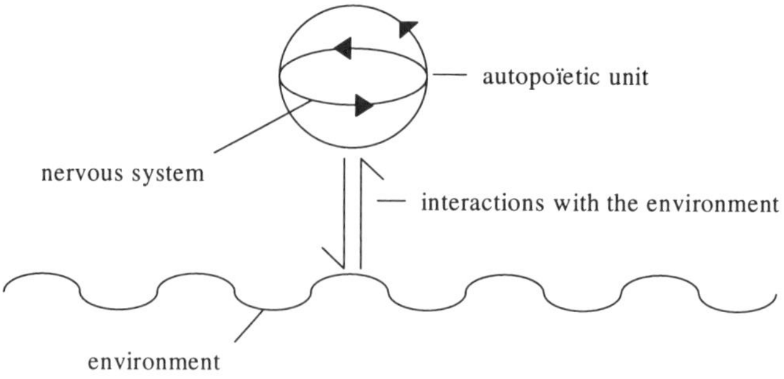

The structural coupling of such multi-cellular neuro-organisms then leads to the concept of meta-systems (*third order autopoïetic units*), which may describe social systems, from social communities of insects to human societies. Firms and enterprises are instances of this type of system (see figure 10.4). A new property of these meta-systems is the progressive building of a common linguistic domain enabling social communication between the member systems, leading to the phenomenon of self-awareness.

Figure 10.4 Diagram of a third order autopoïetic unit and its interactions with the environment (formalism of Maturana and Varela (1987)).

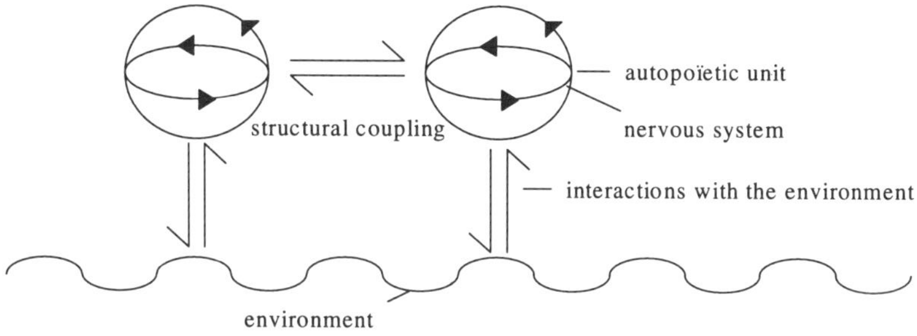

It is interesting to use the Maturana-Varela framework to study the dynamics of learning, since it provides a common base for describing complex systems and their interaction with the environment. It shows that the structural changes in the environment, the enterprise and the human being working in this enterprise are linked together so strongly that it is impossible to consider them separately. Human learning is strongly related to corporate learning and conversely corporate learning is inseparable from human learning, both of them being initiated by environmental changes. To consider only the effects of training on human beings in an enterprise gives a very incomplete picture of a much more complex process. It is important to evaluate what the enterprise, considered as a third order autopoïetic unit, has learned, independently of the learning of each member unit. *The enterprise must be considered as a self-learning organization.* But what does learning mean if applied to an organization? It is the result of the adaptation process to the environmental changes and it is observable in all the internal organizational changes in the enterprise, and in the continuous adaptation of the linguistic domain of the enterprise. These internal and external changes will initiate an adaptation process in each of the human members of the organization.

Traditionally the dissemination of the organizational and linguistic changes had to be done by guided training activities, but this communication channel is very cumbersome, slow and not selective at all. The same training unit is proposed for different human beings. Nevertheless, their personal adaptation to the corporate changes will be quite individual. Moreover, these changes are unidirectional; the learner is considered to be the receptor in a communication process; he is sending feed-back signals, enabling the control of the communication process, without the opportunity of initiating it. Nevertheless, like any autopoïetic unit, he has a self-learning competence continuously adapting his internal structure to the changes in the enterprise and in the external environment.

Frequently, he is the only element of the whole system able to achieve a certain task, and on leaving the enterprise, the system will have lost an important structural unit, because of the enterprise's inability to learn from its employees. It is only recently that organizations have understood the situation and have tried to learn from their member units. Some of the first developments in expert systems were undertaken to formalize the knowledge of top-experts, who were shortly retiring from the system. The difficulty of knowledge acquisition is that very often the expert is unable to express his knowledge correctly, since he has never had the possibility or the need to do so. There is no linguistic domain covering the competence sector of the expert. This competence could be considered inaccessible to the linguistic domain of the enterprise and could remain in the unconscious part of the system. One important learning mechanism for the corporation is to integrate the conceptual distinctions of the expert into the linguistic domain of the enterprise, thus making it possible to exchange messages about these new concepts and to disseminate them to other units in the system. In this way we understand that corporate learning is a complex process involving all the components of the enterprise and being multidirectional. It involves a knowledge acquisition mechanism enabling the widening of the linguistic domain of the organization and communication channels being able to disseminate messages operating within this linguistic domain.

Recent research has shown that knowledge acquisition for expert systems can no longer be seen as a transfer of knowledge from an expert (the *source* of knowledge) to a knowledge engineer (the *receiver* of knowledge). Our IPEX project (IPEX = International Payment EXpert System) has demonstrated clearly that knowledge acquisition is a cooperative process whereby the domain expert and the knowledge engineer are interactively constructing a common linguistic domain which did not previously exist. Once this linguistic domain is available, the expert is able to build progressively on his knowledge. The research has shown that knowledge is constructed at the very moment when it is expressed using the common linguistic domain between the expert and the knowledge engineer (Asselborn, 1993). We tried alternative knowledge acquisition techniques for example, the automatic learning of rules from examples. The decision tree obtained was quite different in form from that built by the knowledge acquisition process involving the domain expert and the knowledge engineer. It could nevertheless be proven that the two trees were logically equivalent (Pichon, 1991).

Computer and networking technologies are providing societies with powerful communication channels, able to transmit and store messages and even to operate complex symbolic transformations on these messages. These new technologies will certainly change the self-learning process of the organization. We are for the moment studying the impact of new groupware techniques on the self-learning potential of the organization.

Unfortunately, *the availability of a computer network is not sufficient to improve the self-learning competence of the organization*, as most of the computer activity operates at the unconscious level of the organization.

Consider the example of a dispute over the result of a complex pay-roll program; nobody in the organization, except perhaps the programmer himself, is able to explain what the program really did. Knowledge about the pay-roll is programmed inside an automatic procedure and has dropped to the unconscious level of the organization, since the computer language used does not belong within the linguistic domain of the organization. If the programmer leaves the firm and if clear and up to date documentation is unavailable, even a computer scientist will have problems understanding what the program is doing. Some firms have overcome this problem by developing expert systems able to explain what a program did and why it produced a particular result. If a person in the organization has a need to learn about the pay-roll he can now do so without any problem. This is possible because the expert system is a computer resource, operating in the linguistic domain of the organization.

This example illustrates that the key to the self-learning competence of the organization is the availability of so-called *knowledge based systems* (KBS), enabling the computerized communication channels to operate inside the linguistic domain of the organization and in doing so to work at the conscious level of the organization.

Ideally the whole linguistic domain of the organization should be covered by a corporate knowledge base: all organizational changes of the system and all extensions to the linguistic domain should be included in the corporate knowledge base. More specifically, the corporate knowledge base should contain a description of the organization itself, of all its components and their couplings. It should contain a description of all the processes, and all the conceptual and organizational rules associated with them; it should even contain a record of previous cases and situations which have generated changes in the organization.

For the moment there are many unsolved problems and clear limits as to what could be integrated into knowledge based systems. In particular, it is difficult to insert common sense knowledge by any means other than by natural language; so it remains clear that the normal structural coupling of the autopoïetic members of the organization is not replaced by a KBS, but is simply completed by an alternative coupling which we shall call an *Intelligent Channel* (I-Ch). The symbolic representation of the organization has to be extended beyond the Maturana-Varela formalism (see figure 10.5).

We can now specify some of the *principles of corporate self-learning*:

- Autopoïetic member units of the organization are linked by an alternative structural coupling through an I-Ch, able to transmit, store and process symbols representing networks of entities in the linguistic domain of the organization.
- All member units have self-learning competence and the possibility of disseminating their knowledge through the I-Ch.
- The act of storing into the knowledge base of the I-Ch (*corporate knowledge base*) can be achieved by the negotiation between member units. This guarantees the adherence of the members to the stored knowledge and a better coherence of the knowledge base. The corporate knowledge base changes continuously and reflects the structural changes

Figure 10.5 Diagram of a third order autopoïetic unit with an Intelligent Channel (extension to the formalism of Maturana-Varela).

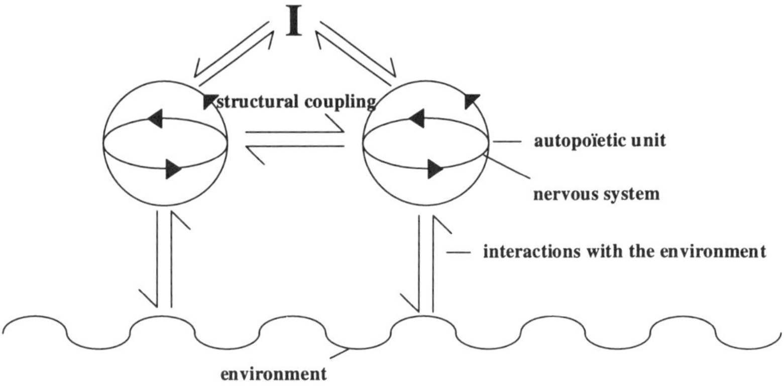

of the organization and of its linguistic domain. Its development is the result of a *cooperative process*, representing corporate self-learning.

- All member units have the possibility of accessing specific parts of the corporate knowledge base through the I-Ch and getting help in their problem solving activity; thus, self-learning through the I-Ch is an incremental process, driven by the member unit and giving access only to those chunks of knowledge which are useful at that moment.

10.3 Implementation of Corporate Self-learning

In the present state of the art, the I-Ch is implemented as a computer system which is not to be considered as an autopoïetic unit. Future technological developments could nevertheless lead to autopoïetic computer systems, thus creating a hybrid organization with human autopoïetic units and machine autopoïetic units.

The symbol processing activities of the I-Ch are assumed by general programs called *Automatic Agents* (AA). Each AA represents a specified interface to the corporate knowledge base, determined by a specific way of accessing knowledge. We will present in more detail three important categories of automatic agents: assistance agents, simulation agents and training agents. In practice, these agents can work in a centralized way or in a very distributed way, being integrated in the work-station of the human unit and accessing a very specialized part of the corporate knowledge base, thus having the function of an *Intelligent Tool* (IT).

10.3.1 Assistance Agents

At every level of an organization, there may be computerized assistance agents designed either for helping human agents or for performing given tasks. The skills of these agents may vary, from providing useful information via algorithms that aid in decision making, to having the ability to give advice on a logical reasoning basis. The human agent considers the computerized agent as an assistant, but also as a means to improve his own knowledge. It should be emphasized that the human agent must be thoroughly acquainted with the strong and weak points of the assistance agent, first, to avoid making wrong decisions, due, for instance, to overestimating its skills, and second, to be able to update its knowledge. Ideally, human and computerized agents should train one another (Asselborn and Jans, 1989).

We have developed Bancomex, an intelligent job aid for bank employees who are expected to give advice about banking services to their customers. It is very interesting to point out that the bank employees, despite the following of traditional training courses, felt a strong need for such a system; as they had difficulty remembering products that were not often sold.

The same system has been implemented using hypermedia (Pemmers and Ingels, 1990) which on the one hand supplies the user with useful information and on the other hand acts as an expert system (Ingels and Pemmers, 1990) advising on a logical reasoning basis. The hypermedia knowledge base is working at a very superficial knowledge level since it is only a network of natural language text and pictures. The expert system knowledge base has a deeper knowledge level, since it is working with rules and frames and has inferencing and pattern matching possibilities. It could be useful to implement an even deeper knowledge base, giving access to the semantics of the linguistic domain. The system is used as a job aid and trainer by the employee in the front office who gives advice to the customers and as a *trainee* by the employee in the back office in the working out of new services in the bank's product line. In another case, the employee in the front office may be confronted by a customer with a problem that cannot be solved by any of the existing banking services. Such cases can be stored in the corporate knowledge base, thus informing the product manager in the back office that new services may have to be created.

In this particular instance, the roles of trainer and trainee have been reversed. As explained before, the different member units communicate via intelligent channels (I-Ch) with the corporate knowledge base.

A second example is the Gessy system (Lescrenier, 1991), developed to assist workers in maintaining complex motor engines for example, in trouble-shooting and in technical diagnosis. The system is based on a description of defects related to possible causes and remedies and can be consulted as a problem occurs. When new situations occur, however, the knowledge base of the system can be enriched by its users (or at least by a selected sub-set of its users). So, again, the human agent and the *corporate* knowledge base are learning from each other.

10.3.2 Simulation Agents

In some situations, for example, creating new services for integration into the product line of a bank, new solutions cannot be retained without prior validation. Thus, the system should behave *as if* a new solution had been adopted, that is, it should be able to simulate its behavior under certain circumstances. Simulation agents use the corporate knowledge base as a model for the whole organization; they effect imaginary changes to the knowledge base and virtually *run the system*. If the results obtained give satisfaction, the new solution can be transferred to the real model, otherwise, other solutions have to be worked out and tested.

For example, Convex (Conzemius, 1993), is a productivity tool for the organization and computerization of administrative procedures. As the knowledge base represents the coupling of member units, any administrative procedure can be modeled and its behavior simulated interactively. When the procedure seems to give satisfaction, all its components for automation as computer programs can be generated more or less automatically. Thus, the simulated and the operational system are the same and statistics about the real system allow the discovery of possible bottle-necks that had not been discovered during simulation. The model of the system can then be adapted, a new solution pursued, its behavior simulated, and finally, the new operational system can be generated.

In Convex, modeling the system means giving a comprehensive description of the tasks, the data that flow between those tasks and the agents who execute the tasks; as the tasks may be manual or automated, the agents can be either human beings or machines. Thus, an important part of the corporate knowledge is described using a formal, comprehensive representation allowing easy access for any purpose.

The Convex system has been applied as a pilot project to the procedure dealing with applications for new telephone connections in the Luxembourg. That pilot project has been very successful; the manual and the automated tasks were implemented very quickly and are now running quite well. Moreover, when a change occurred in the legal environment and the procedure had to be adapted, experts estimated that four months would be needed for adaptation. In fact, Convex allowed the elaboration and implementation of the new procedure within two days.

It is important to mention that any human agent has on-line access to the procedure's description and even has the possibility of simulating its behavior; these features allow him to get acquainted with a new procedure very quickly.

Thus, we can conclude that the simulation agents that are used in Convex enable the whole organization as well as its member units to learn.

10.3.3 Training Agents

Sometimes self-learning will not be possible and goal-oriented learning (or training) cannot be avoided. This is the case when new employees have to be integrated into the organization.

Corporate knowledge ideally covers the knowledge that has to be learned by the new employee; thus, there is a need for effective training via the corporate knowledge base.

The use of an existing knowledge base for effective training is a paradigm for research in the field of *Intelligent Tutoring Systems* (ITS). An ITS is typically based on several expert systems representing

- the domain knowledge, the *expert*: the domain knowledge is encapsulated in the corporate knowledge base;
- the instructional knowledge, the *tutor*;
- the knowledge about the learner, the *student model*: any human agent is described in the corporate knowledge base;
- an instructional environment, that is, elements that create learning situations and support the learner's activity;
- an intelligent interface (Burns and Capps, 1988).

According to Riesbeck and Schank (1991) and also Bloch and Farrell (1988), such training should be case-based.

During the training phase, new employees can be considered as learners in an expert-based training environment (Todd, 1988). They learn first from copying, then move from copying to creative adaptation and finally learn to determine what makes cases relevant in a given situation. Thus, they learn to reason from experience, that is, to practice Case-Based Reasoning (CBR) (Riesbeck and Schank, 1991).

On the job, they are in an expertless training environment. They practice self-organized learning, that is, they are self-aware and understand their own processes, they function purposefully towards goals they have defined themselves and, finally, they evaluate their progress (Todd 1988). Both the human agents, and with them the corporate knowledge base, will learn while trying to find solutions to new problems. The solution to the case most closely resembling it will be tried out. If that is effective, the solution will be added to the corporate knowledge base, otherwise, it will be amended and then added to the knowledge base; this is *success-driven learning*. The unsuccessful solutions are also stored, so that erroneous reasoning will not be repeated; that is *failure-driven learning* (Riesbeck and Schank, 1991). This kind of reasoning needs to call on assistance agents (see paragraph 10.3.1) and simulation agents (see paragraph 10.3.2).

An interesting observation in the field of case-based learning based not on expert systems but only on textual information about cases, is the Exploratory Learning Delivery (ELD) system of Malibu, a project of the European Communities' programme for research and development in Telematic Systems for Flexible and Distance Learning (DELTA) (Sridharan, 1992). Using this system, banking clerks, either already working or aiming to work as company auditors, can be challenged with the case of a virtual company asking for credit. They need to evaluate the risk of giving a credit to that company. For that purpose, they have at their disposal

- any information that can possibly be of interest for their task; access to the information is possible via a powerful information retrieval system with natural language and hypermedia capabilities;
- a set of tools allowing them to compute the information, for example, tools for financial analysis and simulations of other banking applications, text processor and spreadsheet.

As the learners can record the information that has been gathered and finally formalize the conclusions, they can add new information to the *knowledge base*.

It is interesting to note that these employees learn from the corporate knowledge base by using it in a way that is very similar to the way they will use it in practice. This means that the planned goal of the training is very close to the personal goals of the learners and that the acquired skills will be used frequently after the training phase, thus ensuring that the benefits of the training will not be lost. The training system and the production system are completely integrated. Using expert systems for learning is not possible without further improvements in the field of knowledge representation. Burns and Parlett remind us, unfortunately, that the knowledge embodied in expert systems cannot always be readily used for training. To quote these authors, "The knowledge representation in our heads is not the knowledge representation in our computers" (Burns and Parlett, 1991). Expert systems are mostly based on a representation of knowledge that is oriented towards a very specific aim and thus corresponds to a very specific viewpoint; they are "idiot savants." For use for training purposes, however, the knowledge must be represented in such a way as to make it accessible from a variety of very different viewpoints (Fink, 1991), (Suthers, 1988). Acker, Lester, Souther and Porter (1991) and Suthers (1988) claim that representing these multiple viewpoints explicitly is not practical for a large-scale knowledge base. Instead, for example, Acker et al propose to characterize all viewpoints using a small number of view types. During the use of the system, a particular viewpoint can then be isolated by the view type, a concept of interest (main topic of a viewpoint) and a reference concept (related topic). To run an expert-based, organized, mixed-initiative tutoring session, the knowledge base must be augmented by prerequisite relations between topics. The authors call these relations that encapsulate the presentation knowledge and whose construction is very time-consuming a "Stratified Prerequisite Identification Network" (Acker et al, 1991).

10.4 Conclusions

In a professional environment, traditional training approaches are – even when they are adapted by using *self-studying* techniques – of doubtful value and very cost-intensive. Training should therefore be seen in the global context of the whole organization.

We have used the Maturana and Varela approach to describe organizations as self-aware meta-systems with self-learning competence.

The key to corporate self-learning is the availability of a *corporate knowledge base*, included in a so-called *intelligent channel* which allows the whole organization and its member units to learn from each other; this concept is an extension to the Maturana-Varela approach.

Today, the corporate knowledge base is implemented in computer systems and accessed through *automatic agents*; we have presented in more detail *assistance agents, simulation agents* and *training agents.*

We have given examples showing that state of the art technology makes it possible to implement only elements of such a corporate knowledge base but for a full implementation, considerable progress in knowledge representation and, more generally, artificial intelligence techniques would be required.

However, considering the computer system of the enterprise simply as an intelligent communication channel in the structural coupling between human beings, is a completely new approach to corporate computer science. Data bases, documentation systems, knowledge bases and computer software have no meaning by themselves, but are the expression of a subset of the linguistic domain of the organization.

As the survival of the organization strongly depends on the continuous adaptation to a changing environment, the linguistic domain will be dynamically modified. Computer systems, as intelligent channels, should support this continuous reconstruction of the linguistic domain. Today, most existing computer systems can be considered as black-boxes; by their rigidity they are even preventing the organization from learning.

In the future, the constituents of the corporate knowledge base should be built on explicit, transparent, understandable and easily maintainable models focusing on the communication needs of the human actors, rather than on the data processing needs.

References

Acker, L., Lester, J., Souther, A. and Porter, B. (1991). Generating Coherent Explanations to Answer Student's Questions. Burns, H.L., Parlett, J.W. and Redfield C.L. (Eds.) *Intelligent Tutoring Systems, Evolutions in Design*, Hillsdale: Lawrence Earlbaum Associates, 151-176.

Ant, M. and De Cillia, S. (1991). Logique d'une formation professionnelle moderne. *d'Letzeburger Land*, 1991-24.

Asselborn, J.Cl. and Jans, J.M. (1989). Learning Environment in the Professional World. *DELTA Multimedia Journal, 1,* 67-71.

Asselborn, J.Cl. (1993). *Le développement d'un système expert intégré dans une application bancaire (IPEX: International Payment EXpert).* Luxembourg: Centre de Recherche Public-Centre Universitaire, research report CREDI-A-93-010.

Bloch, G. and Farrell, R. (1988). Promoting Creativity Through Argumentation, DECIDER: A Case-based Teaching System. *Proceedings of ITS-88.* Montreal: University of Montreal, 243-249.

Burns, H.L. and Capps, C.G. (1988). Foundations of Intelligent Tutoring Systems: An Introduction. Polson, M.C. and Richardson J.J. (Eds.) *Foundations of Intelligent Tutoring Systems.* Hillsdale: Lawrence Earlbaum Associates, 1-19.

Burns, H.L. and Parlett, J.W. (1991). The Evolution of Intelligent Tutoring Systems: Dimensions of Design. Burns, H.L., Parlett, J.W. and Redfield C.L. (Eds.) *Intelligent Tutoring Systems, Evolutions in Design.* Hillsdale: Lawrence Earlbaum Associates, 1-11.

Conzemius, C. (1993). *CONVEX: Développement d'un système automatisé d'analyse, d'évaluation et de suivi de procédures administratives*. Luxembourg: Centre de Recherche Public-Centre Universitaire, research report.

Fink, P.K. (1991). The Role of Domain Knowledge in the Design of an Intelligent Tutoring System. Burns, H.L., Parlett, J.W. and Redfield C.L. (Eds.) *Intelligent Tutoring Systems, Evolutions in Design*. Hillsdale: Lawrence Earlbaum Associates, 195-224.

Ingels, V. and Pemmers, O. (1990). *Jeunes Adultes*. Luxembourg: Centre de Recherche Public-Centre Universitaire, research report CREDI-T-90-046.

Krier, J. (1991). Priorité au professionalisme. *d'Letzeburger Land*, 1991-24.

Lescrenier, M. (1991). *GESSY, Proposition de fonctionnalités pour la version 3.0 du logiciel*, Luxembourg: Arbed, project report (internal, strictly confidential).

Maturana, H.R. and Varela, F.J. (1975). *Autopoïetic Systems*. Illinois: University of Illinois, Biological Computer Laboratory.

Maturana, H.R. and Varela, F.J. (1987). *The Tree of Knowledge: The Biological Roots of Human Understanding*. Boston/London: Shambhala Publications.

Nyhan, B. (1991). *Eurotecnet Research on Self-Learning and Innovative Training methods*. Luxembourg: Eurotecnet Conference, Innovative Training Approaches.

Pemmers, O. and Ingels, V. (1990). *Hyper-JA*. Luxembourg: Centre de Recherche Public-Centre Universitaire, research report CREDI-T-90-049.

Pichon, E. (1991). *Acquisition de connaissances par induction automatique de règles à partir d'exemples*. Luxembourg: Centre de Recherche Public-Centre Universitaire, research reports CREDI-R-91-069 and CREDI-R-91-070.

Riesbeck, C.K. and Schank, R.C. (1991). From Training to Teaching: Techniques for Case-Based ITS. Burns, H.L., Parlett, J.W. and Redfield C.L. (Eds.) *Intelligent Tutoring Systems, Evolutions in Design*. Hillsdale: Lawrence Earlbaum Associates, 177-193.

Rueda, J. (1991). *An Industrialist's View of the Effective Use of Learning Technologies: the Present and the Future*. Luxembourg: Eurotecnet Conference, Innovative Training Approaches.

Sridharan, M. (1992). MALIBU - Multimedia and Distance Learning in Banking and Business Environments. Huyton A. (Ed.) *DELTA '92*. Brussels: DELTA Central Office, A/46-A/48.

Suthers, D. (1988). Providing Multiple Views of Reasoning for Explanation. *Proceedings of ITS-88*. Montreal: University of Montreal, 435-442.

Todd, R.R. (1988). Self-organized learning within an intelligent teaching system. Self, J. (Ed.) *Artificial Intelligence and Human Learning, Intelligent Computer-Aided Instruction*. London: Chapman and Hall Computing, 197-211.

11 Strategic Management Simulations: the German Case

Klaus Breuer and Siegfried Streufert[1]

This chapter initially considers the rationale and potential value of games and simulations for managerial and executive assessment. Several shortcomings of existing techniques are discussed. In contrast, characteristics of the Strategic Management Simulations (SMS) are described in terms of applicability, reliability, construct validity, predictive validity and other factors. This chapter provides validity information about a German version of the SMS system via a case analysis procedure with two German samples.

11.1 Assessment of Managerial Competence with Games and Simulations

In recent years, computer games as well as computer-based or computer assisted simulations have become a primary resource for executive training and assessment. While many earlier simulation techniques (such as Looking Glass) have tended to focus on interpersonal (and leadership) effectiveness (cf. Thornton and Cleveland, 1990), more recent developments have emphasized decision making competence for executives in both the private and public sectors.

The use of games and simulations for training and assessment has become increasingly valuable. There are at least two reasons for the increased application of these techniques: (1) Executive and professional environments have changed from being more static and stable towards a more dynamic and fluid task setting, and (2) advances in state-of-the-art computer assisted simulations have provided technologies that realistically reflect complex decision making settings. For example, recently developed interactive simulations can expose executives to dimensions of complexity that include challenge, experiences of non-linear processes (exponential growth), of excessive information or work load, rapid event fluidity, uncertainty, delayed feedback and other aspects that are frequently present under real-world conditions. Through the use of simulation techniques, trainees can gain considerable experience in coping with task complexity without risking loss of resources, or staff disruptions that might occur in their *real world* task environment.

Despite improvements in technology, however, many games and simulations suffer from limitations. Two common problems are considered below:

- In most cases, business games or simulations are not based upon the framework of learning-teaching theory. As a consequence, the training objectives of such programs remain unclear or undefined. Moreover, the utility of *abilities* that are to be assessed by these training systems is in question. Evaluation of performance is frequently based upon subjective judgments by trainers or, alternatively, on more or less simplistic scaling methods. "Effectiveness" of participants is often evaluated via variables that are incorporated into the game or simulation system itself (cf. Breuer 1990; Dörner and Reither 1978; Dörner, Kreuzig, Reither and Stäudel, 1983; Funke 1991). In other words, within-system circularity prevents the application of external (real-world) success criteria. Cognitive or learning processes that lead to achievement on the job are rarely considered. While the participant(s) in such games and simulations may report an "enjoyable experience", any assessment of competence and any subsequent training tends to have low validity.
- Most existing simulations can be characterized as "free" (Fromkin and Streufert, 1976), that is, subsequent events are controlled by the prior actions of the participants. This "openness" to the specific characteristics of participant interest and action results in a high variability of event sequences (system status, cf. Breuer and Günterberg 1991; Dörner et al. 1983). Fromkin and Streufert (1976) and Streufert and Swezey (1985) have pointed out that "free" simulations are useful for theory building or in some cases as a "rich" description of reality. Yet the openness of these simulations generates serious problems where the technique is employed for assessment or training purposes: Whenever the participants' subsequent task environments and, consequently, their subsequent actions are confounded with their own prior decision-making processes, comparisons of performance *among* participants or, worse still, comparisons *with a criterion* of excellence become impossible. As a result, reliability and validity of assessment suffer.

These problems, as well as some lesser shortcomings of prior techniques, have been overcome by the Strategic Management Simulations (SMS) which were developed and validated in the United States (Streufert and Swezey 1986; Streufert, Pogash and Piasecki 1988). The SMS procedures are based upon the theoretical framework of Cognitive Complexity (Mandl and Huber 1978; McDaniel and Lawrence 1990; Schroder, Driver and Streufert, 1967;

Streufert and Nogami, 1989; Streufert and Streufert, 1978) and differ from their predecessors in a number of important attributes that are described in greater detail below.

11.2 The Strategic Management Simulations (SMS)

In contrast to free, (sometimes called *open*) simulations, the SMS are *quasi-experimental* in design. Much of the information received by participants is preprogrammed, i.e., each trainee is primarily exposed to a *common* base of informative messages which always arrive simultaneously. Other informative messages which are not of primary importance to the flow of ongoing events (or to the intent of the researcher or trainer) are left to vary to some extent with the prior actions of participants. The latter messages provide the *impression* that the environment is meaningfully responsive to decisions. However, the frequency and time location of these responsive messages are fixed. Their content (e.g., success and failure) can be partly predetermined.

In other words, trainees act within a framework of structural comparability that, nonetheless, allows for sufficient individual variability. This structural comparability permits direct comparisons of performance among participants *and*, of course, direct comparisons of performance with a criterion of excellence. Moreover, the functioning of any participant in one particular scenario can be compared with another performance by the same participant in another SMS scenario (allowing, for example, comparisons of performance prior to and after training).

In three parallel SMS scenarios (Shamba, Woodline County and Astaban) diverse but in each case complex and dynamic decision-making situations, are presented in high fidelity. The three scenarios differ sharply from each other in both their task environment and in the content of their preprogrammed events. As a result, transfer of training upon exposure to several of the SMS scenarios is avoided. Nonetheless, each scenario makes the same demands upon a participant's competence to perform. Parallel demands occur at the same time points during participation.

To support a framework of structural comparability across all participants, the SMS employs a set of principles that differ from other computer-based or computer assisted simulations (Stein-Greenblatt, 1988). These differences are reflected in several basic features that are listed in table 11.1.

As in most other simulations, participants' interactions with the program are recorded by the SMS programs. The resulting records provide the basis for a structural analysis and for the numerical and graphic representation of the decision-making process. The obtained data depict "typical" patterns of a participant's decision-making processes (cf. Streufert, Pogash and Piasecki 1988; Streufert and Swezey 1986). Equivalent characteristic information processing and decision making patterns can be obtained for teams as well as for individuals who are members of these teams as long as (e.g., intact) groups participate in a simulation.

Table 11.1 Comparison of simulation features.

Features of other simulations	*Features of the SMS*
• Fixed (predetermined) model of the simulated environment (outcomes of participant actions are determined by model formulas	• Openness of the environment (outcomes of actions by the participant(s) remain independent of model formulas or of experimenter/trainer judgment)
• Experienced events are the direct (formula based and calculated) consequences of participant actions	• Important experienced events are pre-programmed, other (less important) are left to vary with actions of participants
• Complexity	• Complexity
• Dynamics (internal)	• Dynamics (internal)
• Common starting scenario across participants only	• Starting scenario (very rich) and *natural* subsequent flow of events common across all participants
• Interactions with the simulation by means of entries to variables	• Interactions with the simulation by means of full-text decisions (entered by an assistant)
• Decision-making (problem solving) at predefined intermissions within a sequence of periods	• Decision-making at any time within the flow of the simulation
• Feedback during the simulation by status of system variables	• Feedback during the simulation presents textual responses to decisions
• Simulation outcome determined by final status of system variables	• Outcome reflects multiple performance characteristics of participant(s) in numeric and graphic format that allow assesment in terms of validated criteria of excellence.

The SMS is designed to assess a participants' underlying conceptual style and their associated cognitive decision-making processes in both numerical and graphic formats. Some among the basic measures that are captured by the simulation technique (Streufert, 1991) are listed below:

- the level of differentiation which is applied as part of the decision-making process (breadth);
- the level of integration among decisions (strategy);
- the level of multiple planning;
- flexibility in response to structural changes in the decision-making environment;

- decisiveness in response to structural changes;
- the level of recovery after serious problems are overcome and it is time to return to *standard* decision making conditions.

Measurement of this genre reflects the application of "cognitive strategies", sensu Gagné (1985, 55/56), which are "... the skills by means of which learners regulate their own internal processes of attending, learning, remembering, and thinking." Such processes are often described in term of meta-cognition (Streufert and Nogami, 1989; Suedfeld, 1992) . In other words, the assessment of participants via the SMS is not limited to the measurement of attained levels of achievement, e.g., task specific knowledge gained by prior training or experience. It is not based on judgments provided by observers. Rather, it reflects automated assessment of the basic features of an individual's underlying cognitive competence, i.e., the competence, that he or she is able to apply to a range of complex decision making settings.

Figure 11.1 SMS graphic representation of an individual's decision making process (schema without color information).

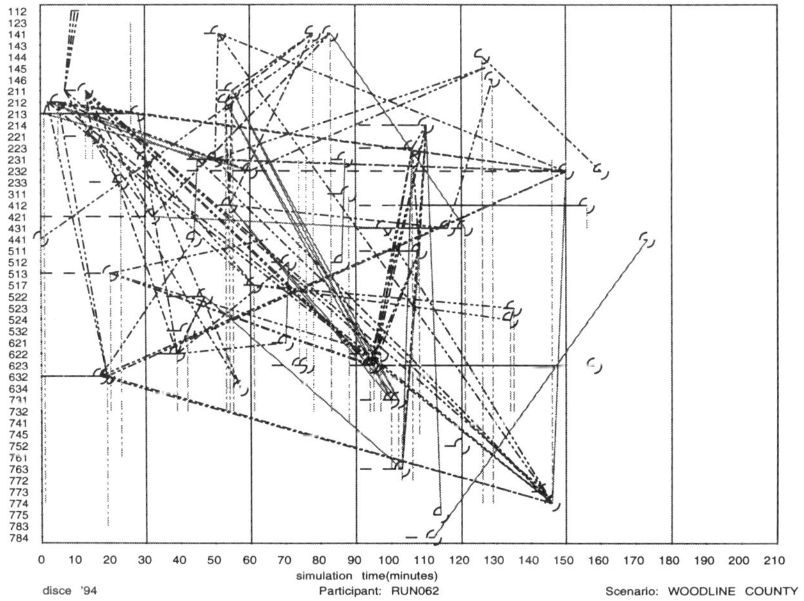

In addition to numerical data on a number of measures, the simulation system generates a graphic representation of decision sequences and of the cognitive basis underlying those sequences. Graphic displays of participants' thought processes and actions provide a useful vehicle for assessment and for debriefing (Streufert, Pogash, Piasecki, Nogami and Swezey, 1988). An example of such a graph is presented in figure 11.1. Validated (Streufert, Pogash and Piasecki, 1988) performance attributes based on complexity theory are reflected both in numerical scores and in the graphic output of the simulation system.

Since prior research has demonstrated that cognitive complexity (and its impact upon task performance) is subject to training (Breuer and Kummer, 1990; Streufert, Pogash, Piasecki, Nogami and Swezey, 1988; Tennyson and Breuer, 1991), the SMS provides an important tool for both assessment *and* training.

11.2.1 The SMS in its German Version

Based on the English language efforts by Streufert and associates, German language versions of the SMS system and of its three simulation scenarios have been developed. Effectiveness of the German simulation procedure was tested and evaluated with participants from the German civil service and industry. The analysis of these SMS *runs* provided evidence that the structural representations of cognitive style and associated performance indicators that were previously obtained with American versions of the SMS, are easily replicated with German participants (Schöpf, 1991).

Subsequently, exploratory research with the German SMS was extended to contrast data from an initial group of rather diverse participants, with a second set of performance data obtained from a group of highly trained executives who were involved in an advanced two-year training program. The obtained validity data are presented below. These data provide evidence for considerable differences between the two groups of participants and, in addition, for moderate individual differences within each group.

11.2.2 Validity of Assessment and Training Simulations

The predictive validity of computer based or computer assisted simulations has often been difficult to ascertain or demonstrate (Schuler and Funke 1991). In the absence of such validity information, the use of complex and demanding simulations in assessment or training settings, is often justified by claims that the simulation contains enhanced (but generally unspecified) diagnostic features. Certainly, simulation based assessments should not merely generate information that can be gained with traditional (less expensive and less time consuming) tests. Of course, where information about the diagnostic capability of any particular simulation or game is lacking, we cannot know whether the assessment merely reproduces knowledge that is otherwise available or, for that matter, whether it generates any validity information at all.

In contrast, validity of the SMS has been repeatedly demonstrated. First, construct validity was established by basing the development of the simulation system within the theoretical framework of cognitive complexity (Streufert and Swezey 1986). The quasi-experimental procedures that are employed, control of information load (flow) during the simulation and performance measures that are calculated by the simulation are all derived from complexity theory and are based on prior research data obtained within that realm. Secondly, the simulation procedure and the measures obtained from simulation participation define the notion of "cognitive strategies" that have become a well known concept in learning-teaching theory (Gagné, 1985; O'Neil, 1978).

Optimally, validity of assessment and training tasks should not be restricted to a very limited domain. For example, if a simulation was specifically designed to predict the success of managers employed in a nuclear power plant, that same simulation would hardly be useful in assessing the performance of governmental social service executives. The SMS avoids such restrictions: it was designed to provide an assessment and training technique across a broad range of managerial professions. Participants are placed into a simulated world where three parallel scenarios (Shamba, Woodline County and Astaban) designed to provide task experiences that on the surface appear "familiar" but, in effect, require cognitive reorientation. Nonetheless, the scenarios permit the development of cognitive strategies on the basis of everyday knowledge. The SMS system does not require previously established domain-specific skills. As a result, competencies that are measured and trained with the SMS are transferable from one executive task setting to another.

Finally, empirical evidence for significant correlations between scores obtained from simulation performance with several indicators of professional success (across a range of managerial job settings) have been repeatedly obtained. For example, Streufert, Pogash and Piasecki (1989) demonstrated on a sample of several hundred American managers that individuals scoring high on several simulation measures have higher incomes (at age), are more often promoted, supervise more other employees and hold higher level positions (at age). Recent data indicate that predictive validity of simulation based performance scores exceeds $r = .60$ (cf. Streufert, 1993).

Establishing Validity for the German SMS Versions

With the validity of the U.S. version established, it became necessary to obtain empirical evidence for the validity of the German SMS. Validity can be considered on the basis of inter- and intra-individual differences that are obtained upon simulation performance (Lienert, 1989, 262). The present chapter primarily stresses an inter-individual analysis.

A number of prior validation efforts for a range of assessment techniques have compared data from novices with data obtained from experts (Funke, 1991). Such an approach can, of course, be problematic whenever low level novices are compared with competent experts: such comparisons can generate results that would be rather trivial. The analysis reported in this Chapter avoids that problem. A first *basic* sample of ten adult participants (cases) was selected with widely varied professional backgrounds (see table 11.2).

A subsequent sample (see below) was selected to differ from some (but not all) members of the first sample. The analysis of simulation participation by the basic sample provided answers to several questions:

- How do participants judge their simulation experiences?
- Is it possible to replicate the structures of decision-making processes obtained in US versions of the SMS with the German versions?
- How do participants react to debriefing about their decision-making patterns?
- Are meaningful individual performance differences obtained which describe the specific decision-making styles of the participants?

Table 11.2 Simulation participants in the basic exploratory sample.

Part.	Age	Sex	Ed. Level	Professional Level
T 01	22	M	Voc. Ed.	Craftsman
T 02	43	M	PhD	Civil Service Executive
T 03	31	M	MS, Economics	Junior Manager in Industry
T 04	27	M	MS, Economics	Senior Student (Diplom/MS)
T 05	37	F	PhD	Senior Researcher
T 06	28	F	BS, Civ. Serv.	Police Superintendent
T 07	49	M	PhD	Executive
T 08	22	F	Voc. Ed.	Secretary
T 09	41	F	PhD	Civil Service Executive
T 10	41	M	MS, Education	Entrepreneur

All ten individuals from the basic (exploratory) sample participated in the German Shamba SMS scenario. Each of the participants was presented with manuals the day before participation in the simulation. The manuals provided all the necessary information about the scenario content. The manuals had to be read on the day prior to participation. Upon arriving at the simulation site the next morning, participants viewed a twenty minute video tape that summarized the content of the manuals, provided information on procedure and increased the realism of the task through a number of visual images about the simulated environment.

Each simulation contained six separate decision-making periods of about one hour each. Ten minute breaks between each of the simulation periods were provided. Overall, participation required about six full hours, providing a rich data base for the representation of each participant's decision-making style.

Briefly stated, the results of the exploratory study can be summarized as follows:

- All participants considered the simulation to be an important self-encounter generator and a significant medium for self-reflection about their personal decision-making processes.
- The decision-making structures obtained with German versions of the SMS were very similar to those obtained with US versions (cf. figure 11.1). The underlying structural components of the decision-making processes were clearly represented and could be easily interpreted. Nonetheless, some hints about potential inter-cultural structural differences between German vs. US participants did become evident.
- Feedback to participants about specific characteristics of their personal decision making patterns, including information about their respective strengths and weaknesses, was accepted by all participants. Participants described this feedback as "rich and informative sources of information." Participants agreed that this information confirmed and extended their own assumptions about their personal abilities. In other words, they considered the information to be useful and valid.
- Meaningful individual differences on all primary measures of task performance matched existing differences in the professional and educational backgrounds of the participants. These differences are quite evident from a perusal of figures 11.3, 11.4, and 11.5 for the assessment of differentiation, integration and *initiative* with participants T01 to T10.

With the plausibility and construct validity of the simulation system established, it is still necessary to provide evidence that the SMS should be considered systematic and valid. For that purpose, the initial exploratory study was extended to generate information about the contrasts among diverse participants. A group of five senior police officers, who had received top rankings for performance and had subsequently been selected for a two-year career advancement program, participated in the simulation. These individuals had already completed one year of *on-the-job* training in different senior positions (guided job rotation) and were now involved in one year of additional training at the German Federal Police Academy. The characteristics of this sample are presented in table 11.3.

If simulation scores reflect performance competence, then one should expect systematic differences between the measures obtained from the sample of highly successful decision makers

Table 11.3 Simulation participants in the promoted sample.

Part.	Age	Sex	Educational Level	Professional Level
P 01	35	M	BS, Civil Service	Assistant Executive
P 02	32	M	BS, Civil Service	Chief Superintendent
P 03	33	M	BS, Civil Service	Assistant Executive
P 04	37	M	BS, Civil Service	Assistant Commander
P 05	35	M	BS, Civil Service	Chief Superintendent

and the measures obtained from the prior basic sample (even though the basic sample did include some persons of higher competence). Moreover, the second sample should generate somewhat (but less) diverse performance levels, since the members of that group had been selected from different organizational backgrounds.

Figure 11.2 Levels of *differentiation (breadth)* in decision making.

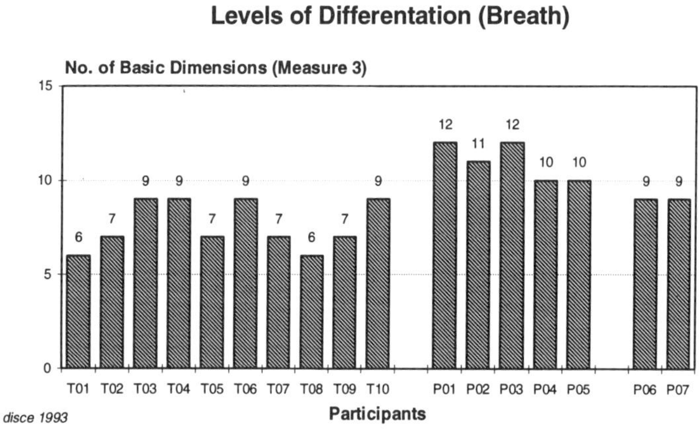

Since the basic sample had also included a few executives who had also experience some success, a comparison between the two samples can be viewed as a relatively conservative test of validity. Measures for the *successful* sample (participants P01 through P05) should deviate systematically from measures assessing the performance of the basic exploratory sample (T01 through T10). The obtained data are presented in figures 11.2 through 11.4.

Figure 11.3 Levels of *integration (strategy)* in decision making.

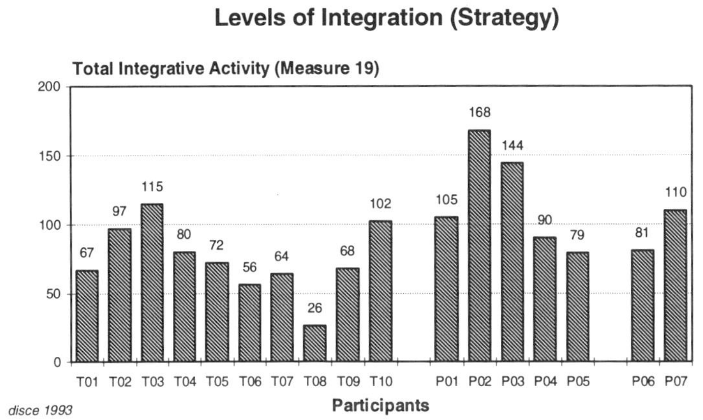

It is evident that the successful sample represents a different population than the basic *exploratory sample*: lower scoring members of the successful sample, generated similar per-

Figure 11.4 Levels of *initiative* in decision making.

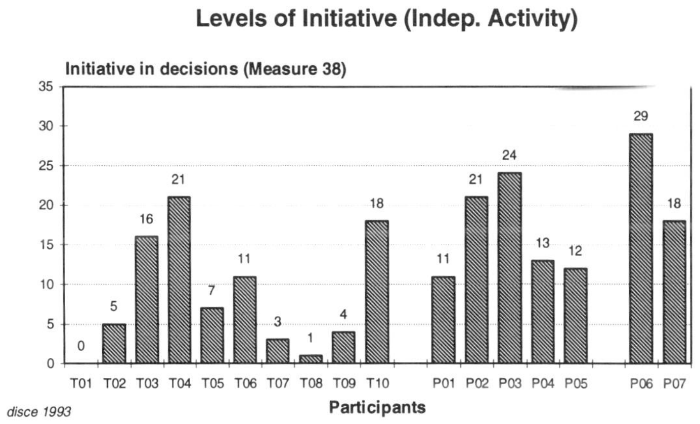

formance levels as the higher scoring members of the basic sample. Clearly, some variance among members of the trained sample did exist, that is, the SMS reflected (theory based) performance differences among individual decision making abilities. Performance scores were not restricted by ceiling effects.

As had been the case for the basic sample, participants from the successful sample provided very positive feedback about the value of their simulation experience. They especially valued the process-oriented information about their performance, and indicated that they had not received any information of this kind following prior participations in other simulations or in real-world tasks.

An extension of this comparative study added two additional senior police officers (P06 and P07). These men had not participated in the career development program. Both held commanding positions in the *new* German states (the former East Germany). Their background included (East German) police officer training. Overall, they had been exposed to different and possibly less effective training and experience. Scores for these two individuals, as one might expect, were located in a range between the basic and the trained sample of simulation participants.

11.3 Conclusions

The present research with the German version of the Strategic Management Simulations has shown, that the procedure generates valid discriminations among participants of different decision-making ability. In other words, the use of the quasi-experimental SMS simulations for assessing an individual's capacity to develop and employ cognitive strategies in response to complex and dynamic decision-making situations is justified.

Other research in the U.S.A. and in Germany (e.g., Streufert, Pogash and Piasecki, 1988) has provided support for the test-retest reliability of measures that are obtained from parallel SMS scenarios. In other words, the SMS can serve as a useful tool in pre-/post test studies, for example as a technique to evaluate the effectiveness of executive or managerial training programs that are designed to improve decision-making abilities.

Moreover, prior research has effectively utilized the SMS system with decision making *groups* (e.g., Streufert, Pogash, Piasecki and Post, 1990). The system may be used to assess and train teams of decision makers that are obliged, for example, to cope with complex, uncertain and fluid task environments.

In all of these applications, repeated and strong evidence for highly favorable responses of participants to their experiences in the SMS simulations and in subsequent feedback settings, is evident. Self-encounters within the complex and dynamic decision-making environments that are provided by the three SMS scenarios are especially valued. The favorable responses are, in part, due to the kind of *experience* which participants tend to gain in this *and* in other simulations, but in another and more important part, they are due to the elaborate feedback system (including numeric and graphic representation of decision-making processes) as well as to feedback that shows how participants performed in comparison to established (validated) multiple criteria of excellence. Those feedback capabilities are unique to the Strategic Management Simulations.

References

Breuer, K. (1990). Lernen mit computersimulierten komplexen dynamischen Systemen. Lechner, E. and Zielinski, J. (Eds.) *Wirkungssysteme und Reformansätze in der Pädagogik*. Frankfurt: Lang, 341-351.

Breuer, K. and Kummer, R. (1990). Cognitive effects from process learning with computer-based simulations. *Computers in Human Behavior, 6*, 69-81.

Breuer K. and Günterberg, A. (1991). *Firma: Die betriebswirtschaftliche Simulation eines Produktionsbetriebs*. Duisburg: CoMet.

Dörner, D. and Reither, F. (1978). Über das Problemlösen in sehr komplexen Realitätsbereichen. *Zeitschrift für experimentelle und angewandte Psychologie, 25*, 527-551.

Dörner D., Kreuzig, H.W., Reither, F. and Stäudel , T. (Eds.) (1983). *Lohhausen. Vom Umgang mit Unbestimmtheit und Komplexität*. Bern: Huber.

Fromkin, H.L. and Streufert, S. (1976). Laboratory Experimentation. Dunnette, M. (Ed.) *Handbook of industrial and organizational psychology*. Chicago: Rand McNally, 415-465.

Funke, U. (1991). Die Validierung einer computergestützten Systemsimulation zur Diagnose von Problemlösekompetenz. Schuler, H. and Funke, U. (Eds.) *Eignungsdiagnostik in Forschung und Praxis*. Stuttgart: Verlag für Angewandte Psychologie, 114-122.

Gagné, R.M. (1985). *The conditions of learning and theory of instruction*. New York: CBS College Publis ing.

Lienert, G. (1989). *Testaufbau und Testanalyse*. München and Weinheim: Psychologie Verlags Union.

Mandl, H. and Huber, G.L. (1978) (Eds.). *Kognitive Komplexität*. Göttingen: Verlag für Psychologie.

McDaniel, E. and Lawrence, C. (1990). *Levels of cognitive complexity: An approach to the measurement of thinking*. New York: Springer-Verlag.

O'Neil, H.F. Jr. (1978). *Learning strategies*. New York: Academic Press.

Schöpf, K. (1991). *Pilotstudie zur Validierung der Strategischen Management Simulation SHAMBA in der deutschen Fassung*. Paderborn: Diplomarbeit.

Schroder, H.M., Driver, M.J. and Streufert, S. (1967). *Human information processing: Individuals and groups functioning in complex social situations*. New York: Holt, Rinehart and Winston.

Schuler, H. and Funke, U. (1991) (Eds.). *Eignungsdiagnostik in Forschung und Praxis*. Stuttgart: Verlag für Angewandte Psychologie.

Stein Greenblatt, C. (1988). *Designing games and simulations*. Newbury Park: SAGE.

Streufert, S. (1991). Zur Simulation komplexer Entscheidungen. Fisch, R. and Boos, M. (Eds.) *Vom Umgang mit Komplexität in Organisationen: Konzepte - Fallbeispiele - Strategien*. Konstanz: Universitätsverlag Konstanz, 197-214.

Streufert, S. (1993). Validated assessment with the SMS management simulations. *Twenty-first International Congress of the Assessment Center Method.* Development Dimensions International, 1-12.

Streufert, S. and Nogami, G.Y. (1989). Cognitive style and complexity: Implications for I-O Psychology. *International Review of Industrial and Organizational Psychology*, 93-143.

Streufert, S., Pogash, R. and Piasecki, M. (1989). Simulation based assessment of managerial competence: Reliability and validity. *Personnel Psychology, 41*, 537-557.

Streufert, S., Pogash, R., Piasecki, M., Nogami, G.Y. and Swezey, R. (1988). Computer assisted training of complex managerial performance. *Computers in Human Behavior, 4*, 77-88.

Streufert, S., Pogash, R. Piasecki, M. and Post, G. (1990). Age and management team performance. *Psychology and Aging, 5*, 551-559.

Streufert, S. and Streufert, S.C. (1978). *Behavior in the complex environment.* New York: Wiley.

Streufert, S. and Swezey, R. (1985). Simulation and related research methods in environmental psychology. Singer, J. and Baum, A. (Eds.) *Advances in Environmental Psychology*. Hillsdale, N.J.: Erlbaum Associates, 99-118.

Streufert, S. and Swezey, R. (1986). *Complexity, managers and organizations*. London: Academic Press.

Suedfeld, P. (1992). Cognitive managers and their critics. *Political Psychology, 13*, 435-453.

Tennyson, R.M. and Breuer, K. (1991). Complex-dynamic simulations to improve higher-order thinking strategies. *Journal of Structural Learning, 11*, 1-12.

Thornton III, G.C. and Cleveland, J.N. (1990). Developing managerial talent through simulation. *American Psychologist, 45*, 190-199.

Notes

1 The development of this chapter was in part supported by Grant ROI DA06170 from NIDA.

12 Computer Support of Operator Training

Piet G. van Schaick Zillesen, Rik B.M. Min, Marcel R. Gmelich Meijling and Ben Reimerink

In recent years, the frequency of use of simulation programs for corporate training in the chemical and food industry has increased dramatically. This increase has been enabled by a rapidly improving availability of the required hardware and software facilities. Charney and Reder (1986) argue that the learning of new skills consists of three components:

- learning the concepts and functionality of the skills;
- learning how the skills should be performed;
- learning to perform the skills in practice (including the recognition of the conditions determining when a certain skill should be performed).

The components are mastered independently. The first two components may be learned in a purely theoretical way. However, practical work is required to master the third component. Usually this component can be mastered by means of on-the-job training. However, usually this component is mastered more efficiently when this on-the-job training is combined with function training in which educational computer simulation programs are applied (Alessi, 1988). Due to this partial replacement of on-the-job training by computer simulation, the costs of the training may be reduced. Furthermore, Alessi states that tasks can be learned faster when an on-the-job training is preceded by a series of simulation programs with a gradually increasing fidelity. This means that the costs of the training may be greatly reduced by two processes: the partial replacement of on-the-job training by computer simulation and the reduction of the total length of the training period.

The major purpose of an educational computer simulation program is to provide learners with the presentation of a system on a computer screen. A system (in the context of educational simulation) is a limited part of reality, selected because of its educational value. In this chapter the simulation program Brine SimUlaTion is described. The system, presented by

Brine SimUlaTion, is a brine purification plant. Brine SimUlaTion is designed for training process operators who control brine purification processes.

Usually high fidelity procedural simulations are used in operator training. These simulations are used for the automation of operators' tasks by means of repetitive execution of these tasks in a simulated working environment. However, the brine purification process is innovated frequently. Automation of operator tasks should be repeated after each innovation. It may be easier for operators to cope with these changes when their mental model of the brine purification process is enhanced. Consequently the enhancement of the operators' mental model was considered more important than the automatization of the operators' tasks. Brine SimUlaTion was designed for this purpose.

Physical simulations, combined with the discovery learning method, are most suited to mental model enhancing (Alessi and Trollip, 1985; Breuer and Kummer, 1990; Gorny, 1988; Kolb and Goldman, 1973). De Niet (1988) developed a physical simulation model of the brine purification process for the purpose of scientific research. The educational application Brine SimUlaTion was based on his model. Brine SimUlaTion enables operators to test and refine their mental model of the brine purification process by means of active experimentation.

A requirement for the method of discovery learning is that the program is used in an open, learner-controlled, context. This open context severely limits the possibilities for the implementing of automatic instructional feedback in the simulation program. However, the learner may use paper materials such as text books, exercises, instructions, and manuals in combination with the program. The learners' activities may be controlled by these paper materials. This type of learning environment, has been called "paper supported simulation environment" (Van Schaick Zillesen, 1990). Min (1987) stated that an educational computer stimulation program cannot be effective if supporting paper materials are absent.

Hartley and Lovel (1984) suggest that adequate instructional feedback can be added to an educational computer simulation program by integrating it with Computer Aided Learning (CAL) materials made with an authoring system. This type of learning environment, has been called "CAL supported simulation environment" (Van Schaick Zillesen, 1990). Until 1988 no authoring system allowed the development of CAL materials with a user-interface similar to that of advanced educational computer simulation programs. Consequently a CAL supported learning environment could not be realized in a convenient way. However, following the publication of Min (1987), a new generation of authoring systems (e.g., Authorware Professional) and Hypermedia systems (e.g., HyperCard) have been introduced. These systems support advanced features such as menu bars, pull down menus, dialogue boxes, interactive graphics, buttons, click-in regions, direct manipulation of objects on the screen and the use of external commands. An adequate simulation environment may be attained by integrating CAL materials, which were generated by means of these authoring and Hypermedia systems with advanced educational computer simulation programs.

Advanced educational computer simulation programs and hypermedia systems share many characteristics. Both CAL-types are meant to be used in a purely learner-controlled context. The philosophy behind the user interface of both CAL-types (direct manipulation of visualized objects on the screen) is similar. The consistency of the user interface and that of the context is almost implicit throughout all parts of the software, when the coaching materials for a CAL supported simulation environment are constructed by means of a Hypermedia system. Furthermore, prototypes of coaching materials can be developed in an extremely fast and highly interactive way using HyperCard, the most usual implementation of a hypermedia system. Consequently an adequate CAL supported simulation environment based on CAL materials produced with HyperCard may be easier to realize than one based on CAL materials produced with an authoring system.

We constructed a prototype of a CAL supported simulation environment by integrating the simulation program Brine SimUlaTion with CAL materials made with HyperCard (Brine tUTor). We called the complete prototype *Brine Purification.* In Brine Purification the simulation module, Brine SimUlaTion and the Hypermedium module Brine tUTor communicate in both directions; the tutor sends information to the SimUlaTion which defines the state (the simulation case, display arrangement and displayed variables) of the SimUlaTion after it has been started; on the other hand Brine SimUlaTion sends information to the tUTor which (after an analysis by the tUTor) defines the feedback given by the tUTor. In this chapter our experiences about the design, construction and testing of Brine Purification are presented. Three topics are dealt with:

- the method, applied for design of Brine Purification;
- a description of Brine Purification;
- the testing of Brine Purification.

In the last section of this chapter, the surplus value of this CAL supported simulation environment compared with a paper supported simulation environment, will be discussed. This discussion will be based on the experience gained, by developing and field-testing Brine Purification.

12.1 Design Method

In recent years we developed a universal design method for educational computer simulation programs (Min, 1987; Van Schaick Zillesen and Min, 1990). The method is designed on a hardware and software-independent level. Furthermore, we constructed several universal design systems (e.g., the RLCS-system, AppleThesis, Thesis, VAX-Thesis, HyperThesis and MacThesis). The systems support the application of our design method on various computers (e.g., MINC, Apple, IBM-PC compatibles, Atari ST, Apple Macintosh). We extended the design system MacThesis (Min, Renkema, Reimerink and Van Schaick Zillesen, 1986; Van Schaick Zillesen and Min, 1987; Van Schaick Zillesen, 1990) to enable the construction of CAL supported learning environments. This extended version of MacThesis (specified by Van Schaick Zillesen and Min, 1990) was used for the construction of Brine Purification.

All educational computer simulation programs designed following our method, consist of three major layers or shells. The outer shell is formed by the educational presentation of the state of the simulated system. During the simulation session, learners interact with this part of the program. Several authors (e.g., Alessi, 1988; Daldrup and Gorny, 1989; Gorny, 1988; Latzina and Wedekind, 1986; Van Schaick Zillesen and Min, 1988a, 1988b; Wedekind, 1985) assign criteria for this shell. Van Schaick Zillesen (1990, 1991) summarizes these criteria. The *heart* of the program is formed by the model code. The model code (often called *compiled model*) is the technical presentation of the simulated system in the computer program. By means of this code the program is able to simulate the behavior of the simulated system. Between the outer shell and the heart of the program there is an interactive interface. On the one hand, the structure of this interface is decisive in the way results of the model code are translated to the learner (e.g., in dynamic graphical displays or in model-driven animations); on the other hand, the actions of the learner controlling the program (e.g., starting the program, inspecting the values of variables or directly manipulating the presentation of simulated objects) are translated to the model code in this interface. Data can be transferred between the simulation programs and other educational software by means of this interface.

The construction of an educational computer simulation program requires the cooperation of experts in many domains such as: mathematical modeling, educational software engineering, instruction, curriculum design and graphical design. Modeling, designing educational computer simulation courseware, implementing the courseware within a curriculum and learning by means of the courseware, make different demands on the technical knowledge of the user. Consequently, all our design systems provide for a separate working environment for each of these activities. The working environments are later referred to as the modeler's environment, the designer's environment, the instructor's environment and the learner's environment. In each working environment only a part of the software can be altered using tools. The part of the software that can be altered and the tools that can be used for this purpose, differ greatly from one environment to another. The environments have been described in detail by Van Schaick Zillesen (1990).

The specification of an educational computer simulation program is complicated by several phenomena. The complications are caused by the great speed at which the technology of educational computer simulation engineering has been developing during recent years. The main complicating phenomena are:

- a rapidly improving hardware performance;
- the development of new theories in the field of user interface design;
- a lack of data originating from research on which criteria for the specification of simulations can be based;
- a limited availability of experts in the field of the implementation of educational computer simulation programs.

The complications mentioned above may make it difficult, or even impossible, to specify an educational computer simulation program completely and correctly, at the start of the construction phase. Consequently models for the construction of educational materials implying distinct phases of product development, such as pilot-research, design, specification, implementation, evaluation and revision (e.g., Koper, 1992; Plomp, 1982), are not appropriate for the construction of educational simulations. The rapid-prototyping model, designed for the construction of innovative software products instead of educational materials, gives more satisfying results (Van Schaick Zillesen, 1991). Zwart constructed an elaborated version of the rapid-prototyping model for the construction of educational computer simulation programs. Moonen (1991, 49) published this model and called it "The OKT-model according to Zwart." When this model is followed, a first prototype is created as soon as possible, based on preliminary specifications. The revised prototype is revised on the results of a formal evaluation by the members of the developmental team. This cycle of revision and formal evaluation is repeated several times. Van Schaick Zillesen (1991) observed that 6 - 12 formal evaluations and revisions are needed before this cyclic phase of program construction is completed. At the end of the last revision the prototype is tested using learners in a real educational situation (summative evaluation).

During the cyclic phase of program construction, the prototype can be adapted to adjust to sudden changes with respect to hardware and software specifications. Furthermore, incorrect specifications (caused by a lack of empirical data or due to a lack of experience) can be corrected with great ease during this phase.

We developed and field tested thirteen prototypes of educational computer simulation programs, in order to evaluate our design method (Van Schaick Zillesen, 1990). The design method proved to be domain independent; instructional simulation software for teaching physics, biology, chemistry, medicine, economy and for training process-operators was developed without difficulty. Furthermore, the design method proved to be learner-population independent. Educational computer simulation programs designed by us, are in use at institutes for vocational training, secondary education, process operator training and higher education.

12.2 Brine Purification

In the eastern part of the Netherlands, there is a layer of rock-salt at a great depth under the soil, which is exploited for commercial purposes. Two types of pipe are used to get the salt out of the soil. Water is pumped into the layer of rock-salt, with the first type of pipe, thereby dissolving the salt. The solution of the salt in the water is called brine. The brine comes up to the surface through the second type of pipe. At the surface, salt is gathered by reducing the brine using an evaporation process. However, the brine contains a few contaminations that have to be removed before the start of the evaporation process. The process by which the contaminations are removed from the brine is called the brine purification process.

The brine purification process is a slow developing process. Consequently it takes a considerable time before the consequences of an intervention in the installation can be observed. For example, it may take 24 hours before an alteration to the flow of a component introduced in the installation influences the quality of the produced brine. Often the team of operators making the intervention is replaced by another team before these results can be observed. In other cases new disturbances may have occurred, causing the operators to make new interventions. Operators rarely observe the results of an intervention independently. Consequently, the operators' mental model of the reactions that take place in the process can hardly be enhanced by means of on-the-job training.

Our educational simulation, which proceeds with a speed of approximately 1000 times real time, enables the operators to get quick, direct, responses to their actions. Furthermore, disturbing factors can be studied independently. Consequently our simulation may be a powerful tool for enhancing the operators' mental model of the processes in the brine purification installation.

12.2.1 Learners' Environment

In the learner's environment the operator controls the simulation in an interactive way. However, the operator is not able to adapt the program itself. The computer is as transparent to the operator as possible. The operator does not have to possess any knowledge or experience about computers, programming or computer science to be able to work with the software.

In Brine SimUlaTion (figure 12.1) three windows are present. In the first window the state of the brine purification plant is visualized by means of a diagram. Operators may control the installation by clicking on the colored parts of the visualization, which represent the structures that can be controlled (taps regulating the flows, concentrations of chemicals on the input side of the installation and reactors that can be put out of order).

Figure 12.1 Screendump of Brine SimUlaTion.

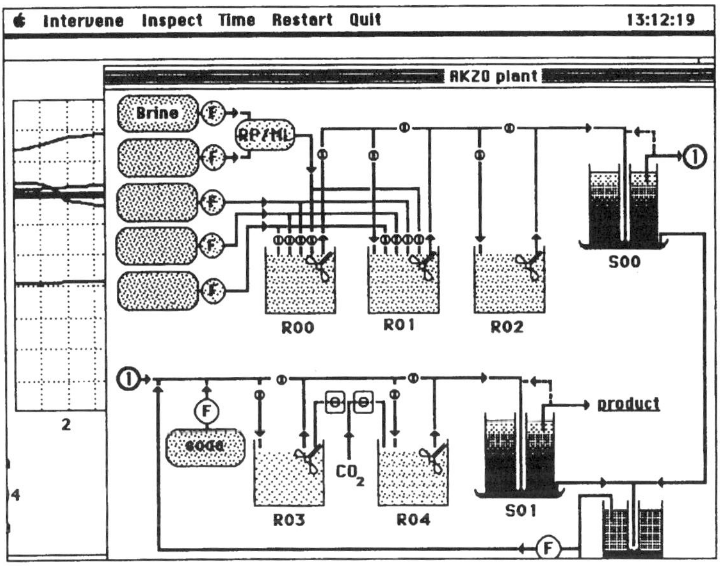

In the second window, a dynamic graph is shown. In this graph time registrations of concentrations in the input are shown. By means of this window, the input of the installation (which is dynamic) can be followed. The user can select the concentrations which are shown, from a menu that appears as soon as the user clicks in one of six colored squares, at the bottom of the window. The color of the square corresponds to the color of the display of the time registration of the selected concentration.

In the third window, a dynamic graph is shown. In this graph, time registrations of concentrations of chemicals are shown at several points in the brine purification process. By means of this window, the proceedings of the brine purification process can be followed. The user can select the concentrations which are shown and the points at which they are measured from a menu. This menu can be accessed in the same way as is described for the second window.

Brine tUTor (figure 12.2) consists of so-called HyperCards. Several types of information (or combinations of these types) are present on the HyperCards of Brine tUTor such as: text, graphic presentations, multiple choice questions and animations. Brine tUTor is organized according to the structure of a cardbox. Four categories of cards are present:

- cards with information on the control of instructions made with HyperCard;
- cards with information about the brine purification process;
- cards with information on the control of the simulation program;
- cards with exercises.

Figure 12.2 Screendump of Brine tUTor.

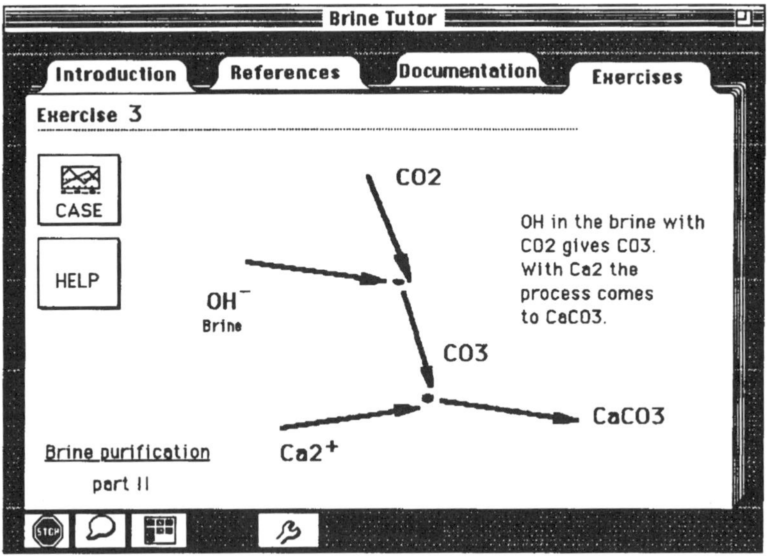

Operators can switch from one card to another by using buttons present on the cards. Furthermore, they can select other cards by means of network-cards, which can be called up with a button positioned underneath the cards. Brine tUTor may give feedback to the operator, based on his actions. Several types of feedback may be given, such as:

- presenting another card with information;
- showing a message on the present card;
- superimposing a window with a message on the present card;

- showing an animation on the present card or on another card;
- changing text on the present card or on another card;
- running the simulation program Brine SimUlaTion.

Figure 12.3 Communication between Brine tUTor and Brine SimUlaTion.

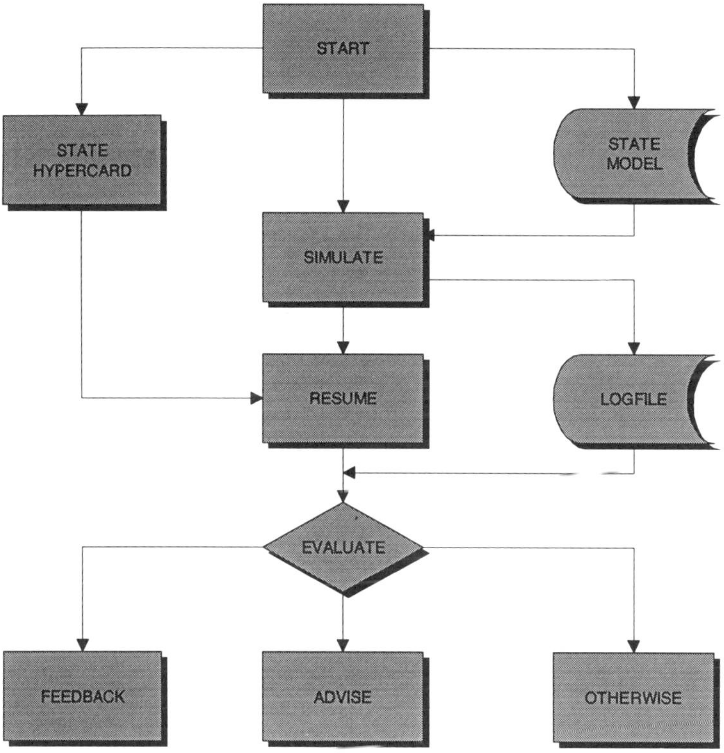

In figure 12.3 a diagram of the system for information interchange between Brine SimUlaTion and Brine tUTor is presented. The state of Brine SimUlaTion, immediately following its loading, is controlled by Brine tUTor. By means of this control system, the simulation case in Brine SimUlaTion is selected, corresponding with the exercise introduced in Brine tUTor. Furthermore, model entities relevant to the purpose of the selected exercise are displayed in the dynamic graphs. Moreover, as a consequence of this control system the screen layout of Brine SimUlaTion is defined; in this way the most relevant information can be shown immediately after the start of the simulation. At the end of the simulation the user's actions during the simulation are analyzed. In this analysis three aspects were checked by means of an evaluation procedure:

- the change of entities, which should be changed in order to do the exercise correctly;
- the value of these entities (by means of range-checking);
- other entities, changed by the user.

Based on the results of this evaluation, feedback is given to the user.

12.2.2 Instructors' Environment

Several problems may occur when an instructor tries to implement an educational computer simulation program in a curriculum. The courseware may use an instructional strategy that does not conform to the instructor's educational philosophy. Furthermore, the language used by the courseware may differ from that used by the operators, or the terminology used in the courseware may not conform to that used in other educational materials (e.g., books) as used by the operators. Moreover, the courseware may present the simulated system in a way that does not appeal to the operators (e.g., the presentation is too abstract or too concrete). The instructor may overcome these problems when he is able to adapt the resources (text, graphic information, cases and exercises) used by the courseware. This is why both Brine SimUlaTion and Brine tUTor have used resources which are easily adapted.

Brine tUTor, as with all materials made with HyperCard, is organized into five user levels. In the learner's environment the user level of Brine tUTor is automatically set on the browsing level. At this level the options available to the user include viewing cards, locating specific information in cards and using the buttons. However, the instructor can change all the properties of the instructions (or even create completely new instructions) in an interactive way by selecting a convenient user level.

Furthermore, we designed tools (by means of HyperCard) that simplify the design of new exercises and the design of new network-cards. An instructor is able to select a simulation case and a set of variables of the brine purification process by using one of these tools. Furthermore, a tool enables the instructor to define rules for the feedback given to the operator at the end of the simulation. The instructor can adapt all the text and all the diagrams produced by Brine SimUlaTion by means of an interactive resource editor.

12.3 Evaluation

Experts familiar with the brine purification process were consulted frequently during the process of product development. Furthermore, a preliminary version of the prototype was tested by five teams (8 - 12 persons) of operators. The prototype was revised based on the comments of the experts and that of the operators. The test procedure was repeated using the revised prototype. After the second test the prototype was revised once again. Furthermore, we developed paper materials with exercises to guide the user during the use of the prototype. The thus improved prototype was tested again. During this test two operators worked with the prototype Brine SimUlaTion, and combined the paper materials. During the computer session the operators were observed. When the operators had completed the last exercise, their opinion was requested on the following subjects:

- the control of the program;
- the paper material;
- the screen design;
- the structure of the software;
- the difficulty of the materials.

On completion of the interview, the software was examined systematically for possible improvements. All comments made by the operators were recorded using an audio-recorder. The test was repeated five times. The results were used for improving the prototype. The thus improved prototype became part of Brine Purification (besides Brine tUTor).

12.4 Method

Experts

For the final test of Brine Purification a group of nine experts from AKZO-Zout Chemie Hengelo (O) was available. All the experts possessed advance knowledge about the structure of the simulated system (the Brine Purification installation) and about the relationships within this system. The experts had no previous extensive experience in controlling the hardware used for the field-test.

Materials

Forms were completed by the experts. These forms consisted of closed questions. The experts were asked to indicate their preferences on a scale of five categories. The evaluation form consisted of four parts:

- Pre-knowledge. In this part of the form the experts were asked about their knowledge of the brine purification installation, the Macintosh computer and the software used during the test;
- General Impression. In this part of the form the experts were asked their opinion on the product (Brine SimUlaTion + Brine tUTor) as a whole;
- The use. In this part of the form the experts were asked their opinion about aspects of Brine tUTor such as buttons and search-help facilities. Furthermore, the experts were requested to note problems of orientation in the information space;
- Simulation. In this part of the form experts were asked their opinion about the integration of Brine SimUlaTion and Brine tUTor.

During the computer session the experts were observed. Furthermore, their interactions with Brine tUTor were logged automatically.

An introductory text was used to inform the experts about the goals and the contents matter of the prototype. It was indicated that the prototype was meant for use in an open context. Initially, the experts were advised to become familiar with the control of the program and to subsequently try to solve a simulation case. Furthermore, they were advised to use the instructional materials to reference any information needed.

Procedure

Only one computer system was available for the test. The experts worked individually. Each expert was allowed thirty minutes. At the start of the session, the expert was asked to read the introductory text. After this, the questions in the *Pre-knowledge* section of the test form were answered. The computer session started as soon as the answers to these questions had been completed. During the computer session the experts were observed. In order to save time, the experimenter was available to assist with explicit requests from the experts. Otherwise, the experimenter did not interfere with the expert during the computer session. As soon as the computer session was terminated, the remainder of the questions for the evaluation were completed.

12.5 Results

The answers of the experts to the questions on the evaluation form are presented in table 12.1. This table shows that the following qualifications are appropriate to the prototype: *clear*, *instructive*, *pleasant* and *interesting*. Furthermore (according to the experts), the prototype can be used as a stand-alone learning tool and the coaching during the computer session is adequate.

During the computer sessions problems were not observed with respect to the control of the prototype Brine tUTor. However, a few problems were reported with respect to the control

Table 12.1 Results of the field-test of the prototype Brine-Purification; answers to questions on the evaluation form (from Van Schaick Zillesen, 1990).

Qualification	*Non-response*	*Mean*	*s.d.*
The prototype is clear (clear = 1.0; not clear = -1.0)	0	0.28	0.38
The prototype is instructive (instructive = 1.0; confusing = -1.0)	0	0.56	0.50
It is pleasant to work with the prototype (pleasant = 1.0; not pleasant = -1.0)	0	0.67	0.42
Working with the prototype is interesting (interesting = 1.0; not interesting = -1.0)	0	0.67	0.42
The prototype cn be used on a stand-alone basis (agree = 1.0; disagree = -1.0)	1	0.56	0.71
The auto-start of cases (immediately showing the required display) is useful (agree = 1.0; disagree = -1.0)	0	0.61	0.69
It is pleasant that paper materials are not needed (agree = 1.0; disagree = -1.0)	0	0.67	0.61
The search tools are useful (agree = 1.0; disagree = -1.0)	1	0.81	0.40
Too much text and too few illustrations are presented (agree = 1.0; disagree = -1.0)	0	-0.50	0.59
I would prefer paper manuals with information about the purification proces and the control of the simulation program (agree = 1.0; disagree = -1.0)	0	-0.28	0.91
The guidance of the user by the prototype is sufficient (agree = 1.0; disagree = -1.0)	0	0.39	0.75
The organization of the prototype (in four functional parts) is clear (clear = 1.0; not clear = -1.0)	0	0.28	0.63
During the use of the prototype I felt lost (lost = 1.0; not lost = -1.0)	0	-0.28	0.72
The indiction of the buttons was clear (clear = 1.0; not clear = -1.0)	1	0.75	0.39
The functioning of the buttons was predictable (predictable = 1.0; unpredictable = -1.0)	0	0.67	0.42
The network tools were useful (useful = 1.0; not useful = 1.0)	2	0.29	0.50
Did you use the information presented by means of the network tools (frequently = 1.0; not used = -1.0)	1	-0.25	0.71
The prototype uses metaphors, like that of a map or a cardbox. The mataphors make the information easier to understand (agree = 1.0; disagree = -1.0)	2	0.43	0.56
Was it clear that the cases of Brine Purification start automatically? (clear = 1.0; not clear = -1.0)	0	0.78	0.46
Brine tUTor gave feedback on your actions during the use of Brine Purification. Did you like this feedback? (pleasant = 1.0; not pleasant = -1.0)	1	0.69	0.45

N persons = 9. A scale with five categories was used for all questions of Brine SimUlaTion. The more diverse control structure of Brine SimUlaTion (consisting of buttons, a menubar, pull down menus and windows) compared with that of Brine tUTor (completely consisting of buttons), may have caused this effect.

The search tools are useful according to the experts. However, most experts indicated that they did not use the search tools (network tool and graphical path tool). Analysis of the log-files showed that these cards were hardly used (one expert used the network tool three times; all the other experts did not use the search tools more than once). According to the experts the buttons were indicated in a clear way, the metaphors making the prototypes easier to understand and the presentation did not have too much text and too few figures (table 12.1).

The organization of the prototype was clear to most experts. Furthermore, only a few of them reported feelings of being lost in the prototype.

In table 12.2 the relative time spent in functional parts of the prototype is presented. The experts spent most of their time studying the simulation part (the prototype Brine SimUlaTion). Most of the time spent in Brine tUTor was spent in functional parts directly related to the exercises (instructions about the exercises and information about the control of the program), while only a few minutes were spent studying the other two parts (information about the brine purification process and information about the control of Brine tUTor).

Table 12.2 Results of the field-test of Brine Purification. Distribution of time during the computer session (in percentages of the total duration of the computer session).

Functional part	*Time (%)*
Simulations programs (exercises)	65.3
Instructions about exercises	10.9
Information about the control of Brine Purification	14.9
Information about the brine purification proces	4.6
Inforamation about the control of Brine tUTor	4.3

The experts liked to work in an environment in which paper materials were not needed (table 12.1). However, when the experts' preference in respect to the guiding materials was asked, the statement that paper materials were preferable was not rejected. Nevertheless, the experts suppose that the prototype can be used as a stand-alone system. Furthermore, the experts indicated that the transfer of information from Brine tUTor to Brine SimUlaTion and vice versa was useful.

12.6 Discussion and Conclusions

In this chapter our experiences as regards the design, construction and testing of a prototype of a CAL supported simulation environments (Brine Purification) are presented. Both the simulation program (Brine SimUlaTion) and the CAL-materials (Brine tUTor) used in this environment could be realized in a simple way. Furthermore, we succeeded in integrating the computer simulation program (constructed by means of MacThesis) with the CAL-materials (constructed by means HyperCard). This integration could also be realized in a simple way.

Operators and experts were able to control both parts of the prototype (Brine SimUlaTion and Brine tUTor) without great problems. However, the user interface of the prototype Brine SimUlaTion was not completely transparent to the experts. Similar problems were not observed when the same prototype was tested with operators in a paper supported learning environment. The user interface of Brine SimUlaTion is not completely consistent with that of Brine tUTor; a sudden change from one user interface to another may shock a user, who is just getting familiar with the first interface. The difference observed between the convenience of the user interface of Brine SimUlaTion used in a paper supported learning environment and that of the same prototype used in a CAL supported learning environment may have been caused by this effect. The importance of a consistent user interface throughout the whole prototype is stressed as a result of the difficulties observed.

A disadvantage of the used CAL supported simulation environment, compared with a paper supported one, lies in the sequential way in which the information about the subject matter is presented. This problem can be overcome by using separate windows, in which information about the subject matter of the program is presented parallel to the simulation programs. Prototypes of CAL supported simulation environments in which the simulation program can be presented parallel to the reference material, may give improved results compared with the present prototypes, especially, when the subject learned by means of the prototype is new to the operators. A new prototype of Brine Purification supports this method of parallel instruction presentation. For this purpose the prototype makes use of the advanced features of the Apple Macintosh Multi-finder system.

The Macintosh Multi-finder system enables the development of structured, integral environments. Multi-tasking operating systems, such as System 7 (implemented on Macintosh microcomputers) and OS2 (implemented on IBM PC compatible microcomputers), share these characteristics. Simulation output can be presented parallel to instruction in separate windows and on separate monitors. Min (1992) developed a theory about the presentation of instruction related to simulation programs. He called this theory "The Parallel Instruction" theory (PI theory). The theory was based on the results of the test described in this chapter and on empirical data gathered by means of constructing and field-testing new prototypes.

A system of providing (delayed) feedback to the user was realized in Brine Purification. This feedback was appreciated by the experts working with the prototype.

Experts working with Brine Purification were free to select their own route. No fixed pattern of exploration could be established. Each expert followed his own route. However, it did not seem that the experts wandered aimlessly, since even difficult reference material was studied intensively. The observed difference between the learning route followed during both tests indicates that the degree of individualization of the learning process can be controlled by the designer of the guiding materials in a simple and effective way.

The promising results of the test indicate that paper materials, inevitable until now for guiding the operator working with a simulation program during the learning process, can be replaced by hypermedia. In this way an almost perfect integration can be achieved. The user interface and the level of coaching by the software, are consistent with the total package (simulation program + guiding materials).

CAL supported simulation environments can be used as stand-alone systems. Instructors and paper materials are, in principle, not necessary during the simulation sessions. The prototypes can be designed in a very effective way by means of the extensive use of interactive software (e.g., HyperCard, MacThesis, MacPaint, PixelPaint). It is very easy to adapt materials produced with HyperCard. Instructors may use this option to adapt the learning environment to the needs of their operators. Furthermore, the instructor can design new exercises in an interactive way by means of tool programs. Calabro (1990) stressed the importance of tools of this kind being made available to hypermedia systems for educational purposes.

The use of hypermedia systems enables the future integration with other CAL materials such as interactive video and expert systems since most hypermedia systems (e.g., HyperCard) offer excellent opportunities for the use of these materials and for data exchange. This approach offers many advantages. Realistic images can be created by means of video-techniques. Interactive, student-controlled, model-driven desktop video programs may be realized following this approach. Furthermore, expert systems may be used for evaluating the pattern of operator-program interactions. The results of these evaluations may be used for adapting the instructional feedback given to the operator. The coaching of the operator during the learning process (the most important problem with regard to educational software used in an open context) may be greatly improved following this approach. A focal point of our present research is the development of a universal design method for the design and the production of educational simulation environments. Important phenomena in the model will be: dynamic specifications (Van Schaick Zillesen, 1992), the use of fast-prototyping techniques, object-oriented coding techniques, repetitive field-testing and the application of parallel instruction theory (Min, 1992). The model will be based on empirical data gathered by means of constructing and field-testing prototypes. Recently we constructed and field-tested prototypes of simulation environments for the support of several courses in food-process technology and biotechnology (Van Schaick Zillesen, Zwietering and Van 't Riet, 1993a, 1993b). We developed new versions of our design systems Thesis and MacThesis, supporting the construction of the prototypes required for this research. A completely new design system is under development. This design system will enable the production of simulation environments that can be used on computers with a MS-Windows operating system. The user interface of these environments will be compatible with IBM's Common User Access standards.

References

Alessi, S.M. (1988). Fidelity in the design of instructional simulations. *Journal of Computer-Based Instruction, 15*(2), 40-47.

Alessi, S.M. and Trollip, S.R. (1985). *Computer Based Instruction, Methods and Development.* New-York: Prentice-Hall.

Breuer, K. and Kummer, R. (1990). Cognitive Effects from Process Learning with Computer-Based Simulations. *Computers in Human Behavior, 6*, 69-81.

Calabro, G. (1990). Hypermedia tools for authoring. *Paper EURIT'90* (published by means of electronic media).

Charney, D.H. and Reder, L.M. (1986). Initial Skill Learning: *An Analysis of how Elaborations Facilitate the Three Components* (Tech. Rep. No. 86-1). Pittsburg: Carnegie-Mellon University, Dept. of Psychology.

Daldrup, U. and Gorny, P. (1989). Modelbildungssysteme im Unterricht. *Log In, 9*(4), 7-12 [German].

De Niet, G. (1988). *Kwaliteitsbeheersing in continue chemische processen.* Ph.D. thesis, University of Twente, Enschede [Dutch].

Gorny, P. (1988). Didactic and Software-Ergonomic Aspects of Dynamic Modelling and Simulation Systems. Lovis, F. and Tagg E.D. (Eds.) *Computers in Education* (291-297). Amsterdam: Elsevier Science Publishers B.V. (North-Holland).

Hartley, J.R. and Lovel, K. (1984). The Psychological Principles Underlying the Design of Computer-Based Instructional Systems. Walker, D.F. and Hess R.D. (Eds.) *Instructional Software, Principles and Perspectives for Design and Use.* Belmont: Wadsforth Inc.

Kolb, D.A. and Goldman, M.B. (1973). *Toward a typology of learning style and learning environment.* Cambridge: Mass. Institute Tech.

Koper, E.J.R. (1992). *Premises for the development of high quality educational software.* Plomp, Tj., Pieters, J.M. and Feteris, A. (Eds.) *European Conference on Educational Research*, Book of Summaries, Vol 2, 634-637, University of Twente, Enschede.

Latzina, M. and Wedekind, J. (1986). Simulationsprogramme: Systematische Beschreibung und Bewertung. *Log In, 5*(5/6), 35-41 [German].

Min, F.B.M. (1987). *Computersimulatie als leermiddel: Een inleiding in methoden en technieken.* Schoonhoven: Academic Service [Dutch].

Min, F.B.M. (1992). *Parallel Instruction, a theory for educational computer simulation.* Interactive Learning International, 6(3); 177-1.

Min, F.B.M., Renkema, M., Reimerink, B. and Van Schaick Zillesen, P.G. (1986). MacTHESIS: A Design System for Educational Computer Simulation Programs. Moonen, J. and Plomp, Tj. (Eds.) *Eurit'86: Developments in Educational Software and Courseware* (689-691). Oxford: Pergamon Press.

Moonen, J. (1991). *Toegepast Onderwijskundigen: Architecten of Ingenieurs?* Dijkstra, S., Krammer H.P. and Pieters J.M (Eds.) *De onderwijskundig ontwerper* (47-60). Amsterdam: Swets & Zeitlinger B.V. [Dutch].

Plomp, Tj. (1982). *Onderwijskundige Technologie: Enige Ervaringen.* University of Twente, Enschede [Dutch].

Van Schaick Zillesen, P.G. (1990) *Methods and techniques for the design of educational computer simulation programs and their validation by means of empirical research.* PhD. thesis, University of Twente, Enschede.

Van Schaick Zillesen, P.G. (1991), Ontwerpen van Educatieve Computersimulaties: Een gezamenlijke taak voor onderwijskundigen, modelbouwers en docenten. Dijkstra, S., Krammer H.P. and Pieters J.M.(Eds.), *De onderwijskundig ontwerper* (187-198). Amsterdam: Swets & Zeitlinger B.V. [Dutch].

Van Schaick Zillesen, P.G. (1992). *The Simultaneous Production Model; a model for the construction, testing, implementation and revision of educational computer simulation environments.* Paper presented at European Conference on Educational Research (ECER), University of Twente, Enschede, Symposium on Didactics and Educational Computer Software (organizer A. Dirkzwager). Published in the ERIC database, University of Syracuse.

Van Schaick Zillesen, P.G. and Min, F.B.M. (1987). MacTHESIS: a design system for educational computer simulation programs. *Wheels for the Mind of Europe*, *2*, 23-33.

Van Schaick Zillesen, P.G. and Min, F.B.M. (1988a). Onderzoek naar computersimulatiemethoden en animatietechnieken ten behoeve van onderwijs en opleiding. Been, P.H. and Koster, K.B. (Eds.) *Modellen en empirie* (115-127). Bijdragen aan de Onderwijsresearch (20). Amsterdam: Swets & Zeitlinger [Dutch].

Van Schaick Zillesen, P.G. and Min, F.B.M. (1988b). A design system for educational computer simulation programs used in secondary education in the Netherlands. Lovis, F. and Tagg E.D. (Eds.) *Computers in Education* (265-269). Amsterdam: Elsevier Science Publishers B.V. (North-Holland).

Van Schaick Zillesen, P.G. and Min, F.B.M. (1990). Towards an Interactive Design Method for Educational Computer Simulation Programs. *Paper EURIT'90* (published by means of electronic media).

Van Schaick Zillesen, P.G., Zwietering, M.H. and Van 't Riet, K. (1993a). *Computer support of Food and bioprocess engineering education.* Computers Educ.

Van Schaick Zillesen, P.G., Zwietering, M.H. and Van 't Riet. K. (1993b). *The use of computer simulation for biotechnology education.* Biotechnology Education.

Wedekind, J. (1985). Einsatz von Mikrocomputern fuer Simulationszwecke im Unterricht. Mandl, H. and Fischer, G. (Eds.) *Lernen im Dialog mit dem Computer* (210-217). Tuebingen: Urban and Schwartzenberg [German].

13 Delivery Systems for Corporate Training in the Future

Alexander J. Romiszowski

This chapter is about delivery systems for corporate training in the future. First, we will describe electronic networks and human resources development. The next section is about the changing face of human resource development. Subsequently, we answer the question why to use hypertext for electronic seminars and cases. Next we will describe seminars and case studies in a hypertext environment. Finally, we will give some future directions.

13.1 Electronic Networks and Human Resources Development

13.1.1 Telecommunications and the Workplace

The development of telecommunications and digital data transmission is revolutionizing the way that business is performed. People are working and communicating ever more by means of computer based workstations that support databases, electronic mail and a host of other information tools. There is less need and less time available for face to face meetings, than in the past. In addition, the costs of electronic communication are rapidly falling, at the same time as the costs of transport and subsistence associated with conventional meetings are rising sharply. Many corporate organizations are already taking these trends into consideration in their policy on communication. They are demanding that conventional meetings between people based at different sites be justified in terms of what aspects of the proposed meeting cannot be effectively handled by telephone, teleconferencing, electronic mail, fax, or some combination of such media.

As electronic communication networks become more ubiquitous, easier to use and more powerful, the trend towards electronic, *networked*, business communications will grow rapidly. As a result, people will spend an increasing proportion of their time at workstations and proportionately less in live meetings (Vallee, 1982; Zuboff, 1988).

13.1.2 Telecommunications and Human Resources Development

This trend is also liable to spread to meetings with educational or human-resource-development aims. The U.S. telephone company AT&T, for example, has already moved towards the massive use of teleconferencing in place of conventional classroom-based courses for most of its sales and management training needs. Over a period of some five years, the use of telephone-based training (so called Teletraining) in AT&T has grown exponentially. There are over 400 centers around the U.S.A. that can be linked in any combination so that local groups can participate in learning activities with other groups. In addition, of course, any individual can be linked into a network for audio teleconferencing. The multi-way audio is further supported by various media now available for the rapid transmission of text and graphics: for instance fax, slow-scan video and electronic mail. The resultant *audiographic* systems for teleconferencing are relatively cheap to set up and use and they are proving to be surprisingly effective. The major part of sales and management training in AT&T is now delivered by this method (in 1989, over 69,000 employees participated at least once in some form of teletraining) and results overall are considered to be quite satisfactory (Chute, 1990).

Of course, the rapid expansion in use of electronic teletraining will be driven, as always, not so much by effectiveness, but rather by economic factors. AT&T has reported an overall reduction in the costs per student hour of training of more than half. This cost saving comes almost entirely from savings in travel and subsistence costs when employees participate in centrally organized *place-based* courses, as well as from reduced loss of productivity, due to a reduction in the time that employees are away from their jobs (Chute, 1990; Chute, Balthazar and Poston, 1988). In some respects, AT&T is an exceptionally good candidate for teletraining, being the *owner* of the telecommunication system and operating on a continental scale (Chute, in his cost saving estimates, uses an average figure of $400 for the travel costs of one employee participating in a centrally organized course).

However, given that the annual human resources development budget of corporate U.S.A. is estimated at some 25 to 30 billion dollars in direct costs, but over 100 billion dollars if travel and lost productivity costs are included, there is a tremendous economic opportunity available to any company that cuts down on conventional training, replacing it with teletraining.

13.2 The Changing Face of Human Resource Development

13.2.1 New Forms of Educational and Training Needs

There are also other pressures, both organizational and philosophical, that are increasing the amount of autonomy, self-directedness and responsibility that employees have in respect of their own education and development. From the philosophical side, there is the viewpoint that people should have more control over what they learn and how they learn it. These viewpoints are embodied in the principles of modern adult education, or andragogy. They also reflect earlier humanist traditions. They are further strengthened by the modern concepts of continuing or *permanent education*, which spring from the realization that change in society, and particularly in the workplace, is now so fast that everyone is of necessity involved in a process of lifelong updating in relation to the workplace, this need for updating may in some respects be very specific and personal for each individual. Hence the growing popularity of the *Open Learning* concept as a modular approach to education that can take anyone from wherever they are at present in a given domain, to wherever they need/want to be, relatively independently of the needs/wants of other people (Paine, 1988).

From the organizational side, there is the growing realization that the needs of individuals for job-related education and development are so varied and personal that it is totally impractical to satisfy them by means of a program of standard course offerings. Furthermore, there is such a proliferation of technical information published, that may (or may not) be of importance to certain employees, that the conventional approaches to the handling of information resources by some form of library and information/abstracting service, are breaking down. It has become necessary for all key employees (for instance technical and executive) to take on more responsibility for keeping themselves up to date on new developments that might affect their field of work.

13.2.2 New Forms of Educational and Training Methods

Given the increasingly competitive nature of business in the international marketplace and the critical importance that access to and use of up-to-date information and methods plays in a company's competitiveness, it is not surprising that the concept of human resources development as *self-development* is taking root. This concept sees keeping up-to-date and employable as the responsibility of every employee. The employer's responsibility is to make this possible, by helping to identify the needs of the individual and by facilitating access to the resources necessary to satisfy those needs. This will ever less frequently call for lengthy courses organized either within the company or by outside providers, but will instead make much more use of networking, access to external databases and electronic libraries, small specialist group teletraining and self-instruction in all its forms (Eurich, 1990; Kearsley, 1985; Romiszowski, 1988).

As the trends outlined above expand through the business community, similar trends will be seen in relation to adult education, especially in the growing use of distance education in formal educational institutions. To some extent, similar economic factors may lead to a greater use of distance education and electronic networking as the communication media as support to conventional courses. This will be brought about partly by organizational and pedagogic benefits that such systems can offer conventional courses and partly because it will be seen to be the duty of education to use such systems in order to prepare its graduates for the realities of a workplace where they will be obliged to use them.

13.2.3 Learner-Directed Conversation in Distance Education

This last point really brings home the importance of examining now, how to get high quality educational experiences and effective learning from electronically networked communication. The particular focus of this chapter is on the effective implementation of group discussion, or *conversational*, methodologies on electronic telecommunications networks. This focus is particularly important, as we know much less about how to converse effectively on electronic networks, than we do about electronic self-instruction. There is a long history and fairly developed technology of the design, development and delivery-at-a-distance of self-study materials in several different (including electronic) media. There is much less known about the running of effective group-discussion sessions at a distance. Such teaching methods as seminars (where a group critiques and comments a prepared paper or presentation) or case-studies (where groups exchange ideas on how to explain or deal with a problem situation) are traditionally implemented in small or medium sized groups, led by skilled and experienced *facilitators*. Much of the success of these teaching methods is ascribed to the facilitators and the skill with which they focus discussion, guide the approaches adopted by the participants, use the natural group dynamics to stimulate interest, participation and deep involvement, pull together what has been learned in the final debriefing discussion, and so on. Can such participatory discussion methods be effectively orchestrated at a distance? How might this be done?

The answers to such questions are vital if we are to learn just how we can utilize the new electronic communication media for education and training. If we cannot use these media for effective participatory group discussions, then there is a serious limit to the extent to which we can use distance education methods effectively. On the other hand, if the economic and other pressures outlined above force our hand into using distance education on a massive scale, then there is a serious limit on the effectiveness of courses in subject areas that are particularly reliant on small group discussion for effective learning.

Although the above-mentioned scenario refers particularly strongly to the context of human resources development in the corporate world, the questions are also of importance to the educator, particularly the adult educator. The work which is reported in this chapter has been performed to date with groups of students on graduate courses. It will still be necessary to extend this work to the corporate world. However, the basic questions remain the same and the main thrust will continue to be to seek more effective methods for using the new communication media and in the process reduce what might be termed the *loneliness of the long distance student.*

13.3 Why Hypertext for Electronic Seminars and Cases?

13.3.1 Two Paradigms Compared

In order to answer this question, let us review a little theory and also some of the research that is already available on this topic. To start with the theory, it may help to compare and contrast two alternative paradigms, or maybe philosophies, which are current in education – the *instructional* and the *conversational* paradigms. These are summarized in tabular from in table 13.1.

The instructional paradigm is the one that has driven much (though by no means all) of the research and development of the past 30 years that has been performed under the label of educational (or instructional) technology. The conversational paradigm may be seen as the basis of much of the work done on small group work, group dynamics, so-called experiential learning and so on. Very often, those working in these areas see little connection between their approaches and methods and those of the instructional technologists. There are of course some very important areas of overlap, for example, the prolific and excellent work on simulations, role play and case study methodology that has been done by educational technologists, but by and large the enthusiasts for one or other of these paradigms have kept apart, professionally speaking.

There is no reason why this should be so. Firstly, there is no question of considering these two approaches as mutually exclusive, or that one is *right* and the other *wrong*. They are complementary approaches and each has its role to play in educational and in training systems. Secondly, many real life teaching methods may be in part instructional and in part conversational. Thirdly, there are useful theoretical models of the conversational process as a teaching methodology that have originated on the *instructional* side of the artificial *divide* that seems to separate researchers in our field. One such model, or rather theory, is Gordon Pask's

"Conversation Theory" (Pask, 1976, 1984). The work described here is based to some extent on this theory. One hoped-for outcome of this work may, therefore, be a closer integration of research and development on teaching.

Table 13.1 Instruction versus conversation.

Paradigm:		*'Instruction'*	*'Conversation'*
OBJECTIVES: (OUTPUT)			
	(why?)	specific pre-defined products standard	general negotiable processes variable
MESSAGES: (INPUT)			
	(what?)	designed	created
	(when?)	pre-prepared	on-line
	(who?)	instructor	participants
	(whom?)	one-to-many	many-to-many
INTERACTION: (PROCESS)			
	(focus)	behaviors	ideas
	(analysis)	criterion-ref	contents-structure
	(feedback)	corrective	constructive
	(complexity)	one-layer thick	interwoven layers
DISTANCE EDUCATION:			
example		Correspondence courses	Teleconferencing Videoconferencing
		Computer Mediated Communication (CMC)	

In relation to distance teaching specifically, one may notice at the bottom of table 13.1 that the more conventional *study module* or typical correspondence course model may serve as a good example of the instructional paradigm. Teleconferencing, both audio and video based, is on the other hand a good example of the conversational paradigm in action, as also is Computer-Conferencing, as it is most commonly practiced. Computer-Mediated-Communication (CMC) has, however, a number of guises. When a computer network is used directly between one student and a distant tutor in order to reinforce a set learning task in algebra and to troubleshoot the student's difficulties on the prescribed problem set, the interchange of messages, although constituting a conversation, may well follow the instructional paradigm in most aspects. A student accessing a computer based instructional package on algebra is having a sort of conversation with the package, but most people would not consider this a good example of conversational education.

13.3.2 Hypertext: Instructional and/or Conversational

To turn to hypertext environments, we can see this versatility of CMC in being able to support both conversational and instructional procedures. The joint cooperation on the analysis and development of a hypertext document satisfies all the basic requirements of a conversation between the participants.

The study of a hypertext version of a maintenance manual for an airplane in order to learn a particular set of troubleshooting procedures satisfied the requirements of instruction. It is possible that different nodes of a single network could perform instructional and conversational functions respectively. Indeed, one of the implementations described in this chapter does just that. This versatility of CMC in general and hypertext systems specifically makes them particularly interesting systems to study with a view of their rational adoption in training (Horn, 1990; Romiszowski, 1990b).

This *versatility* of hypertext is a potential advantage which is an addition to others mentioned in the literature, such as: a synchronous communication, ability of attract more and richer comments and contributions from students, a permanent record of study, including student comments and annotations, non linear study, random access and so on. It is one potential advantage that is little mentioned, as most authors stress either the nonlinearity and student-directedness of the user process, or the influence of structure inherent in the content on the authoring process. The work reported here is seeking to use the physical characteristics of a hypertext environment to shape the teacher/learner interactions in particular ways.

13.3.3 Problems of Structure and Control in CMC

In order to give some background to the work, it is necessary to mention, very briefly, some earlier work which attempted to use a simple, unstructured, electronic communication system for seminars at a distance. Several computer-seminars (this word is preferable to the more common term *conferences* in this context) were organized during 1988 and 1989. The first of these linked two graduate student groups, one at Syracuse University in the U.S.A. and the other at the University of Twente in the Netherlands, to jointly discuss a position paper on the impact of the use of new emerging technologies in education on the role and the process of instructional design. Some 40 students debated this issue for some six weeks on a standard electronic mail network (bitnet). In many respects the experience was a huge success, but two specific problems were observed. These were labeled the problems of *structure* and *control* (Romiszowski and De Haas, 1989; Romiszowski and Jost, 1989).

The problem of structure is that participants who take part over a long time period by occasionally logging onto an ongoing discussion on electronic mail have difficulty in maintaining an overall view of the content and structure of the previous discussion. The messages are received in chronological order and seldom is it clear to which previous messages they relate, until they have been read. They are then stored in one (also chronologically organized) *notebook*, unless the participant decides to do something special like storing different messages in different *topic* files or notebooks.

Existing mainframe based systems do not have very convenient or versatile methods of storing the structure of the incoming stream of messages. Our students, in general, did not develop any personal structure for storing the messages. As a result, they lost the *big picture* of what had been discussed. Several of the students were asked, after the experience, to draw a structured outline of the content of the whole seminar. Each student's memory of the content and structure of what was discussed was different on important points.

The problem of control refers to the ease or difficulty with which the seminar organizer can keep the participants on task. What tends to happen in this form of discussion over time is that most participants respond to messages as they read them, thus extending the discussion on some hot issue that someone else has just mentioned. If this issue happens to deviate from the originally intended discussion topic, the chances are that discussion will, from that point onwards, ignore the formally assigned task and wander ever further into other topics. This phenomenon can of course also be observed in face to face group discussions. Also, it is not always an undesirable thing to let participants have their head in a discussion just to see where it leads.

However, if for some reason there is a specific issue that is to be addressed, excessive digression should be controlled by the group leader, facilitator, or by some other means. Our observation in the electronic seminar was that it became more difficult to bring discussion back on track than would normally be the case in a conventional meeting. Requests and reminder messages from the distant leader were largely ignored. In the case of the seminar theme of this first experience, the premises of the issue (whether certain new technologies will in fact be used in education) were challenged and this led the discussion from technical to economic questions, to equity in relation of the *haves* to the *have nots* and so on.

13.3.4 Software for Maintaining Structure and Control

Several similar electronic seminars were run, confirming that the problems of structure and control were inherent to the methodology. A review of the literature concerning educational computer conferencing revealed that others had experienced similar problems and the only way to diminish them that had been tried was to develop special software for computer conferencing. This would usually embody some form of learning institution metaphor, with a structure that replicated large group conference rooms for mainline discussions, small seminar rooms for interesting, but peripheral issues raised by participants and meeting rooms for personal interchanges with just one or two colleagues.

CoSy and Participate are examples for such systems that are now commercially available. We reviewed experience with both these systems and also gained some practical experience of our own. It seems that the participants still do not place their messages very accurately in the most appropriate *space* in the conferencing structure prepared for them. It is necessary to have a moderator, who reads all incoming messages and decides on the most useful place to store them. The resulting structure imposed on the discussion is thus the moderator's. Also the moderating task is very time consuming and must be performed in a regular, disciplined manner if it is not to bring the whole conference or seminar to a halt. It was for these reasons that we turned to HyperCard, to experiment with other ways of storing an electronic seminar discussion in a structured manner.

13.4 Seminars and Case Studies in a Hypertext Environment

13.4.1 The HyperCard-Based Seminar Network

Figure 13.1 shows the structure and the functioning of our first version of a HyperCard-based *shell* for small group seminars. The basic structure consists of an individual stack of notecards for each of the participants. Each card also has a button for each of the other participants. Clicking on a participant's personal icon takes you out of the stack you are currently reading into that other participant's stack. You have also to indicate the card number of that stack that you wish to access. Any participant who has a comment that links to a given card in another participant's stack indicates this by registering that card's number in his personal icon *mailbox*. Any other participant then knows that a link has been formed and can follow that link, if desired, by clicking on the mailbox icon and typing the required card number. Learning time to master the use of this system is some two minutes.

The sample cards in figure 13.1 are from a seminar-based course that ran through one semester. Each participant (there were seven) prepared a position paper on some specific topic of their choice within a wider predefined topic (in fact the same one that was used in the first e-mail conference described above). Each participant stack therefore contained their own position paper, that would be spread over some six to ten cards, care being taken to separate each important point on a separate card.

This ensures that although one card may give birth to links to a bunch of other cards written by other participants, all these cards will be related thematically. In this way, it was hoped to automatically build one group-developed structure of the whole of the discourse.

Figure 13.1 The structure and the functioning of the first version of a HyperCard-based shell for small group seminars.

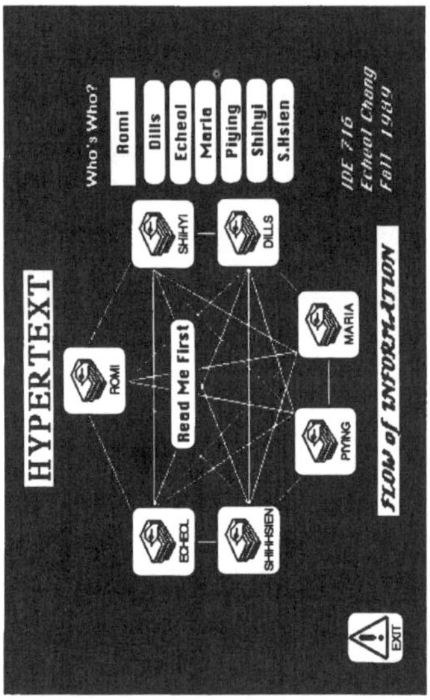

1.1 The Hypercard discussion environment-home card

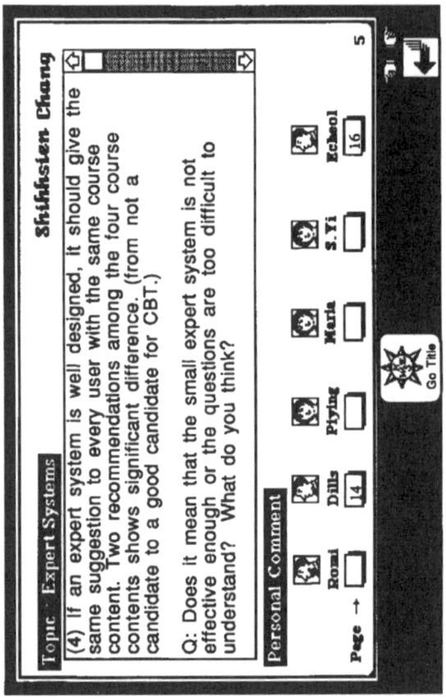

1.3 Fifth card of the discussion paper

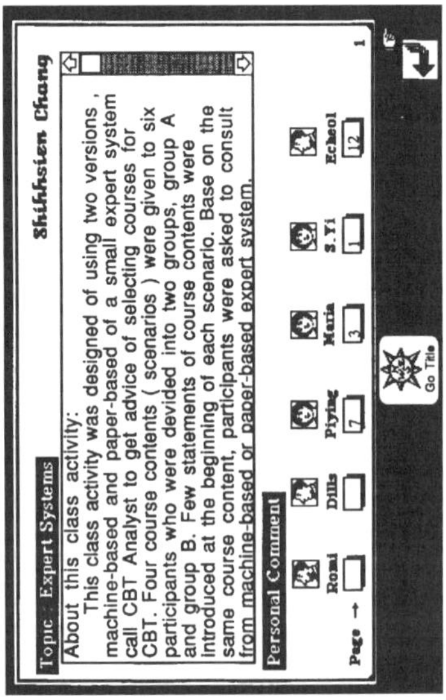

1.2 First card of a discussion paper

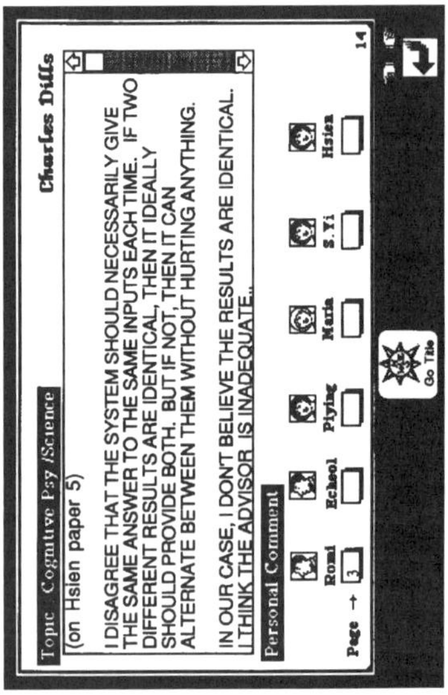

1.4 Another participant's *comment* on the discussion paper

13.4.2 The HyperCard Simulation of a Mainframe Based System

In order to be able to perform some comparative studies in a relatively controlled environment, we also developed a HyperCard-based shell that operated just like a file-exchange system that can be implemented on most mainframe computers (note this did not emulate e-mail, but rather the file sending and manipulating capabilities offered as standard on many machines: e.g., XEDIT on the IBM mainframes). These systems will allow the split-screen scrolling of two files for comparison purposed. Our HyperCard version does just this, but the screen design quality and ease of learning to operate the system are comparable to the network *shell.*

Figure 13.2 shows an excerpt from a seminar that was run on this system. Note that the comments made by all participants on the position paper are stored in the lower window of the card. However, as the position paper is again so written as to have only one topic per card, all related comments, and the point to which they relate, are available in one card. In addition, participants may *open space* between two previous comments already registered, in order to place the new comment in as close proximity as possible to other related items.

The resulting discussion record is *chunked* by theme or sub-topic, to the extent that the original position paper being commented was sub-divided by the original author across a series of cards in the stack. In this respect, the HyperCard version is potentially superior to a similar implementation on a typical mainframe-based system, where the position paper is all in one file and, if at all lengthy, readers have to make references in their comments to specific subtopics or the use some artificial strategem such as numbering all lines and referencing their comments by line number.

However, the reader comments are not individually linked in an electronic manner to each other. Any structure that emerges is largely created by the reader of the comments file. The contrast between the two shells is that one exhibits some of the features of an electronically cross-referenced hypertext and the other does not.

13.4.3 A Structured Case-Study Discussion Environment

Another training methodology that depends heavily on relatively open-ended and rather *deep* conversation between participants and course leaders is the case-study. The object of the case-study methodology is to engage the participants in analysis and evaluation of a given case, in order to develop their skills in handling a range of similar real-life situations later on, or alternatively, to create a better and deeper understanding of the general principles that are illustrated by the facts of the case presented.

Figure 13.2 Excerpt from a seminar.

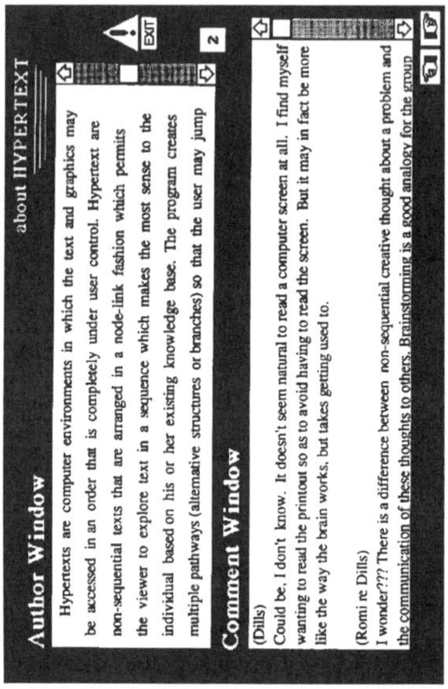

2.1 The second card in a discussion stack on "Hypertext"

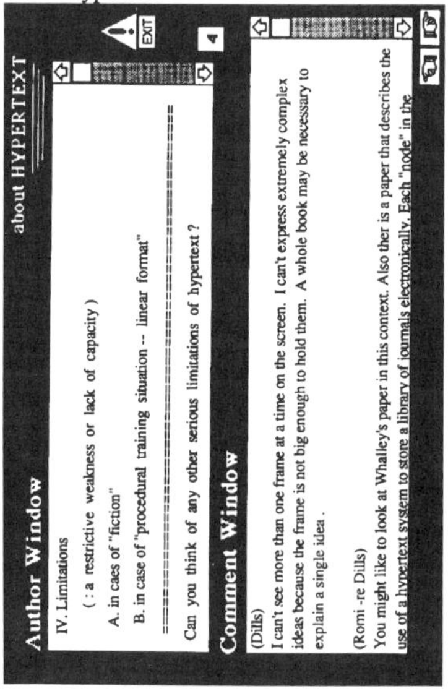

2.2 The fourth card and early comments

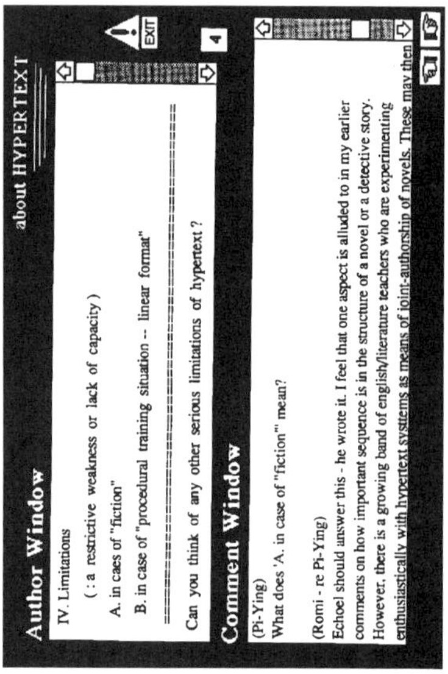

2.3 The fourth card and later comments

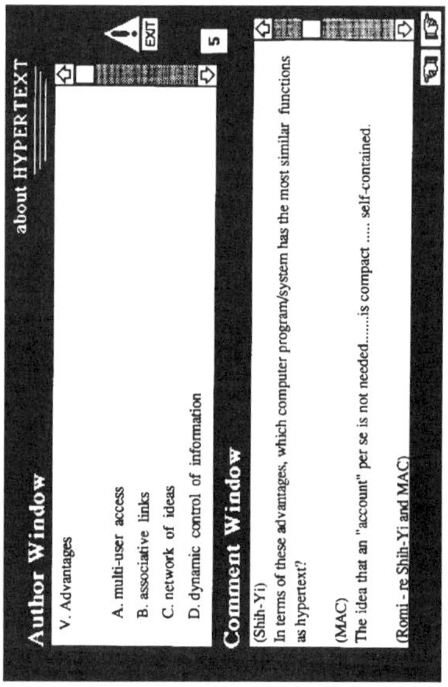

2.4 The fifth card

Learning must go beyond the specific case itself in order to be useful. When the cases are drawn from the learner's real-life experience, the learners are effectively engaged in a process of "reflection-in-action," as described and advocated by Schön (1983).

When they are imaginary, or drawn from other people's experience (e.g., Harvard Business Cases), they engage the learners in a similar reflective process, that has the aim of preparing the participants for future challenges of a nature that is modeled by the case material.

At a recent conference, Barnes (1990) argues very convincingly that the key to the effectiveness of a case-study exercise is the quality of the case *discussion*, and this depends in turn on the quality of the case discussion leader. One unfortunate result of this is that effective learning from case-study exercises is not always achieved. Also it is always instructor-intensive and, therefore, relatively expensive. This factor unduly limits the use of the case-study method. At the same conference, I presented a viable approach to overcoming the frequent unavailability of a competent case-discussion leader, as well as increasing the efficiency of the available leaders, by means of a networked case-study discussion environment (Romiszowski, 1990a). This is a *hybrid* system that combines some of the best aspects of computer-based learning for presentation and initial discussion of the case materials, with some of the best aspects of computer-conferencing, to provide opportunities for reflective discussion of the deeper implications of the case, between various participants and a discussion leader who may be separated by both distance and time.

The computer-based-learning element is constructed according to the principles of the "Structural Communication" methodology of "conversational self-instruction" (Egan, 1972; Hodgson, 1974; Pusch and Slee, 1990; Romiszowski, 1986). The computer-mediated case discussion elements can be implemented on any existing electronic network capable of ASCII file transfer, and may be set up to operate as a one-on-one discussion between a participant and the discussion leader, or as an open discussion between the leader and a group of participants.

An example of the case discussion in action is shown in figure 13.3. The case is concerned with the analysis of the causes of a human performance problem and the recommendations of appropriate solutions. The participant has already studied the basic *facts* of the case and is now invited to construct a solution to the problems encountered. This solution is constructed by selecting all the items considered relevant from an extensive (20 or more item) *menu* of plausible courses of action. This allows the participant a great amount of freedom as there are thousands, possibly millions, of different combinations of response components. The computer analyzes the response, using a small expert system that replicates the technical expertise of the discussion leader, identifying significant patterns in the response that may be worthy of comment.

Figure 13.3 An example of the case discussion in action.

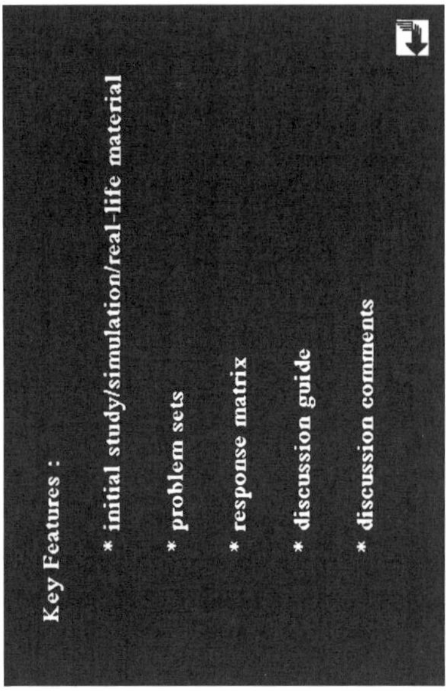

3.1 Characteristics of Structural Communication

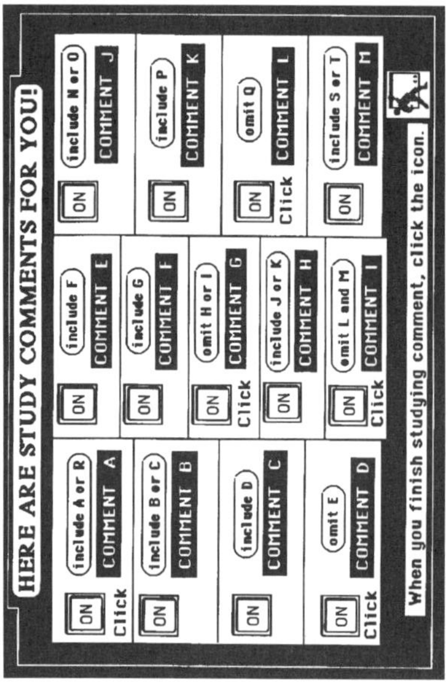

3.3 The Discussion Guide

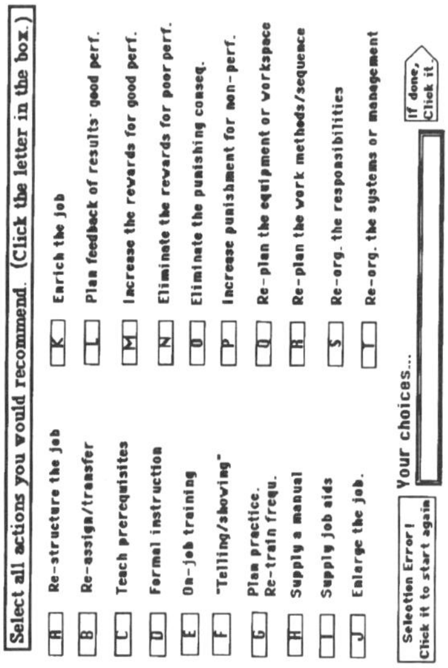

3.2 The Respone Matrix

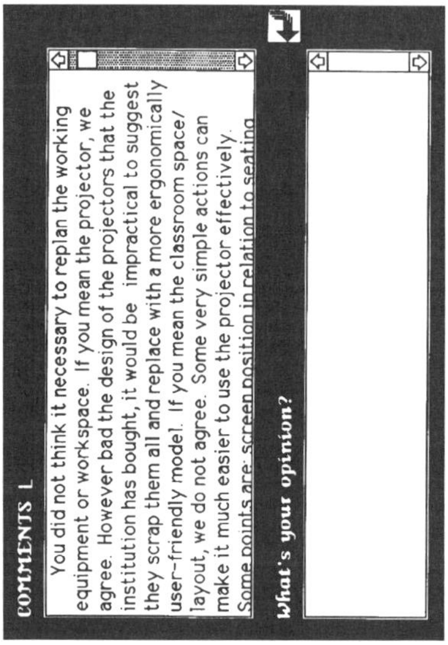

3.4 A Discussion Comment Card

In this way, the participant is directed to a series of *feedback comment* screens where certain aspects of the case are further discussed and alternative viewpoints and solutions are compared.

It is at this point that the participant may *interject* in the discussion, with an original comment or a specific question. This student-generated comment is transmitted to a distant discussion leader, and to other participants if so desired. Discussion then continues on the electronic network.

Ongoing research with this system has shown great potential. We have concentrated, on investigating the educational effectiveness of such an approach. Some of our findings are summarized here. Further details have been published elsewhere (Romiszowski and Corso, 1990; Romiszowski, Jost and Chang, 1990).

- A typical case discussion exercise on this *asynchronous* mode, may stretch over a period of two or more weeks. Typical participants, however, will spend a total of some three hours, spread over some five or six log-on sessions. The total time devoted to the exercise by the typical student is similar to the time that would be spent in a face-to-face, *synchronous* classroom-based case-study exercise.
- However, every student is participating actively during every log-on session. Students are not excluded from the discussion by those who tend to dominate any conversation. As a result, the total amount of discussion, as measured by the volume of commentary and the number of different student-generated comments, tends to be much greater than is achieved in a conventional classroom setting.
- The quality of the student-generated discussion is also superior, as basic questions related to understanding the case and its implementations are handled automatically in the initial Computer-Based-Learning phase. Students use the network to extend the discussion to a deeper level and make more carefully planned comments.
- The acceptability of this technique was reflected in student reaction questionnaires, in which over 80% of the respondents expressed preference for the computer-based case studies over similar exercises studied in conventional classroom discussions. It is important to note that the respondents were adult students on full-time university courses, who had experience of and easy access to both modalities. Their preferences were thus reflective to the intrinsic aspects of studying cases in these two modalities, rather than extrinsic aspects related to scheduling, distance or accessibility problems.
- The efficiency of the technique was reflected in the ability of one case discussion leader to handle the conversation of over 100 students, on three different geographically distant campuses, over a whole semester. This entailed dealing with some 300 individual student messages per week in the initial stages, and a progressively smaller number as

the students settled into using the networking system productively, to raise only important and relatively *deep* issues related to interpreting or solving the case.

- The acceptability of the technique to discussion leaders is dependent on their willingness and ability to communicate by means of computer-conferencing systems as opposed to face-to-face. However, in cases where these prerequisites are met, we have observed a high level of satisfaction on the part of the discussion leader, particularly with the enhanced quality of the discussion, the avoidance of discussion of basic questions related to understanding the case material, and the enhanced possibilities for involving all the participants actively in the discussion.

13.5 Future Directions

13.5.1 Current and Future Research

The research summarized above has concentrated on establishing the practically and educational effectiveness of using electronic networks for *conversational* but clearly *focused* learning activities over distance. Current work is following two routes.

- The further investigation of the most effective and efficient approaches to the use of networks as a medium of conversational learning/teaching. One current project is investigating certain aspects of students' learning style in relation to the effectiveness and acceptability of network-based learning. Another is investigating enhancements and improvements to the learning environments that we have created so far.
- The implementation of working pilot projects over considerable distances and over significant periods of time, to investigate the cost-benefit factor of our approach in real educational and HRD settings. One project will link university students across three continents in collaborative conversational learning, through electronic seminars and case-studying exercises. Another will supply an on-line learning service to personnel in a corporate setting.

The ultimate aim of this research program is to construct cost-effective working models of future systems of adult education and retraining, that would be accessible to participants from their workplace or home, on a flexible *open learning* basis, and would be capable of operating under either the *instructional* or the *conversational* approaches.

13.5.2 Future Directions in Training and Development

The trends outlined at the beginning of this chapter suggest that as computers and networks become increasingly used both for work and for communication, the pressure will mount to use them increasingly for education and training. We are already quite skilled at developing computer-based-instructional packages that effectively teach all manner of content. We also have the technology to efficiently distribute such packages to end users by means of electronic networks.

The trends also suggest that as business success increasingly depends on so-called *knowledge work*, the workforce will increasingly depend upon the abilities of locating existing knowledge, evaluating its relevance to the work in progress, and using relevant knowledge creatively to solve the problems or further the goals of the enterprise. This implies that the importance of learning specific content as part of initial training will diminish, as the *shelf-life* of the content diminishes, but the importance of developing creative thinking and problem solving skills will increase. Therefore, a further implication is that teaching techniques that are based on the *conversational* paradigm, such as small group seminars or case-studies, should be increasingly important in future HRD.

Taking these two trends and all their implications, together, we may expect to see increasing use of computers and networks for the delivery of *conversational* as well as *instructional* courses. The totally electronic vocational training system may only be a year or two away from reality. At this time, we are not so skilled at designing effective conversational courses for delivery at a distance. Nor have we given much thought to the design of the student-system interface for efficient delivery of such courses.

The importance of the research and development program outlined in this chapter is to discover *now* how to best implement conversational learning exercises on the networked delivery systems that we may well be using for much of our training and development effort in the *future*.

References

Barnes, L.B. (1990). Case method leadership: some thoughts of an ignorant expert. Klein, H.E. (Ed.) *Problem Solving With Cases and Simulations*. Proceedings of the Seventh International Conference on Case Method Research and Case Method Application. Produced and distributed by the WACRA. Waltham, MA: Bentley College Press.

Chute, A.G. (1990). Strategies for Implementing Teletraining Systems. *Educational & Training Technology International, 27* (3), 264-270.

Chute, A.G., Balthazar, L.B. and Poston, C.D. (1988). Learning from Teletraining. *American Journal of Distance Education, 2* (3), 55-63.

Egan, K. (1972). *Structural Communication.* Belmont: Fearon Publishers.

Eurich, N.P. (1990). *The Learning Industry: Education for adult workers.* Princeton, NJ: The Carnegie Foundation for the Advancement of Teaching.

Hodgson, A.M. (1974). Structural Communication in practice. Romiszowski, A.J. (Ed.) *APPLET Yearbook of Educational and Instructional Technology.* London, UK: Kogan Page.

Horn, R.E. (1990). *Mapping Hypertext.* Lexington, MA: Lexington Institute.

Kearsley, G. (1985). *Training for tomorrow: distributed learning through computer and communications technology.* Reading: Addison-Wesley.

Paine, N. (1988). *Opening Learning in Transition: An agenda for action.* London: Kogan Page.

Pask, G. (1976). Conversational Techniques in the Study and Practice of Education. *British Journal of Educational Psychology, 46.* Reprinted in Hartley J. and Davies, I.K. (Eds.) (1978), *Contribution to an Educational Technology, 2.* London: Kogan Page.

Pask, G. (1984). Review of Conversation Theory and a Protologic (or Protolanguage). *Educational Communication and Technology: A Journal of Theory, Research, and Development, 32* (1), 3-40.

Pusch, W.S. and Slee, E.J. (1990). Structural Communication: a forgotten application of cognitive theory to instruction. *Instructional Developments, 1* (2). Syracuse, NY: Syracuse University School of Education.

Romiszowski, A.J. (1986). *Developing Auto-instructional Materials: from programmed texts to CAL and interactive video.* London: Kogan Page.

Romiszowski, A.J. (1988). *The Selection and Use of Instruction Media* (2nd Ed.). London: Kogan Page.

Romiszowski, A.J. (1990a). The case study methodology: interactive media and instructional design. Klein, H.E. (Ed.) *Problem Solving with Cases and Simulations.* Proceedings of the Seventh International Conference on Case Method Research and Case Method Application. Produced and distributed by the World Association for Case Method Research and Application (WACRA). Waltham, MA: Bentley College Press.

Romiszowski, A.J. (1990b). The Hypertext/Hypermedia Solution – But What Exactly is the Problem? Jonassen, D. and Mandl, H. (Eds) *Designing Hypermedia for Learning*, 321-354.

Romiszowski, A.J., Jost, K.L. and Chang, E. (1990). A Hypertext Approach to Structuring Computer-Mediated Seminars and Case Studies. In D.W. Dalton (ed), *Proceedings of the 32nd Annual International Conference of the Association for the Development of Computer-Based Instructional Systems*, 419-434.

Romiszowski, A.J. and Corso, M. (1990). Computer-Mediated Seminars and Case Studies: Possible future trends for in-service training and development by means of interactive distance education. Paper presented at the 15th World Conference on Distance Education, Caracas, Venezuela.

Romiszowski, A.J. and De Haas, J. (October 1989). Computer Mediated Communication for Instruction: Using E-mail as a Seminar. *Educational Technology.*

Romiszowski, A.J. and Jost, K.L. (1989). Computer Conferencing and the Distance Learner: Problems of Structure and Control. Paper presented at the 1989 Conference on Distance Education, University of Wisconsin.

Schön, D.A. (1983). *The Reflective practitioner.* New York: Basic Books, Inc.

Vallee, J. (1982). *The Network Revolution: Confessions of a scientist.* Berkeley, CA: And/Or Press, Inc.

Zuboff, S. (1988). *In the Age of the Smart Machine: The future of work and power.* New York: Basic Books, Inc.

APPENDIX

Overview of the Studies on Behavior Modeling

OVERVIEW OF THE STUDIES ON BEHAVIOR MODELING

Author(s)	Purpose	Key Variables	Design/Methods	Sample	Effects
Baldwin (1992)	Test positive and negative models and multiple scenarios	Reaction; Learning test; Retention test; Video taped reproduction; Audio taped generalization	Post-only	Business students 72-Trained	Significantly greater generalization with positive and negative models than with only positive models
Bandura and Cervone (1983)	Test the hypothesis that self-evaluative and self-efficacy mechanisms mediate the effects of goal systems on performance motivation	Goals and performance feedback; goals alone; feedback alone; neither factor	Baseline assessment, followed by random assignment within groupings to treatment conditions	45 men and 45 women drawn from an introductory psychology course	Goal systems gain motivating power through self-evaluative and self-efficacy mechanisms activated by cognitive comparison
Baron (1970)	Investigate the effects of attraction toward a model and model's competence on adult imitative behavior	Ratings of models by the subjects	2X2 factorial design based upon two levels of attraction (low,high) and two levels of model's competence (low, high)	48 undergraduate psychology students at University of South Carolina	Attraction produced no effect upon the learning of imitation
Burnaska (1976)	Determine if behavior modeling improved interpersonal skills	Observations; Ratings by employees	Post-only (observations) Pre-post (ratings)	General Electric Middle Managers 62-Trained 62-Control	Trainees received significantly better ratings
Byham, Adams and Kiggins (1976)	Investigate transfer of training to the work place	Ratings on interpersonal skills from subordinates	Pre-post	Financial accounting supervisors 8-Trained 8-Control	Trainees received significantly better ratings

Author(s)	Purpose	Key Variables	Design/Methods	Sample	Effects
Dowling and Frantz (1975)	Investigate the relationship between imitative learning and the quality of an interpersonal relationship	Ethnocentrism as measured by a revised version of Adorno's 36-item Ethnocentrism Scale	2x2 design using facilitative conditions (positive, negative) and ethnocentric model (ethnocentric, nonethnocentric) and control	72 college students in 10 discussion groups	Facilitated models generated significantly more imitative learning and persisted over a 3-week follow-up period
Goldstein and Sorcher (1974)	Determine impact of interpersonal skills training of foremen on worker efficiency and productivity	Subordinate productivity	Pre-post	General Electric foremen 100-Trained 100-Control	Significantly higher subordinate productivity for trained foremen
Hards (1981)	Determine impact of Supervisory Skills Training on supervisor/employee interactions and on-the-job performance	Supervisory Knowledge and Skills Test Employee Rating Survey Manager Rating Survey	Pre and post ratings	Hospital department heads and supervisors	Definite and positive effect on both the acquisition of knowledge and skills and on supervisory performance
Kazdin (1974)	Determine effectiveness of covert modeling and reinforcement in increasing assertive skills	Four(4) self assessment measures of assertiveness; behavior role-playing test of assertiveness	Post only; Self ratings; 'blind' judges	Subjects responded to advertisement. 12-modeling plus reinforcement 11-modeling 11-no model control 11-delayed treatment control	Support the therapeutic efficacy of covert modeling as a treatment technique

Author(s)	Purpose	Key Variables	Design/Methods	Sample	Effects
Kazdin (1975)	Investigate effects of covert modeling and imagery assessment on assertiveness	Self-report inventories of assertiveness; Role-playing test; assertiveness rating by 'blind' judges	2x2 design using number of models imagined (multiple vs. single) and model reinforcement (imagining positive consequences vs. imagining negative consequences); Assessments pre and post treatment	Subjects responded to advertisement; 11-single model/ reinforcement 11-single model/ no reinforcement 11-multiple model/ reinforcement 11-multiple model/ no reinforcement 10-nonassertive-model/control	Imagining effects multiple models or model reinforcement enhanced behavior change
Kloba (1975)	Determine effectiveness of microcounseling employing a high status model vs. no status attributed to model	Dependency-interdependency; Factor E Scale of the Junior-Senior High School Personality Questionnaire; Ratings by judges using the Open Ended Comments Rating Scale	Factorially modified posttest only-control group design	104 high school sophomores	High status models in microcounseling can increase training effectiveness
Kloba and Zimpfer (1976)	Determine effects of model status and independence	Ratings by trained judges on Open-Ended Comments Rating Scale	2x2 post-only design using model status (high vs no status) and level of trainee dependence (independent vs. dependent)	52 high school sophomores	High-status model or independent trainee led to higher ratings

Author(s)	Purpose	Key Variables	Design/Methods	Sample	Effects
Komaki, Barwick and Scott (1978)	Determine effects of behavior analysis used to improve worker safety	Injury frequency rate; Observational codes by trained observers	Multiple baseline design; measurement over 25 weeks	142 wholesale bakery employees	Safety performance substantially improved over baseline
Latham and Saari (1979)	Determine effects of behavior modeling on supervisors' interpersonal skills	Knowledge tests, ratings by superiors, ratings during role play, reaction ratings	Post only	Paper company foremen 20-Trained 20-Control	Highly favorable reactions; trainees significantly better than control on knowledge tests 6 mos. after training; on role play 3 mos. after training; supervisors' rating 1 year after training
Mazzarese (1984)	Determine effects of demographic variables and psychological characteristics on behavior change	Ratings by trainees, their manager and their subordinate	Pre, post-score and post-post-score	102 participants 102 managers 102 subordinates	Sixty days post training, participant with abstract learning styles improved more than those with concrete learning styles. More improvement appeared for those with an external as compared to internal locus of control
McDaniel (1985)	Evaluate effectiveness of behavior modeling for supervisory training.	Ratings by trainees, employees, and superiors.	Pre and Post - Trainees Post Only - Employees and supervisors	187 - Supervisors 443 - Employees 178 - Managers	Positive change found in use of skills between end of training and 7 month evaluation
Meyer and Raich (1983)	Evaluate behavior modeling to improve effectiveness of salespersons	Sales performance of participants	Average per-hour commissions 6 months before - 6 months after training	Sales associates with retail firm 58-Trained 64-Control	Trained group increased sales by about 7%, while control group decreased sales by about 3%

Author(s)	Purpose	Key Variables	Design/Methods	Sample	Effects
Mills (1985)	Determine effectiveness of positive and negative models in learning communication skills	Recall of key actions; trained observer rating; reaction measures	Pre and Post with four conditions: 1. Positive - positive 2. Positive - negative 3. Negative - positive 4. Negative - negative	38 undergraduate students	Conditions 1, 2, and 3 show advantages over Condition 4
Moses and Ritchie (1976)	Determine effects of behavior modeling on supervisor's performance in handling employee problems	Rating of role play in an assessment center	Post-only	Supervisors 90-Trained 93-Control	Trainees showed significantly better performance two months after training
Newman and Fuqua (1988)	Comparative study of positive and negative modeling in counselor training	Counselor Rating Form Counselor Evaluation Rating Scale	3 treatment groups: - negative modeling only - positive modeling only - half negative and half positive modeling	47 graduate students	No significant differences in rating among groups
Porras and Anderson (1981)	Effects of modeling - based training	Plant performance indices, labor relations data and perception of supervisory behavior elicited from plant personnel.	Pre and Post Questionnaires with trained and control groups	Manufacturing operation of a forest products company. Trainees – all supervisors at one plant, plus 30% of employees reporting to each supervisor; Control – all supervisors at two plants, plus 30% of employ-	As compared with control, significant improvement in rating of supervisors' behavior; improvement in plant performance; some positive effect on plant labor relations

Author(s)	Purpose	Key Variables	Design/Methods	Sample	Effects
				ees reporting to each supervisor	
Porras and Hargis (1982)	Determine preconditions, both individual and organizational, most highly related to change in organizational behavior.	Ratings of supervisors' skills, psychological characteristics, and demographic variables	Pre and Post questionnaires with trained and control groups	Supervisors 20-Trained 13-Control	Role clarity, control over the job, feelings of competence on the job, self-actualization, and self-regard were all significantly positively correlated with behavior change as predicted. Role conflict and overload and job-generated stress were significant negative correlates of subsequent change. Demographic variables failed to reach predicted significance levels
Russ-Eft (1985a)	Evaluate behavior modeling training for workers	Ratings of workers' behaviors	Pre and post training questionnaires	16-Trained and their coworkers 14-Control and their coworkers	Significant improvement in skill for trained group
Russ-Eft and Hurson (1987)	Investigate the impact of behavior modeling training	Training and project costs in terms of time and materials; Project completion; Dollar benefits to the organization	Questionnaires and interviews both pre and post training; used discounted cash-flow method	42 supervisors	Estimated 35% rate of return averaged over all 42 participants

Author(s)	Purpose	Key Variables	Design/Methods	Sample	Effects
Russ-Eft, Krishnamurthi and Ravishankar (1994)	Determine the cost benefit of training	Costs determined using trainee's time away from work; trainer's time for preparation and training; actual materials used; salary plus fringe for designing the sessions; Certification costs using benefits determined, skill gains, amounts of time spent on skill areas, and salaries	Pre - post ratings; Dollar value assigned to behavioral improvements	42 trainees	Positive net benefit in dollars
Russ-Eft and Mazzarese (1990)	Compare skill gains of supervisors with high management versus low management support	Trainee ratings of management support; ratings of supervisory skills pre and post training	Self and manager ratings pre and post training	Supervisors 14-Trained 11-Control	Significant improvement in skill for trained group. Trainees rating high support showed more significant gains than trainees rating low support
Russ-Eft and Zucchelli (1987)	Determine the impact of positive and negative models	Subjects recognition and recall of key behaviors; performance of key behaviors rated by 'blind' judges	3x4 design using Time (1,2, and 3) and conditions: 1. Positive - positive 2. Positive - negative 3. Negative - positive 4. Negative - negative	20 managers and administrative personnel	Conditions 1, 2, and 3 performed better than Condition 4
Schoening (1981)	Assess the effectiveness of behavior modeling to improve interpersonal problem solving skills in managers	Judges ratings trainees' skills; Trainees' reactions	Video tapes of role playing exercises pre and post training.	16 Managers and supervisors of an electronics manufacturer	Judges found significant change as result of training. Trainees rated the training as being moderately effective

Author(s)	Purpose	Key Variables	Design/Methods	Sample	Effects
Sevy and Olson (1982)	Assess knowledge and skills acquired from a behavior modeling program	Supervisor-employee interactions skills	Skill Audit after training; Supervision questionnaire having subordinates rating trainees' behaviors	Grocery store supervisors 17 Trained 18 Control	Significant improvement in knowledge from skill audit, but not from skill ratings
Sorcher and Spence (1982)	Determine effectiveness of behavior modeling on improving race relations in South Africa	Change in attitudes; behavior observations; and structured interviews	Pre and post training measures; 'double-blind'data collection and analysis' multiple measures	6 trained supervisors with 51 employees; 6 control supervisors with 80 employees	No significant change in attitudes or behavior observations; significant improvements in reported behaviors from structured interviews for trained group
Taylor (1992)	Determine relationships between implementation characteristics and measures of training success	Training directors' ratings of supervisors's reactions, learning, and skill use	Examining correlations between implementation characteristics and training success	285 training and personnel directors from U.S. companies with at least 3,000 eployees providing interpersonal skills training	Significant positive correlation between immediate supervisor support for training and supersvisors' reactions, learning, and skill use; significant positive correlation between top management support for training and supervisors reactions
Trimble, Decker and Nathan (1985;1991) Experiment 1	Effects of positive and negative models on trainee learning	Recall, recognition, and distinctiveness of key behaviors	Post only 2x3 mixed design using time (1 and 2) and condition: 1. Positive - positive 2. Positive - negative 3. Negative - negative	54 volunteer undergraduate students	Significant increase from Time 1 to Time 2 in recall and recognition; significant interaction between time and condition: At Time 1, subjects in conditions 1 and 2 out - performed those in condition 3; - At Time 2, recall was same among conditions; but

Author(s)	Purpose	Key Variables	Design/Methods	Sample	Effects
					recognition was better by subjects in condition 3
Trimble, Decker and Nathan (1985;1991) Experiment 2	Effects of positive and negative models on trainee learning	Recall, recognition and distinctiveness of key behaviors, role-play behavior and trainee reaction	Counterbalanced design with 4 conditions: 1. Positive - positive 2. Positive - negative 3. Negative - positive 4. Negative - negative	84 volunteer undergraduate students	No differences between positive only and mixed models on trainee performance
Werner, O'Leary-Kelly, Baldwin and Wexley	Test pre- and post-training interventions on training outcomes	Trainee reaction (immediate and delayed), learning retention, behavioral reproduction, behavioral generalization.	Post only 2x2 factorial design: 1. No pre or post intervention 2. Pre intervention, but no post intervention 3. Post intervention, but no pre intervention 4. Both pre and post interventions	150 volunteer undergraduate students	Post-training goal setting led to less favorable immediate reactions but more favorable delayed reaction. Goal setting enhanced learning retention and behavioral reproductions. No impact of pre-training motivation

Author Index

Subject Index